Aesthetic Critical Inquiry
Andrea Feeser, Series Editor

THE LAUGHING STALK

Live Comedy and Its Audiences

Edited by Judy Batalion

Parlor Press
Anderson, South Carolina
www.parlorpress.com

Parlor Press LLC, Anderson, South Carolina, USA

© 2012 by Parlor Press
All rights reserved.
Printed in the United States of America

SAN: 254-8879

Library of Congress Cataloging-in-Publication Data

The laughing stalk : live comedy and its audiences / edited by Judy Batalion.
    p. cm. -- (Aesthetic critical inquiry)
  Includes bibliographical references.
  ISBN 978-1-60235-242-1 (pbk. : acid-free paper) -- ISBN 978-1-60235-243-8 (hardcover : acid-free paper) -- ISBN 978-1-60235-244-5 (adobe ebook) -- ISBN 978-1-60235-245-2 (epub)
 1. Stand-up comedy. 2. Performance--Psychological aspects. I. Batalion, Judy.
  PN1969.C65L37 2012
  792.7'6--dc23
                                2011044537

Cover design by David Blakesley.
Cover Image: Juan Muñoz, *Towards the Corner*, 1998. © Tate, London, 2011. Used by permission.
Printed on acid-free paper.

Parlor Press, LLC is an independent publisher of scholarly and trade titles in print and multimedia formats. This book is available in paper, cloth and Adobe eBook formats from Parlor Press on the World Wide Web at http://www.parlorpress.com or through online and brick-and-mortar bookstores. For submission information or to find out about Parlor Press publications, write to Parlor Press, 3015 Brackenberry Drive, Anderson, South Carolina, 29621, or email editor@parlorpress.com.

Contents

Illustrations	vii
Acknowledgments	ix
Introduction: Difference at Work: The Live Comedy Audience *Judy Batalion*	3

Locating Live Comedy

1 Creating the Audience: It's All in the Timing *Alice Rayner*	28
2 Room for Comedy *Iain Mackintosh*	40
3 The Stand-up as Stand-in: Performer-Audience Intimacy and the Emergence of the Stand-Up Comic in the United States since the 1950s *Matthew Daube*	57
4 A Comedic Tour de Monde *Shazia Mirza*	82

The Cult-ure of the Audience, and Audiences of Culture

5 Audienceship and (Non)Laughter in the Stand-up Comedy of Steve Martin *Lesley Harbidge*	96
6 Hoyle's Humility *Gavin Butt*	116
7 George Lillo's *The London Merchant* and the Laughing Audience *Diana Solomon*	124
8 Laughter in the Final Instance: The Cultural Economy of Humor (Or why women aren't perceived to be as funny as men) *Rebecca Krefting*	140

The Industry, or, the Audience in the Making of the Comedy Show

9 Rhyme or Reason: Trying to Draw Some Conclusions about Comedy Audiences *Sable & Batalion*	157

10 Choosing Comedy 165
    Julia Chamberlain

11 Seven Steps to the Stage: The Audience as Co-creator of
   the Stand-up Comedy Night 174
    Kevin McCarron

12 Hecklers: A Taxonomy 186
    Nile Seguin

13 The Comedy Clubbers: Photographs 189
    Sarah Boyes

14 *Audience* 194
    Michael Frayn

Live Comedy in Context

15 *Ugly Betty* and the (Live) Comedy Audience 202
    Elizabeth Klaver

16 Watching Me, Watching You: Sitcom and Surveillance 220
    Frances Gray

17 Obscene or Absent: Literary versus Comedy Audiences 235
    AL Kennedy

18 *The Daily Show*'s Studio Audience 248
    Scott Jacobson

19 It's My Show, Or, Shut Up and Laugh: Spheres of
   Intimacy in the Comic Arena and How New Technologies
   Play Their Part in the "Live" Act 253
    Kélina Gotman and Samuel Godin

20 High Time for Humor 271
    Andrea Fraser

21 *Inaugural Speech* 279
    Andrea Fraser

About the Editor 291

Illustrations

Figure 1.1 Pierre-August Renoir, *At the Theatre*.	10
Figure 2.1 Audience Seating Plan, Olivier, Royal National Theatre, London.	42
Figure 2.2 Olivier, Royal National Theatre, London.	43
Figure 2.3 Tony Blair at a Party Conference.	54
Figure 2.4 George Michael at Wembley Stadium.	54
Figure 7.1 William Hogarth, *The Laughing Audience*.	125
Figure 9.1 Jerome Sable and Eli Batalion.	158
Figures 13.1 to 13.4 Sarah Boyes, The Comedy Clubbers: Photographs.	*190–193*
Figure 14.1 Plan 1 and Plan 2 for Michael Frayn, *Audience*.	*200*
Figures 21.1, 21.2, 21.3 Andrea Fraser, *Inaugural Speech*, video stills.	*289–290*

Acknowledgments

While I had known that a stand-up set could be four minutes, I had not realized that a book about stand-up sets could take the better part of a decade to complete (and it's a good thing I hadn't!). Myriad people were involved in making this collection, from brainstorming to polishing stages, and they all deserve acknowledgment. Sadly, most won't get it.

Enormous thanks to Andrea Feeser, the series editor, who offered me the chance to propose a book, helped me develop the idea at every stage, offered answers to my endless questions, and read countless drafts of each essay. Thanks to all the contributors for their dedication, hard work and extreme patience; thanks to their agents and representatives; and thanks to the comedy writers whose inspiring work did not, for whatever reason, end up in the collection. Thanks to David Blakesely at Parlor Press for his persistence and advice, and Terra Williams for her editorial eye. Thanks to Dominic Johnson, Robbie Praw, and Xavier Ribas for suggesting potential contributors. Thanks to the Courtauld Institute of Art Research Forum for awarding me a postdoctoral fellowship during which time I completed the bulk of my editorial work. Thank you to every audience that I've been part of, as well as those that I interacted with as a performer, even the ones—especially the ones—who loathed me, thereby making me work to understand them. And thanks, of course, to Jon Lightman, my most brutal and most constant audience, for being crazy enough to share his life with a performer/academic/writer.

The Laughing Stalk

Introduction

Difference at Work: The Live Comedy Audience

Judy Batalion

> *Life is a comedy for those who think . . . and a tragedy for those who feel.*
>
> —Horace Walpole

LIFE IS A COMEDY FOR THOSE WHO THINK

This collection of writing explores live comedy audiences, considering the meaning and composition of an audience in today's global world, and the ways live audiences represent a magnified series of intimate relations and emotional expressions including love and hate. This is a book about the stage and the seats, the sorts who are in/on them, and how difference plays itself out between them. Informed by my work in academia and stand up—my dual experience as a cultural critic and performer—this project offers observations and analysis based in two very different discourses that hopefully help flesh one another out. I begin this multi-dimensional exploration with two anecdotes.

During the summer of 2006, I was at the Edinburgh Festival, one of the world's largest performing arts and comedy congregations, where I saw the one-man show *The Naked Racist*, by Canadian comic Phil Nichol, who had just won the UK's premiere comedy prize. Nichol proved to be a performance powerhouse, beginning his spectacle with a rock-star-styled guitar solo, and throughout, dazzling the audience with high-octane anecdotes about his personal confrontations with prejudice, expressing his disdain for the ploys of world leaders, as well as for those who are uncritical and blindly follow these leaders and promote war. Nichol's philosophic means of protesting violence—and in particular the American public's support of George Bush—was via nudity, and through the hour, he progressively stripped down to reveal his all. Moreover, he charmingly encouraged the three-hundred-member audience to join in the action! Lo-and-behold, all around me gaggles of comedy fans, rapt by Nichol's energy, began to remove shirts, shoes and hats. With Nichol in the lead, they stood up, throwing their extraneous clothing to the wind, like hippies tossing flowers. Indeed, Nichol ended the show by inviting a slew of naked comedians—not known for their stunning physiques—to bear floral headdresses and dance in the aisles.

Amongst this spectacle and frenzy, however, I remained seated, in a smug, knowing sort of way, even aware that my resistance might be ruining the joy for my neighbor (who, admittedly, didn't seem to notice me as he rolled off dirty socks and swigged four pints of beer). I patiently waited for the brilliant moment I was sure would come—the moment when Nichol would self-consciously announce his own tactic, and reveal to the audience how, despite his noble plea for peace, he had still managed to rile them, to use his charisma to influence crowd behavior, just as he accused politicians of doing. Surely, the irony of the situation was not lost on him, and I figured he won this major arts award because he would so cleverly reflect back to us what he was critiquing—he would show his audience that they too were implicated, that one protest just leads to another, how herd dynamics are unrelated to political wing. But, to my genuine surprise, Nichol said nothing. The curtains went down, but the frenzy oozed beyond the show and into the bar, and I left the comedy venue feeling nervous. I was amazed at how quickly an emotion can spread, and at the intensity with which mood and ideas can be socially experienced. How was this show different from a political rally, except that it didn't announce itself as such? I was frightened by the crowd mentality, the political statement that had been taken uncritically and unselfconsciously and turned into a vibe for all-night partying and, likely, drunken sex.

The next powerful—but perhaps opposite—comedy audience experience occurred in October 2008. Sarah Silverman performed her long-awaited London debut show at the Hammersmith Apollo, a three thousand-seat theater. Silverman had become famous in the US for her brand of non-PC humor, which uses racial stereotypes and crass sexual description to, her audience believes, ironically display their inherent unfoundedness. (This type of post-PC humor characterizes the work of several American comedians, like Dave Chapelle and Lisa Lampanelli.) I enjoyed much of Silverman's work, which I had seen in her film *Jesus is Magic*, and attended the show to hear her new material, curious how middle-class PC England would respond to her "mouth." I wondered what a post-colonial culture that was obsessively worried about expressing any form of prejudice would make of her jokes about starving African babies.

But once again I left a comedy show amazed; in this case, because the audience's response to the gig was not based on the material. The audience here was instead focused on how short her set was and how shoddy the warm-up had been considering the high price of the tickets (the act broadcast a couple of flat jokes via webcam from L.A claiming he was too ill to come to London). During an awkward encore—in which Silverman returned to the stage with no material but some quite funny improvising, and in which people squirmed in their seats in discomfort—and then after the show, for weeks in media reviews, she was panned for "disrespecting her British audience." Blog entries turned markedly un-PC and anti-American (i.e., another Yank comes to England to rip us off) and the small British-Jewish media community was upset at how she had "represented" Jews in the public eye. Everyone was offended that a British opening act was not invited to do a spot, and they blamed her for being both arrogant and uncomfortable. "But what did you think of *the jokes,* of her shtick, the non-PC stuff?" I asked friends and colleagues. None of that mattered. People were mad that they didn't get what they paid for, and that she didn't play to them. Comedy is thrilling for the risk it offers, but audiences don't like it when they lose. Perhaps her fans like her controversy when it's about someone else. Silverman's racy material was not controversial, but her show (purposefully?) was. Indeed, perhaps she was (consciously or not) accomplishing precisely what was lacking for me in Nichol's piece: she undermined the performer's charisma, causing friction with the crowd, enabling a variety of responses and affects instead of uniform adulation.

What intrigued me in both comedy experiences was how much my impressions of the show had much less to do with the performer, performance, and act, and much more to do with the audience—how it (re)acted, what it valued, how self-conscious it was (or not), and how easily moods travel through a group. These experiences reminded me how powerful the audience is, how it is both a homogeneous force, and yet a heterogeneous mix (my own reaction in contrast to others'). In both cases, these were foreign-born performers in Britain—one, a Canadian man who lived in London, the other, an American Jewish woman who was visiting from L.A.—and even though both shows were filled with fans, the identity politics appeared relevant: British audiences seemed to respond to the acts based on preconceived notions that Americans (and for some, Jews) are the over-dogs, who can and should be criticized. In Nichol's case, he did the criticizing, "on the same page" as his audience; in Silverman's case, she became the criticized, because she was different.

Both performers had travelled the globe—a British person would only know Silverman's work through non-live media—and yet a huge number of people gathered to see her, just as a huge number gather at Edinburgh. Indeed, comedy is thriving in the US, the UK and Canada. But what comprises these growing participating audiences? *Who* is listening? The comedy audience is not a mere segment of the public at large; it is a group that has elected to come together intentionally. Any comedy performer will tell you how hard it is to perform to an actual public—a space where people are walking in and out, where they have not paid and do not know what they are getting into, a space with no cohesive mood nor identity. A comedy audience, on the other hand, is a group held together by a desire to have an emotional experience and one shared mainly with (irrelevant) strangers, by their desire to be that comedy audience.[1] Where does this desire emerge? What is so appealing about being part of a live comedy audience? I ask this especially today, when so much comedy is available on the internet and television,[2] and when *an audience* is often filled with members from across the globe and diverse racial, religious, gender, age, and class strata.[3]

Despite these media and global conditions, people still assemble to see live comedy and experience social and emotional arousal, and are greatly affected by it. What does a live comedy audience and its desire for the intensified and engineered emotional exchange in a live comedy show represent about our culture? If live humor is a creator and signifier of community, in that it often works by the comic showing the audience *who we are* through defamiliarization (thereby assuming initial familiarity and elements of shared identity), how is there solidarity among and between performers and audiences in hybrid, global, and different milieus, and what is solidified? Do the members of a comedy audience really laugh together? How does a live comedy audience work?

Laughter Literature

These are the questions that catalyzed this collection of diverse writings, questions I couldn't find answered elsewhere, neither in humor nor theater studies, where the former largely neglects the audience and the latter largely neglects humor.

Numerous journalists have bemoaned the analysis of comedy as taking away from the joke. (On the other hand, analyzing love, sex, and romance is fine; why, in our culture, is there more at stake in a joke than in a relationship?)[4] Scholars, however, have been more confident and explored humor and laughter from a variety of perspectives, but these perspectives invariably neglect the audience and the physical experience of comedy—location, gesture, background music, demeanor. Much humor scholarship, including publications in the eminent *HUMOR: International Journal of Humor Research*, focuses on the structure of jokes, their strategies, and ethnic classifications.[5] Literary and cultural studies, on the other hand, often consider laughter and its social significance, but their arguments usually focus on it abstractly, as a form of rebellion; they do not consider actual sentient audiences. A more recent trend is to write about the appropriateness of jokes and PC-culture, but again, no attention is paid to a live listener. Humor has become a hot topic in visual arts in the past few years, and often in relation to cross-cultural understanding, but analysis is usually focused on the making of a joke in the artwork (which might up its market value). Performance studies have tended to consider pain and masochism over humor and pleasure, and most theater studies focus on scripts. Aside from a few scientific and social scientific analyses of *in situ* joke telling and laughter patterns in social contexts, there has been little study of the recipient of the joke.[6]

In Freud's oft-cited and foundational consideration of humor, the essay "Humour," he explains that the joke has three parts: the teller, the object, and the hearer. Almost none of his analysis addresses the hearer. In fact, he dismisses the hearer, classifying him (to Freud, it's a him) as "a copy" of the teller. In Freud's earlier seminal work, *Jokes and Their Relation to the Unconscious*, he describes a joke as comprising the joker, the mocked, and the recipient—two of three are audience. Freud acknowledges the importance of the audience, but does not speculate on how these two elements of audience relate to each other, nor on how they affect the joke-maker. But a comedy interaction includes them, and many layers: the two-way nature of the performer-audience interaction (including how the audience influences the performer by intervening, contributing to and detracting from humor, and even how the performer watches the audience); the relations between performers themselves (who form an audience for each other onstage); and the relations between audience members (who perform for and watch each other). Further, inter-performer relations may influence inter-audience relations and vice versa. Complex and multidirectional networks are involved.[7]

Though most considerations of humor have not addressed its recipients, a handful of theater studies texts do contemplate the live audience; however, none of these consider comedy. The late-1980s saw Susan Bennett's pioneering of the "materialist" approach. In her book *Theater Audiences: A Theory of Production and Reception,* she points out that theater is often studied as English, with a focus on the text of the script, but argues that instead, it be studied as the live and fully experienced event that it is, including consideration of the audience composition, its apparent homogeneous response, and the active relationship between spectators and performers. Bennett points out that audiences often enjoy coming to a particular theater rather than a particular play. Ric Knowles expanded her line of thinking in his 2004 book, *Reading the Material Theater,* which takes up questions of cultural difference and the importance of location and material pragmatics, including backstage, rehearsal, and reception spaces.

In a different strand of theater studies, Herbert Blau's 1990 text *The Audience* also considers live theater audiences, questioning the meaning and possibility of the heterogeneous audience group in postmodern culture, suggesting that this decentered group comprises decentered subjects, and highlighting the complex dynamics that occur in the live transmission of a theater piece. As Blau argues, the contemporary audience is an intensified representation of a heterogeneous group, and it always was—we are falsely nostalgic for a community that never existed: theater always emerged from difference. Blau expounds that contemporary life is like theater in that it is a constant performance, thereby bending the audience-performance binary. Blau argues that the audience is a constructed consciousness, held together through a mutual desire to be an audience. While his study is more a cultural assessment about the meaning of theater and audiences rather than an in-depth "material" analysis of audience dynamics, it is helpful in questioning the nature of contemporary live gathering, and highlighting the nonhomogeneous nature of audiences. Similarly, Philip Auslander's edited collection, *Performance: Critical Concepts in Literary and Cultural Studies*, also addresses the mixed makeup of an audience, and includes a section on "audiences/spectatorship," with essays about the ethics, responsibilities, expectations, and pleasures of the spectator, the nature of the audience as a group held together by its desire for a united consciousness, and how audiences are heterogeneous, genre-specific, and change over time.[8]

Finally, on a different note, this collection has been influenced by the "material" psychoanalysis of the late Teresa Brennan. In *The Transmission of Affect*, Brennan argues for the predominance of mood over thought, and the study of the physicality of psychology. One's mood, which she claims is contagious, is generally of more influence than what ones thinks or perceives, such that a person's reactions to received information are based on their emotional state rather than on the content of the information. Brennan also explores the physical ways in which mood is transmitted through a crowd, including pheromones, and subconscious response.

This collection takes into account these considerations of crowds and audiences—their material and heterogeneous nature—and marries them to the comedy audience, attempting to provide an elaborate contemplation of live humor *in situ* today, exploring the representation of affective experience set in a physical context. In bringing these "material" studies to humor studies and comedy, where emotions for the audience are heightened, where social catharsis is experienced (live comedy is often the sole media for the articulation of group anxiety—for years, the stand-up stage was where talk of a fear of a terrorist attack on London was heard), where all is more vulnerable, this anthology explores the *palpable* audience: why, how, and who is coming together for an intensified emotional event? The essays examine the nexus of audience/performer social dynamics that play out in the comedy room as well as the meaning of a comedy audience in today's media-entrenched, capitalist, and global culture. Unlike those who have explored the joke and its maker, this book aims to explore an anthropology of the listener/viewer, considering how the teller and receiver affect each other, and the short-term transmission of emotions among strangers.

Figure 1.1 Pierre-August Renoir, *At the Theatre*. © The National Gallery, London. *Renoir at the Theater: Looking at La Loge,* the 2008 Courtauld Gallery exhibition of Impressionist paintings, included numerous canvases depicting theater boxes, including this 1876-77 painting by Renoir. The

work, and the show, explored the hierarchies and strands of looking that occurred in nineteenth-century theaters, in particular the gazing that went on between audience members who examined each others' seating, clothing, and social positions. The actual performance formed the backdrop to the primary intra-audience spectacle.

A LIVE STORY, A LOVE STORY

The culture and make-up of the contemporary comedy audience, and questions of inter-culture and emotional transmission, stem from my experiences as an audience member and cultural critic, but were most pungently raised by being onstage. As a performer in London, the audience flabbergasted me. It was always so different from what I expected, and certainly from the show before—a comic's routine is anything but routine, a set not set. Responses to jokes, character, and gesture would be vastly different one night to the next. It made very little sense. Why did the audience seem to offer a homogeneous response, and why did audience members respond more to each other than to the material, which often did not change? I could not understand why an audience with young American women, who I would have thought empathized with me (a Canadian female), scowled through my stand-up act, when an audience of British firemen, with whom I assumed I shared few reference points, laughed at each line. Why would an audience warm up to an act and then become hateful, or respond "joke by joke" instead of with constant laughter? I could not grasp why at times they were giving, and at others difficult, "British and cold," off-putting and off-put. Nor could I comprehend why these characteristics seemed to have nothing to do with the actual people who comprised the group. The audience members' response generally seemed to be less about *who* they were, and more about the particular night, setting, my shirt, the line-up, my confidence, and their assumptions about who I was.

I wanted to understand their capricious reactions, and more important, know how to mold or influence their responses. As most performers (especially of stand-up) and how-to comedy guides will tell you: the audience is everything; if they're not laughing, there's no show. You can't practice stand-up in your bedroom; audience reaction is integral to the performance. If there's no laughter, it's not a joke. There is no honeymoon period: you have to make them laugh right away.⁹ The performer relies on laughter, but if she doesn't understand the audience, how is she to ensure it?

I'm sure this sense of bewilderment was especially enhanced and articulated by living and performing in a foreign culture (which was the case with Nichol and Silverman), mainly because cultural differences and audience expectations caught me off guard. Though I ascribed to the school that what was really, truly funny, could be universally funny, I always accepted national and cultural subtleties. I had been aware that there were differences in North American and British senses of humor, having to do with expectations and what was considered normal behavior that could then be subverted through comedy (the particular element of privacy and shame in British culture, and its presence in British comedy, is addressed in this collection by Frances Gray). I had also been aware that blatant cultural differences in audience practice do make a difference to performances; i.e., British audiences drink much more alcohol (while, as Iain Mackintosh discusses, American ones eat, causing lethargy); British comedy shows often take place in rooms above pubs with neither a stage nor lighting-rig and a more casual atmosphere; many comedy shows are inexpensive and sometimes free. British television and radio (their specialty) airs endless discussion programs—Brits are used to listening to people talk sans visual effects. Further, I noted that Brits seemed to respond better to the awkward and scruffy rather than the polished and brash—they love Larry David, and hate Jerry Seinfeld.

But while I was trying to figure out how to work to these conditions, not to mention overcome overwhelming performance anxiety, other "difference" factors crept up on me. After my first series of audition shows in 2005, I was approached by producers who immediately commented upon how American Jewish I appeared (i.e., "If I booked bar mitzvahs, I'd call you all the time"). Considering that I am Canadian, and that my Jewish identity was the last thing on my mind and in my set, this left me flummoxed. I came to realize that Jews were not in the public eye in Britain, and rarely on television "out" as Jews, as apparently, I had been.¹⁰ I became aware I was being taken by the audience for something that had not been my intention to convey. I saw what the other saw of me, became self-conscious, and wondered even more about the audience and what it wanted. How would this new information about their impressions of me feed into my act and impressions of them? Did it matter what they saw in me, could I play to it, and should I? What else did I *not* know? I did not know if every British audience had the same expectations and presumptions, and continued to perform in a haze, seeking guidance, like someone who is dating and desperate to understand why her date didn't email back. I felt like I had cultural autism.

I became fascinated by this audience, this other, that behaved in ways I could not always control nor comprehend. I studied repeated elements of audience behavior, and began to realize certain things: a comic needs for the front row to laugh, and needs to match the energy of the room. I also began to think about relationships and intimacy practices. The English are very private; they don't discuss success and are self-deprecating in an emotionally covert way. As Jane Walmsley characterizes in her brilliant book *Brit-Think, Ameri-Think*, American comedians present themselves as the only sane ones in a crazy world, even if the joke is ultimately on them, whereas Brit comics present themselves as the crazy ones in an otherwise ordered world (121–126). Performing onstage, and conducting my intensified anthropological investigation, helped me begin to understand the culture I lived in and how I was seen in a foreign mirror. In many ways, stand-up is like a first date between the audience and performer. It is part casual, part rehearsed, an attempt to connect, perhaps to show off. Sometimes it's impassioned, sometimes it's cold.

The "love" between actor and audience is often considered to be a false love, an attention the actor *needs;* the need is downgraded, characterized as debased, even abject.[11] But of course, the audience is involved in the love relationship too, and, as suggested by Eric Fromm, love is an activity, a giving, a verb. "Love" can be seen as the process of understanding and accepting difference. On the other hand, there is also "hate" for an audience, a subject which is less handled by scholars. The comedy encounter is an intense one, and in ways, an intensely aggressive one, as can be seen by its rhetoric: the comedian who "dies," "kills," and "storms." The two-way and ambivalent performer-audience emotional experience is real, and part of the complex performance dynamic that includes identity politics and cultural expectations, as well as the different layers of performer-audience inter and intra relations in the room.

In commissioning this collection, I considered the comedy audience and the whole comedic encounter—where there is a degree of codependence, as a joke *needs* a laugh in order to be a joke—as a site in which love and hate are played out. It is a space where the intense emotions that accompany every intimate relationship (including anxiety, prejudice, and ambivalence) are expressed in an amplified and artificial way so that they are both dangerous and ultimately safe. This might be similar to the more oft academically considered relationship between the psychoanalyst and the analysand, experienced inside the analyst's consulting room. Here, the transference occurs—the patient projecting their problematic feelings onto the therapist (and the counter-transference, when the therapist does the same to the patient)—inside a safe and contrived space.[12] This book does not necessarily look at the therapeutics of performing as catharsis, nor the mic as couch, but more, the two-way constructed intimacy that takes place in a very particular physical location. By looking at comedy this way, we can learn about performer-audience relations including the needs and desires of the audience, and as such, consider the meanings of audiences in today's cultures, and what audiences might tell us about these cultures—their ways of loving, hating, relating—especially in mixed urban locales. How do comedy audiences serve as representations of culturally specific practices of intimacy, and how do they help form culture, and perhaps, new types of intimacy? In some ways, I am focusing on a magnified emotional scenario of trust, desire, and disdain in order to ask about intracultural intimacy and aggression, about how to really accept and deal with the other, about difference at work.[13]

WELCOME TO THE BOOK

From the dual position of "comedemic," I have selected the writings in this text, the acts in this show, which themselves span a wide range of disciplines and geographical, professional, and cultural locations, in order to probe the live comedy audience from all sides. This anthropology of the audience weaves together the following thematic strands:

1. The material and physical experience of comedy and of the listener, and of the state of audiencehood, looking at place, time, gesture, and setting as part of the comedy encounter; and, along with this, the ways mood can physically spread in a crowd.

2. Meanings of the live group today, sometimes in relation to secondary or mediated audiences, or the audience that spills onto the street after the show.
3. Interculturalism, and the consideration of how humor, audience practices, listening practices and intimacy practices differ across cultures (be they defined in national, class, gendered, or racial terms).
4. Love, hate, responsibility, rebellion, and the emotional dynamics of the constructed comedic relationship.
5. The "intra-audience" and "intra-performer" dynamics, considering the nexus of relationships that plays out in a comedy room, including those between audience members and between co-performers.[14]
6. The relationship between comedy and academia.

This collection contains the writings and "speakings" of a diverse array of professionals, mainly working as academics in universities, or comedy performers and producers working in the industry. This anthology, then, merges works from two very different worlds—the self-conscious and the crass. Though I would argue that comedy comes from intellectual play ("Life is a comedy for those who think . . ."), and that production of comedy and a thesis probably use similar critical faculties, the norms of communication in each world are different, and their professionals adhere to different language codes. While academia tends to be very careful about speaking in cultural characterizations, performers live off them, and the industry deals with them in pennies and numbers. In the comedy business, race, class, and gender is untheorized and "functional." Identity politics is not debated—it is. Both academia and comedy are ultimately investigative; they are attempts to observe and make sense of the world so as to reveal truths, but these truths emerge in different discourses, and might be thought to be of different sorts.

These discourses may be jarring when read together—academics are surprised by the comedian's candor; practitioners are bored by academics' elusiveness—but hopefully, in juxtaposition, they complement each other, filling the other realm's lacks. Shifting between two universes—the university and "the circuit"—calls attention to what is suppressed in each. What do they each, and sometimes both, use as strategy and conceal in defense? Perhaps pain, pathos? Laughter can be a cathartic response—it can expel pain, or manage agony by converting it to pleasure. Similarly, one might think of academic study as a way of organizing and controlling the experience of negative emotion and turning it into thought or theory. Academia and comedy might emerge from malaise, and function as a strategy for dealing with it. They both might be ways—albeit very different ones—of experiencing pain, not alone, but collectively.[15]

The difference in language systems was certainly jarring to me as a performer. Having spent many years in academia, I was taken aback by the unmediated response of my comedy audience. I was used to academics who responded to a paper with an obscure and irrelevant question meant to show off their own research, but I wasn't used to "Hey, d-Jew ever work in a d-Jewo?" This collection seemed to attract a breed of academics who, like myself, do practice comedy—and I often wonder if turning to comedy is a way of dealing with the repressions of academic language and thinking. We comedemics are split people, perhaps unlike classic academics, used to shifting between different audiences and as such keeping audience on the forefront of our minds.

There are different truths, and different ways of relaying them. Some of the comedians in this collection reflect explicitly about the audience, and others address the issue in creative terms. Some scholars deal with audience as a cultural representation that holds a particular historical and social meaning, and some analyze the live audience and its social dynamics, thereby shedding light on cultural practices. This book is a cultural study rather than a professional guide, but it could ideally help performers in a more abstract way. Academia and comedy are both critical, but produce different pleasures in their audiences—I hope this book will produce as many pleasures as possible.

THE RUNNING ORDER

The book comprises four sections. The first sets out a context for the live comedy audience. "Locating Live Comedy" includes writings about the space, place, history, and physicality of laughter and audiences, drawing most heavily on the "material" approach. The book opens with Alice Rayner's essay on the nature of the comedy audience. A scholar of performance studies, Rayner has worked on the relationships between comedy and morality, and has interrogated both comic and audience responsibility. In this chapter, she considers the audience's identity in a temporal framework, emphasizes the importance of timing in many aspects of the workings of humor, and opens up questions about the agreements implicit in a community.

In "Room for Comedy," theater architect and former producer Iain Mackintosh takes us through the technical requirements of designing spaces for comedy theater. He highlights the importance of the color, size, and shape of a room, and the softness of the audience's seats, arguing that every actor knows how important these things are, but few architects do. He stresses how important it is that a space be clothed for comedy if it is to promote live laughter, and as such, how an audience is deeply influenced by its surrounds, which emerge from and hold its own cultural meanings.

Matthew Daube's essay also sets a context for live comedy by addressing the emergence of stand-up in the US. Daube interprets stand-up as a reaction to 1950s capitalist mass industry—a desire for individuality and the intelligence of the individual, which is projected by audiences onto the comedian, who is "almost just like them." Through a series of case studies, he traces the development of the "casual" relationship between the audience and the comic since the 1950s, situating live stand-up as a specific art form with its specific audience.

British Muslim comedian Shazia Mirza discusses identity politics around the globe, focusing on how being a woman and a Muslim impact upon her audiences in different places. In this piece, live comedy audiences are considered for their intercultural differences.

The anthology's second section, "The Cult-ure of the Audience, and Audiences of Culture," contains essays that explore specific case studies of particular comedy productions, focusing on the audiences' cultural concerns, their cult-ish behaviors, and the cultures from which they emerge.

Film scholar Lesley Harbidge investigates the audiences of Steve Martin's live gigs, before and after he reached cult status. By considering the various ways in which Martin's audiences (or, fans) did *not* laugh at his comedy, focusing on Martin's fluctuating performance of "himself" and a "character," and analyzing the layers of interaction between performer and audience members and between audience members themselves, Harbidge dissects the dynamics of live performance in small venues versus in large stadium spaces.

Art and queer theorist Gavin Butt explores the queer audience. In his interview with the transsexual British comedian David Hoyle

(The Divine David), who hosted a weekly live "magazine" talk-show in London, he poses questions about the aggression felt and played out between performers and their audience, and between performers themselves. The interview also considers the therapeutic role of live performance, and the difficulties of culture-clash.

English scholar Diana Solomon studies a historical case, relaying how eighteenth-century British audiences enjoyed the stand-up-comedy-like after pieces to theater shows. These after pieces, which Solomon refers to as "mini stand-up routines," were tailor-made for the performers, and designed to arouse the audience; they were also usually given by women, and included direct audience address. Like Harbidge, Solomon addresses the dynamics involved when a performer—in this case, a woman—flips out of role and into "herself," and suggests why this type of performance may have been appealing. We might extrapolate from this essay to reflect upon why live stand-up, with its direct audience address, might be so appealing to contemporary western audiences—though, contemporary audiences seem to like women comedians less.

Or so would argue performance studies academic and stand-up Rebecca Krefting in her essay that responds to Christopher Hitchen's claim that women are not funny. Krefting resists traditional gendered explanations of comedy—i.e., biology or differences in performance technique—and instead, addresses the American cultural resistance to female comedians by invoking a Marxist analysis of production and economics, thereby exploring the expectations and desires of American capitalist culture.

The essays in the third section, "The Industry, or, the Audience in the Making of the Comedy Show," address how the audience forms an integral part of the live comedy show, largely from the perspective of those who work on and behind the stage.

Sable & Batalion, a film and theater-making duo who toured the world performing their own brand of hip-hop comedy theater, discuss their worst audiences, their best audiences, and experiences performing in a niche genre—how do audiences and the industry deal with unique brands? The partners also address the intra-performer dynamics of the duo, and how the audience impacts upon and is impacted by their relationship.

Julia Chamberlain, an established UK comedy promoter and new act competition judge, addresses how she "produces" a comedy audience, the work she thinks an audience will like, what goes into her curation of a show and arbitration of taste. In our correspondence, she characterizes different types of audiences from an industry perspective, and analyzes which comedians are best suited for which venues.

Kevin McCarron is an English lecturer and stand-up comedian who produces a chain of stand-up clubs across the UK, is a regular professional MC, and led a pedagogical project investigating the relationships between academic instruction and stand-up. McCarron discusses how the audience comes into play in all the stages of writing and performing a joke live.

Also considering the inevitable role of the audience in live comedy performance, Canadian stand-up and TV writer Nile Seguin presents a short comedic analysis of hecklers, and the disruptive and helpful roles they play in a live event.

For her piece, photographer Sarah Boyes staged a comedy event in Brighton, UK, and recorded portraits of audience members, laughing, pausing, bored, and leaving the club, pointing out the dramatic shifts in emotion through even a short gig.

Michael Frayn's play *Audience* is a classic British farce and comedy of embarrassments. This excerpt of the play explores the experience of audience members when watching a play, including the anxieties and pleasures felt by the writer of the piece, who is also an audience to his own work.

The final section, "Live Comedy in Context," addresses liveness in relation to other media (television, film, and the internet), and comedy in relation to other spheres (high art and literary domains). In doing so, these essays point to particular characteristics of comedy audiences—their expectations, pleasures, and fears. To several of these authors, the comedy audience is a cultural representation, a residue and marker of greater sociocultural trends.

English professor Elizabeth Klaver provides a detailed analysis of the once highly popular, but now discontinued American television series, *Ugly Betty*, and compares its televisual techniques with those of live comedy, investigating the specificity of each medium in its ways of discussing gender, class, and ethnicity, and of relaying humor.

While Klaver's essay looks at the "American dream" that attracted audiences to *Ugly Betty*—i.e., the rags to riches tale, English comedy scholar and playwright Frances Gray considers the experience of live audience-ness in contemporary British culture, where humor is based on embarrassment, on being found out. Gray reflects upon surveillance cameras and surveillance culture in the UK at large, and how the increased experience of "being watched" affects the national British psyche and its comedic output.

AL Kennedy, novelist and stand-up comedian, reflects on the differences in audiences who turn up to a literary reading, and the ones that turn up to a stand-up comedy club. She considers these audiences' differing desires and expectations in various national contexts.

Scott Jacobson, American TV writer, chats with me about the role of the studio audience in the making of *The Daily Show*, reflecting on how he simultaneously wrote for an immediate live crowd and an enormous television viewership.

Performance studies lecturer and dramaturge Kélina Gotman, and composer Samuel Godin, consider the distances between different layers of live comedy audiences. Examining the strata of comedy reception—live, live shows via film, live shows broadcast on the internet, and the futuristic possibility of live internet shows—Gotman and Godin examine how new technology and live media interact today.

Finally, the book ends with another welcome, this one addressing high art, academia, and humor. In the script, "Inaugural Speech," performance artist and UCLA professor Andrea Fraser performs her version of an opening ceremony to a "high art" event, switching roles and playing with her audience. In the preceding conversation, she describes the role of jokes in her unique brand of art-critical live performance work, in which humor is her strategy for critiquing art and scholarly institutions from within. She discusses the use of humor as strategy in the avant-garde, and offers consideration of her different types of audience members: in-the-know and naïve.

Overall, this book comprises a series of essays, or a varied set of acts, from the US, Canada, and the UK, and from an array of disciplines that's even more diverse—from the more expected performance studies to architecture and professional hip hop actors. Many of them focus on stand-up, possibly due to its current currency, or perhaps it is a heightened example in which the live comedy audience can be explored; others consider comedy theater, performance, and music. These writers likely write with very different audiences in each of their minds, but I hope as an audience you might stretch your receptions to accommodate ideas from different fields, forming a new hybrid audience. You might question whether academic pieces or humorous ones seduce or reinforce their audiences in different ways. After all, this whole collection is really a discussion about relating, empathy, and the porous boundaries between one and the other.

Finally, though I was unable to include them in this anthology, the following related subjects deserve further investigation: smiling and comedy gestures and bodies; humor and violence; slapstick and visual humor; crowd theory and theories of leadership; improvisation; psychoanalytic analyses of audience behavior and of the audience-performer encounter (perhaps as a form of intersubjective third-space); the translation and evolution of humor over time; the purpose-built comedy club; the "weak" performer and failed jokes; gendered behavior within the audience; and the history of national audience practices (e.g., why do the French call "bravo"?). Ultimately, I aimed to focus on the live audience, and the essays I chose were those that best dealt with the subject.

So, depending on whether you are at a desk/on a train/in bed, put your feet up/down/across, turn off your email/phone/self-conscious radar, turn on/on/on the lights, remember not to distribute any of these essays without copyright clearance, and please welcome to the stage, *The Laughing Stalk: Live Comedy and Its Audiences.*

Notes

1. This idea is taken from Alice Rayner, "The Audience: Subjectivity, Community and the Ethics of Listening," *Performance: Critical Concepts in Literary and Cultural Studies,* Ed. Philip Auslander (London: Routledge, 2003) 249–268.

2. Philip Auslander questions the meaning of "liveness" in today's mediated world in his book, *Liveness,* which was reprinted in 2008 with a new section that addresses liveness in the context of new media. While many of my questions about live comedy audiences overlap with his concerns about live audiences in general, Auslander's interesting argument verges on the negative, whereas the tone of this book is more exploratory. Auslander foresees the "death" of liveness, and its imminent end due to mediated technology, claiming that liveness is now only experienced in relation to mediated culture (i.e., we respond to theater based on how we were taught to respond to TV shows), and that people can just watch any show on YouTube. But I stress that they don't *just* watch a show on YouTube. People still voluntarily go out and pay to see a live show—and in particular, live comedy—and this anthology attempts to explore why, how, and to what end. Philip Auslander, *Liveness: Performance in a Mediatized Culture,* 2nd ed. (Abingdon: Routledge, 2008).

3. John Limon, whose work on stand-up is discussed in footnote six, claims that the original comedy audience in 1950s America was largely male and heterosexual. I wonder, is that still true? John Limon, *Stand-Up Comedy in Theory, or, Abjection in America* (Durham: Duke, 2000).

4. The question that journalists do seem happy to tackle is whether women can be funny—a flurry of such editorialized articles appears in some glossy every few months. This gender concern might reflect a cultural confusion about women's social position, power, and authority (where being funny is generally equated with being in control). This theme is addressed in Rebecca Krefting's essay in this collection.

5. Jason Rutter also levies this critique on humor studies, and recommends more *in situ* study of joke telling in "The Stand-Up Introduction Sequence: Comparing Comedy Comperes," *Journal of Pragmatics* 32 (2000): 463–483.

6. Humor studies usually focus on the joke and its logic (see, for instance, *HUMOR: International Journal of Humor Research*) and the analysis of ethnic humor (see for instance the work of Avner Ziv). Humorous stances and their meanings have also been analyzed in English studies, again focusing on the making and meaning of the joke. See for instance: Alice Rayner, *Comic Persuasions: Moral Structure in British Comedy from Shakespeare to Stoppard* (Berkeley: University of California Press, 1992).

Recently, several cultural studies of humor have been published. These works generally address the cultural context and conditions of humor, including PC-ness, appropriateness, and the cultural meanings of jokes, thereby invoking the audience, but rarely addressing it specifically. See for instance: Graeme Dunphy and Rainer Emig, eds., *Hybrid Humour: Comedy in Transcultural Perspectives* (Amsterdam: Rodolpi, 2009)—this book considers the humor of ethnic minorities in twenty-first-century Europe as a means of connection and subversion, and so acknowledges the recipient community that shares the joke, but only in an abstract sense; Stephen Wagg, ed., *Because I Tell a Joke or Two: Comedy, Politics and Social Difference* (London: Routledge, 1998); Sharon Lockyer and Michael Pickering, eds., *Beyond a Joke: The Limits of Humor* (New York: Palgrave Macmillan, 2006); Jan Bremmer and Herman Roodenburg, eds., *A Cultural History of Humor: From Antiquity to the Present Day* (Cambridge: Polity, 1997); and Philip Auslander, "Comedy about the Failure of Comedy: Stand-Up Comedy and Postmodernism," *Critical Theory and Performance,* ed., Janelle Reindt and Joseph Roach (Ann Arbor: University of Michigan Press, 1992)—this last text is a cultural study and one of the few performance studies texts that deals with comedy performance. The most elaborate recent academic consideration of stand-up comedy is John Limon's *Stand-Up Comedy in Theory, or, Abjection in America* (Durham: Duke, 2000), which is cited by many authors in this collection and which considers, in psychoanalytic terms, the development of stand-up comedy alongside the history and culture of America since the 1950s. Another new text that addresses stand-up, Peter Robinson's *The Dance of the Comedians: The People, the President, and the Performance of Political Standup Comedy in America* (Amherst: University of Massachusetts, 2010), considers the powerful "dance" that takes place between performer and audience in a live performance act but, focusing on the performer and his performance, does not provide a rigorous assessment of the audience.

On the other hand, humor has long been considered in feminist literary studies, mainly theorized as a site of female rebellion—humor and laughter enable aggression, self-awareness, and solidarity. Though laughter usually implies an audience, these studies focus on it in the abstract, considering its meaning rather than the setting of the act. See for instance: Frances Gray, *Women and Laughter* (London: Macmillan, 1994); June Sochen, ed., *Women's Comic Visions* (Detroit, MI: Wayne State University, 1991); Jo Anna Isaak, *Feminism and Contemporary Art: The Revolutionary Power of Women's Laughter* (London and New York: Routledge, 1996); Helene Cixous, "The Laugh of the Medusa," *New French Feminisms,* Ed. Elaine Marks and Isabelle de Courtivron (New York: Schocken, 1981); Susan Suleiman, *Subversive Intent* (Cambridge, MA: Harvard University Press, 1990); Linda A Morris, ed., *American Women Humorists, Critical Essays* (New York and London: Garland, 1994). Many of these feminist texts draw on writings by literary, cultural, and psychoanalytic theorists including Bergson, Kristeva, Rabelais, Barthes, Bakhtin, Baudelaire, and Benjamin. These theorists write about laughter, but again, usually consider it abstractly, in terms of a libidinal response, and for its revolutionary capacity and as a subversive strategy, rather than *in situ*. This "simplistic" subversive stance is criticized by Sean Zwagerman in *Wit's End: Women's Humor as Rhetorical and Performative Strategy* (Pittsburgh, PA: University of Pittsburgh, 2010), who acknowledges the importance of considering the recipient dimension of the "speech act," but he, too, focuses on the strategic use of humor by the user.

Humor has been increasingly studied in the visual arts over the past few years (including comic strips), resulting in several exhibitions and books. In 2008, London Hayward Gallery's *Laughing in a Foreign Language* examined the translation of humor across cultures (e.g., do jokes make sense in different contexts?) and the social position of the foreigner in these global times (e.g., can humor help us to understand the other? can laughter help all of us deal with global pessimistic gloom by functioning as a form of rebellion?). Again, though the consideration of foreignness implies an audience, the focus was on the art and its humor. Similarly, several recent books consider the intersection of the serious and the humorous in contemporary art, focusing on how visual art tells jokes and what kind of jokes it tells. See for instance: Sheri Klein, *Art and Laughter* (London and New York: IB Tauris, 2007); Jennifer Higgie, ed., *The Artist's Joke*, in the series Documents of Contemporary Art (London and Cambridge: Whitechapel and MIT Press, 2007). Other art historians who write about performance art have considered the "contract" between performers and audience, but not in a comedic context, and they have not considered the contracts among the audience members themselves. See for instance, Kathy O'Dell, *Contract with the Skin: Masochism, Performance Art, and the 1970s* (Minneapolis: University of Minnesota Press, 1998).

Humor is also addressed in countless monographs on comedians and particular comedy clubs and TV shows, and in stand-up comedy how-to guides (of which there are many). See for instance the recent: Richard Zoglin, *Comedy at the Edge: How Stand-Up in the 1970s Changed America* (New York: Bloomsbury USA, 2008). Humor has been the object of study by an array of psychologists and scientists who address humor in development and in animals. Neuroscientist Robert Provine's, *Laughter: A Scientific Investigation* (New York: Penguin, 2000) examines laughter patterns, and might be the most relevant to this study. Provine's work is addressed by Lesley Harbidge in this collection.

7. Freud became concerned with the issue of dynamics in the psychoanalytic relationship, and considered transference and counter-transference and the ways in which ideas and emotions are transmitted in both directions between patient and analyst; these same considerations can be applied to the relationship between comedian and audience. Further, while people presume comedians are immature and want attention or crave approval, and scholars like Limon characterize comedians as being abject, of hating their lives and needing an identity break from them, I wonder if we can't think of comedy audiences as also being abject and desperate: after all, they come to the shows. Again, they are integral to the process. The relationship is co-dependent. The dynamic is two-way.

8. Most cultural, media, and theater studies texts consider television and film audiences more than they do live audiences. For instance: Will Brooker and Deborah Jermyn, eds., *The Audience Studies Reader* (New York: Routledge, 2002). However, some texts have indeed explored live audiences. The "materialist" approach to live theater is relayed in Bennett and Knowles. Both texts draw on the late 1970s/early 1980s works of Keir Elam on the semiotics of theater and Anne Ubersfeld on intra-audience relations. William Gruber's *Comic Theaters: Studies in Performance and Audience Response* (Athens: University of Georgia, 1986) pre-dates Bennett, and argues that comedy theory needs to consider the comic theater, and the verbal and visual elements of comedy. The book, however, focuses on an analysis of plays rather than a study of audience. This "material" discussion also resonates with Giuliana Bruno's oeuvre on cinema, in which she addresses not the film scripts or representations, but the actual cinemas in which they are screened. See Giuliana Bruno, *Atlas of Emotion: Journeys in Art, Architecture and Film*

(London: Verso, 2002). A similar way of thinking also appears in the History of Science discipline, with studies on laboratory architecture. These texts focus on the space in which the scientific activity occurs, arguing that the architecture impacts upon scientific results and thinking in general. See for instance, Owen Hannaway, "Laboratory Design and the Aim of Science," *ISIS* 77 (1986): 585–610.

A handful of psychologists explore the dynamics of live performance. See for instance, Harry Levi Hollingworth, *The Psychology of the Audience* (New York: American Book Co., 1935); and Kevin Dunbar and Isabelle Blanchette, "Analogy Use In Naturalistic Settings: The influence of Audience, Emotion and Goals," *Memory and Cognition* 29 (5), July 2001: 730. A small number of plays about comedians, including Trevor Griffiths's *Comedians* and Terry Johnson's *Dead Funny* touch on audiences.

The study of the audience also appears in historical considerations of theater that were mainly published from the early 1980s to the early 1990s; for instance, there are several texts that address Shakespearian audiences, the audience of revolutionary Paris, Ancient Greek audiences, and audiences in Soviet Russia and antebellum America. A recent and relevant publication that addresses historical theater audiences is Bridget Escolme's *Talking to the Audience: Shakespeare, Performance, Self* (London: Routledge, 2005), in which she considers the contemporary English audience's interests in Shakespeare and the trend for audience interaction, focusing on the audience aside, and otherness and awkwardness in the live encounter.

A few theater scholars have explored the topic of audience participation in theater. See for instance: Susan Kattwinkel, ed., *Audience Participation: Essays on Inclusion in Performance,* in the series Contributions in Drama and Theater Studies (Westport: Greenwood, 2003).

Alongside theater studies, the focus on the live audience was also taken up a decade later in the visual arts, principally by Nicolas Bourriaud in his influential 2002 *Relational Aesthetics* (Paris: Les presses des reels, 1998). This book comments on the increased number of "high" artworks that demand live audience interaction in the museum and focus precisely on the issue of human interrelationships. Bourriaud's contemplation, however, hones in on the internet-based culture that produced this art trend, rather than on actual audience activity.

Sociologist and game theorist Jason Rutter, mentioned in note five, has written several texts on the *in situ* analysis of live comedy audience behavior in the UK (and in particular in pubs), as well a dissertation, "Stand-up as Interaction: Performance and Audience in Comedy Venues," University of Salford, 1997.

My searches have also revealed a random smattering of audience-related texts from diverse fields and perspectives, but none address comedy. These texts include Walter A. Davis, *Psychoanalysis, Modern American Drama and the Audience* (Madison: University of Wisconsin, 1994), which introduces a psychoanalytic framework for audience studies, but does not address comedy nor the dynamics of live performance; Howard R. Pollio and Charles Swanson, "A Behavioral and Phenomenological Analysis of Audience Reactions to Comic Performance," *Humor: International Journal of Humor Research*, 8.1 (1995): 5–28; Evan Cooper, "Is It Something He Said: The Mass Consumption of Richard Pryor's Culturally Intimate Humor Author," *The Communication Review*, 3 (2007): 223–247, which focuses on a particular comedian case-study; Paul Hare and Herbert Blumberg, *Dramaturgical Analysis of Social Interaction* (New York: Praeger 1988); S.I. Salamensky, ed., *Talk Talk Talk: The Cultural Life of Everyday Conversation* (London: Routledge, 2001).

Several comedian "how-to" guides do address the audience as a factor the comedian must consider. See reference in footnote nine.

9. See for instance, Steve Allen and Greg Dean, *Step by Step to Stand-Up Comedy* (Westport: Greenwood, 2000). Limon discusses the fact that if there is no laughter, then the joke is not actually a joke.

10. The lack of Jewish presence in the British comedy world and media and it's apparent "non-marketability" has been addressed in the UK Jewish media. Other writers have traced anti-Semitic sentiment in British comedy audiences. See Jamie Glassman, "Have You Heard the One About the Jews?" *London Times*, 15 August 2006.

11. This love or need for attention rarely emerges in discussions of other professions, but I wonder if a similar claim can't be made for many of them, including academia, where the student-audience can easily "fall in love" with the professor (who might indeed desire attention like the comedian does). Blau and Limon discuss this love; to both, it is debased and abject.

12. See for instance, Mignon Nixon, "On the Couch," *October* 113 (2005): 39–76.

13. Live performance as a negotiation of difference is discussed by Blau, who argues that theater never emerged from a collective impetus but from division (1–49), and Auslander, who discusses the ambivalence of the audience member who both identifies with and differs from the performer (*Liveness*, 64–67).

14. These "intra-audience" dynamics are alluded to in studies of theater boxes (e.g., the Courtauld), and are discussed in some material theater studies as well as in Blau's argument that audiences are heterogeneous. In the realm of comedy, this is discussed in Rutter and in Limon, briefly, when he mentions that Richard Pryor's audiences were divided in that black audience members and white audience members laughed at different elements or understandings of the same joke. Here, he suggests heterogeneity, but the "science" studies and theater box studies look more specifically at how audience members interact with each other.

15. Both Limon and Blau address pain. To Limon, pain is about *I* whereas laughter is about *We*. To Blau, pain is the most basic and truthful emotion. Freud considers that one function of laughter is as a means of catharsis (*Jokes*).

WORKS CITED

Auslander, Philip, ed. *Performance: Critical Concepts in Literary and Cultural Studies*. London: Routledge, 2003. Print.
Bennett, Susan. *Theater Audiences: A Theory of Production and Reception*. 2nd ed. New York: Routledge, 2003. Print.
Blau, Herbert. *The Audience*. Baltimore, MD: Johns Hopkins University Press, 1990. Print.
Brennan, Teresa. *The Transmission of Affect*. Ithica, NY: Cornell University, 2004. Print.
Freud, Sigmund. *Jokes and Their Relationship to the Unconscious*. Trans. James Strachey. London: Penguin, 1991. Print.
—. "Humour." *The Standard Edition*. Vol. XXI. Trans. James Strachey. London: Hogarth, 1961. Print.
Fromm, Eric. *The Art of Loving*. New York: Harper, 1956. Print.
Knowles, Ric. *Reading the Material Theater*. Cambridge: Cambridge University Press, 2004. Print.
Walmsley, Jane. *Brit-Think, Ameri-Think: A Transatlantic Survival Guide*. New York: Penguin, 2003. Print.

1 Creating the Audience: It's All in the Timing

Alice Rayner

Alice Rayner is professor of critical theory and dramatic literature in the drama department at Stanford University. Her research interests include the phenomenology of theater as well as comedy, genre theory, rhetoric, psychoanalysis, and hermeneutics in the analysis of texts and performance. Published books include *Comic Persuasion* (University of California Press, 1987), *To Act, To Do, To Perform: Drama and the Phenomenology of Action* (University of Michigan Press, 1994), and *Ghosts: Death's Double and the Phenomena of Theatre* (University of Minnesota Press, 2006). She has written several essays on the ethics of listening and the morality of comedy.

The good teacher writes a thoughtful caution in the margin of the student's paper: "What do you mean by 'audience'? Be specific." The student persists, perhaps resists: "You know—THE audience, ANY audience," though what she probably means is the collective version of ME. This good teacher's demand to dismantle the assumptions behind any projection of just what *the* or *an* audience might see, hear, think, feel, believe (especially believe), or more generally perceive, much less *be*, is a perpetual tug against unfortunate students' naivety. She wants naturally to keep her students from imagining an audience as the collective version of themselves. Yet the habit of imagining a collective response persists.

In 2001 Richard Wiseman, a professor of psychology at the University of Herfordshire, in conjunction with the British Association for the Advancement of Science, inaugurated a web-based project called the LaughLab to discover the "world's funniest joke." The LaughLab took submissions of jokes—largely from Europe and America, but apparently from seventy different countries—and surveyed participant responses to a random selection of jokes sent in. While claiming to be searching for the world's funniest joke, the research analyzed primarily demographic details of humor according to gender, age, and nationality. Wiseman, along with "team members Helen and Emma," who vetted the jokes for offensiveness (the "disgusting ones"), managed to collect, according to Wiseman's website, forty thousand jokes and one and a half million ratings. By these ratings, Wiseman was able to identify what was funniest to women, what to men, what to nations, and finally to discover the world's funniest joke.[1]

After the publicity on this remarkable finding there were a number of articles written in the popular press. Some years after the experiment, comedian Lewis Black on his own History Channel/YouTube, staged an encounter with Professor Wiseman. Black objected to the claim that he had found the world's funniest joke.

> It's not the world's funniest joke. It's not even close to the world's funniest joke. . . . First of all the thing about humor it, ultimately, it's subjective. What you find funny the person next to you won't find funny, and the person next to you might find half funny. And the thing is everyone is right. It's your sense of humor. . . . As much as you guys try, science can't deal with comedy.

Wiseman himself objects: "Well if you don't do what we did to understand comedy, what do you do?" Black shakes his head, looks at such a hapless, hopeless idiot, and walks off: "You go tell jokes." This is followed by a man holding his hands over the ears of a young boy, telling the joke: "Why was Helen Keller such a bad driver? . . . Because she was a woman." The boy doesn't get it. Who in the audience cringes? Which is the joke there: about Helen Keller, about blind people, about women, about cruelty and tastelessness, or about people who tell tasteless dumb woman jokes?

Research via YouTube is a suspect, but the performance of Black's objection—of the comedian to the scientist—points toward what in other terms (or in other venues with slightly more discrimination than either the History Channel or YouTube), might most generally be described as the "problem" of the audience, which is not all that different from the problem teachers find with student references to what audiences think or feel. Who or what constitutes an audience? What sense of an audience distinguishes the specialized interests and criteria of the social scientist from those of the stand-up comic? Similarly, what justifications belong to the teacher, who would cut out all reference to the audience, and the student who refers all things to the audience?

To take a position on audience, whether of *the* or *an* audience, is already to posit a very specific model of communication and reception. That is, many of the difficulties in identifying, pleasing, constituting, or otherwise accounting for the person or group of people who attend to one's speech arise from the image of the audience as the target, even the end point of a performance. In this model, an audience is the object of the speaking: the ear, collective or individual, implicit or explicit, at which the joke, the speech, the act, is aimed. As an object, the, an, or *some* audience is the proper concern of social science for certain kinds of data (who laughs at what), of politics for certain kinds of appeal (what words or images raise fear or sympathy or concern and, especially votes), as much as it is of comedy (what jokes work in which town, for which kind of person). At that point, the comedian becomes another kind of social scientist with radically different measurements of both the joke (a bomb, a giggle, a gut-buster) or the audience (they were dead tonight). Both the social scientist and the comedian target an audience on the basis of a certain *ethos* where attitudes or habits, feelings, perceptions, or assumptions produce what is known as the *character* of a community, a nationality, a gender, an age. From such notions of character, which include gender, age, nationality, and/or community, further assumptions, prejudices, or identifications become what Judith Butler calls the "sediments" that constitute identity. Out of that sedimentation comes the ethos that inaugurated concern or interest in the first place. The demographic details that describe that community, however, can certainly be statistically and usefully correct, but they do not necessarily take up the more difficult and elusive sense of the way perceptual habits and value systems intersect to generate the character of both individuals and groups. Indeed, character itself might well be considered to be a retrospective identification of habits and values.

What I hope to trace here briefly is the circularity in the model of objectivity that makes the study of audiences interesting, but inconclusive, if not impossible. From the comedian's stance ("As much as you guys try, science can't deal with comedy") to the statistician ("according to the data, jokes containing one hundred and three words are the funniest"[2] and "people found the jokes funniest at 6:03 in the evening, and least funny at 1:30 in the morning'"), both the joke and the audience resist the objectification that determinant definition requires. Even if the figures are accurate, the statistician there is making a pretty good joke that, if it needs explaining, has to do with what Arthur Koestler identified as the "bifurcation of conflicting codes." In this case, the conflict is between the specificity of the time (6:03 p.m.) and its correlation to the degree of humor, with the alternative sense that humor is necessarily surprising, unexpected. This is not to say that very interesting, even true things cannot be said of jokes or audiences or the system of values out of which laughter rises. It may well be useful information to know, or at least believe, that out of ten countries, Canadians found the fewest jokes funny and Germans found the most. My point is not to diminish the findings of Professor Wiseman's study—he publishes in peer-reviewed journals presumably far more rigorous than the web. The point, rather, is to indicate a relatively recent example of humor as a topic of social science that tries to identify a demographic order to humor. But I must admit I find the statistics themselves very funny.

As though to answer that attempt, Lewis Black takes the position that humor is largely, if not utterly, individual, subjective. While this may temporarily counter the claims of the social scientist, it does not account for what can be called the collective character of humor that typifies, if not identifies, a nationality or a community or more broadly, an ethos. Or, to locate that collectivity in physiology, the notion of humor as a subjective matter does not account for the contagion and expansiveness of laughter that spreads through an audience. While this may not apply to the joke told one-on-one, a laugh is diminished, if not absent, in an audience of one (here thinking of the smoke-filled night club on its last legs). At the same time, even that one-to-one relation between a performer and a solo audience may constitute enough of a bond to form a community of two.

What to make of these extremes between the broad demographics of the social scientist and the radical individuality of the comic? How does either of these extremes, or the relationship between them, locate the ethos of humor that might typify a community *or* an individual, a community *and* an individual? Or, what is the problem with choosing between them to define or refuse to define humor? One of the difficulties in addressing these questions comes from the sense that each question calls for a difference in *kind* for response. There is a category error in expecting that the stance of the comedian will ever directly address the concerns of the social scientist. Yet humor remains as a persistent gauge of character in both individual and collective conditions.

One path through the impasse begins at what might be called the acute point of laughter rather than the structure or content of a joke. That is, a joke may be made out of very specific cultural terms that are deeply embedded in history, language, place, and identity, or at a moment specific to time and place. Making a joke out of those terms, however, calls for an equally specific sense of opposition or contradiction. That is not to say these terms account for all humor, but when Koestler identified humor as a matter of the "bisociation of conflicting codes," he brought both the collective, cultural context and the individual event of humor into play. Laughter, in Koester's terms, is a kind of explosion in the brain: the physiological response to an impossible logic, whether that logic is physical, linguistic, or abstract. The collision of codes produces the response. Koestler manages to trace the model of such a collision from humor through science and into art in an accounting for the appearance of new perceptions.

In another context, Catherine Clément identifies the moment or experience of that collision as a syncopation (*syncope*) or gap that eludes consciousness (which includes fainting and laughing as well as certain ways of thinking). And the sense in which the moment and the experience are identical belongs to the anomaly that constitutes humor in the first place as the bisociation or gap. The cliché that "it's all in the timing" is a looser way to make this point, indicating not just the need to get the rhythm of a joke "right" to make it work. A well-timed punch line works not just in time but also as a relation of temporal elements. As pieces collide in the telling, the joke explodes *out* of time (as long as it's *on* time). For Koestler, that gap at the boundaries of logic and sense is generative and it constitutes the space of new discoveries. The components of the explosive device, however, are entirely variable: clearly identifiable in some cases, fully anomalous in others, appealing to biology, to language, to assumptions, to details, to daily life, to universal conditions, to history.

What does this have to do, then, with the contradiction in the identity of humor somewhere between the social collective (nation, ethnicity, community, gender, or group) and the individual anomaly (that's *not* funny; or it *is*, to *me*)? Where is the sense that humor and by extension comedy are thoroughly ethical, which is to say they belong to a specific historical time and place and therefore to the character or ethos of a nationality, a group, a community (social science) and at the same time independent of that collective (subjectivity)? Part of the difficulty in addressing the all-or-nothing range between the subjective and the collective ethos comes from the assumption that an audience is a pre-existing entity that in some sense lies in wait for the oncoming joke. At the level of entertainment there is clearly a degree of reality to that formulation. But to *think* of audience in those terms is to bypass a more fundamental relationship between humor and its audience, namely its temporality. In the notion that "it's all in the timing" lies not only a matter of rhythm in the telling of a joke but of creating an audience at a given moment in time out of the conditions of the joke itself.

Suppose, that is, that the audience is not simply a body, collective or individual, waiting to be amused, but an after-effect of the new perception created by the perceptual contradictions or logical impossibilities or various forms of bisociation belonging to the joke. In this view, the joke makes the audience, if only at the mundane level at which those who do not "get" the joke are not the audience for the joke. To put it another way, an audience is not just a pre-existing condition but also a consequence arising from the very gap in the fabric of thought and perception identified by a joke, making the joke itself a generative tool for creating an audience. This does not eliminate the validity of the premises of the social scientist or the comedian; Wiseman and Black can both be right. Identifying who laughs at what remains feasible to the extent that the demographics, defined character, or social values encompass *other* conditions that make some jokes perceptible to some people and out of the ken of others. Those other conditions tend to elude science. At the same time, the scientist's identification of an audience has to occur after the fact, leaving humor itself unpredictable, temporal, a matter of occasion, an event. What eludes the scientist and the comedian are those "other conditions" that constitute the event.

While the laughter bound to a joke can situate either a broad demographic or an individual, the event escapes in time. Even as the joke locates the collective or the individual, however, it displaces them: they will not necessarily last into the next joke. What is hilarious today may be dull tomorrow, worse in repetition. What the crowd finds uproarious, the individual finds distasteful. The audience forms as though by accident, though it is made, not found. They disappear and disperse as a community at each moment. They may re-form at another moment, may laugh at another joke, but they will be in some sense a *new* community. A joke may pull together any number of strands—from social habits or verbal games to sexual or scatological anxieties, from aggression to sympathy—but as a temporal event, content is only part of its condition and consequence. Without discounting the effects of a specific content, the temporality of humor, its coming and going, its disappearance, and its brief creation of an audience all reflect a profound instability in terms of identity, both of the humor itself and its audience. Certainly a joke requires a kind of readiness or a receptive set of conditions. That readiness, however, may simply be a matter of a tipping point of a certain build-up in false consciousness. There is a reason for the contradictory notions of an audience, and humor puts those contradictions into clear relief to the degree to which it destabilizes the continuity of what is known, what is conventional, what is perceived. Puritanical fears of humor are not so off base in the recognition of humor's destabilizing force, though it is usually misrecognized as immorality.

Laughter creates community, however temporary, but that community does not inevitably exist prior to the event that creates the laughter. The fluidity, even the loss, of community marks the connection of humor to a more radical sense of how community itself is a temporal process and not a stable entity. When, more generally, comedy as a genre integrates individuals into a social fabric, the joke extends to the illusion of temporal completeness: the happy couple is "done," however much hope resides in the moment.

Temporality, in one sense, invades the demographic, though time is never really external to either the structure of a joke or its occasion, so the invasion does not come from the outside. The temporality of a joke is both surreptitious and obvious: perhaps most obvious when the joke does not work twice. It was funny the first time, not the second and not at all the fiftieth, unless it is. In the case of the nasty joke above that follows the Black/Wiseman encounter, however, it was not at all funny to *me* as female, capable driver, sympathetic to blindness, American, of a certain age—until I accidentally laughed. The "accidental" aspect of the laugh ruins the logic that my situation will determine my response. The laugh invaded not just my sensibilities but also the demographic description of my position: of who ought or ought not to laugh as well as *when* I accidentally laughed. It certainly was not at all funny when reproducing it in writing here, and not really all that good in memory. It becomes a little better, however, when I imagine telling it to someone else, though even that would depend not just on whom I told it to, but on when I told it, not to mention on my timing in the telling. A very bad joke can be *made* by the timing of the telling. That alone is enough to suggest that the effects of a joke have at least as much, if not more, to do with time as with content. Time, in this case, perhaps any case, acts more as a function in a relationship between elements (joke teller/audience/event) than as an entity. Indeed, a major difficulty in talking or writing about time belongs to its inevitable conception in language as an entity, where the physicist or the mathematician can perhaps more usefully designate time functionally, formulaically. The rules by which language and grammar bind the functions and dynamics of temporality severely simplify the human understanding of those dynamics.

If time is as crucial to effecting laughter as subject matter and the juxtapositions (or bisociations of Koestler) within a joke, a new kind of pressure falls upon questions of ethics. From the perspective of time, a specific subject matter may well, even necessarily, be local and specific to identifiable circumstances, but in the timing, those very circumstances are what explode in laughter. When the timing is right, the laughter resists the norms of "decent" behavior. Such timing belongs to the vitality of something like a fifth dimension that is neither *in* time nor out of it. Timing is not something outside, like an ingredient added to a recipe, yet it is not identical to the terms of a joke (women, drivers, women drivers, blind people, or in the world's funniest joke—see note 1—operators, hunters, mental density, double meanings). Subject matter may very well be offensive, yet in some circumstances, even thoughtful, sensitive, high-minded people may laugh at the offense. Indeed, thoughtful, sensitive high-mindedness tends to be the very element that most forcefully explodes at a given moment. What constitutes the kinds of norms "ethics" implies turns into abnorms in a joke. Certainly Henri Bergson's notion of *élan vital* identifies the value in the abnormal turn against the constrictions of normative ethical behavior. Does this mean that laughter really is as antithetical to social morality as the Puritans fear? It probably does, insofar as morality rests on defined and definable principles. If laughter and jokes have a place within consideration of ethics, then, another kind or category of ethics needs to be identified outside or beyond definable values and relations. This makes comedy, humor, and joking, suspect and dangerous at the same time that they evince multiple dimensions in the relationships that constitute ethics.

Temporality constitutes one of those dimensions, not as an abstract aspect of time but as a material condition of a certain joining or mutuality in the pleasure of a well told, good joke. The comedian who says an audience is hot or cold, is with her all the way or just not there, indicates the sense of the difference between being in or out of the temporality to which a joke belongs. Akin or analogous to space but not spatial, tied to the understandings of a given culture or gender or race or community but not identical to them, employing norms of sense-making to make them appear nonsensical, the explosion of a laugh, like Clément's syncope, breaks into a dimension of mutuality in excess of or beyond the mutual understanding that created the joke or humor in the first place. The convulsion, the faint, the laugh: physiological responses both outside and within the usual four dimensions. This dimension, whose evidence is laughter, rests within the mundane, normal world, but fractures it from within, resting unquietly in both utopian ideals and totalitarian rigidity, whose extremes determine the range of politics and religion, sexuality and decorum, automatism and chaos, which are the home fields as much of jokes as of ethical distress. Content or subject matter can doubtless identify the specific historical, social, and political circumstances in which a joke operates. The hunter's joke would make no sense where cell phones are not ubiquitous. There is no question here that content is conditional to humor, but while the content must certainly cause laughter, and it certainly identifies the mutual understanding between a joke and its audience, content does not sufficiently explain why timing is the crucial detonator for a laugh and why a joke needs the formal devices of time.

Anyone who has had to explain a joke knows the sense of failure in making a connection to her listener. Some cross-cultural impasse may well account for that failure, but just as likely the timing of the joke was off and the explanation, while clearing up confusion, carries no punch. When the timing is *on*, a bond between joke teller and audience intensifies, at least for the duration of a laugh. Not a long time, to be sure, but duration is not the issue. The language of laughter, as many have pointed out, is consistently violent: the punch line, the knockout, a killer, dying with laughter, exploding with laughter. That language does not exactly suggest a particular *bond* between two people as much as an attack. Without necessarily denying the element of attack, especially in the relationship between a stand-up comedian and audience, I suggest the violence is not between the joker and audience but within the structure of the joke that explodes or tears apart the fabric of cognition. The explosion may well reduce to some physiological explanation, to the sense of release, even to a sense of discovery of the new territory that interests Koestler. My focus here is rather on how the temporality—or rather a disruption of temporality—creates the impact, the instant that one gets the joke and the explosion of laughter blows a hole in the specifics of circumstances. What surrounds that hole may be fully explained, but the explanation stops short of the event. The temporal dimension—the sudden and surprising grasp of humor—rises from within a structure, yet also escapes the constraints of temporal sequence as though coming from outside time. It is as difficult to step outside and identify the onset of laughter, as it is to name the *now* of the present, yet each is existentially actual. The contradictory logic of such now/not now, of the immeasurable present, does a certain kind of violence to ordinary time frames. Yet that moment, perhaps measured at best in nanoseconds, forges a bond of community in excess of the shared assumptions that created the joke in the first place. That is to say, the community of a joke forms around such temporality even while it is attached to shared identifiable ethos. The excess of laughter, peculiar to human interactions, constitutes a unique dimension of community formation where standards of mundane behavior and perception may be suspended, altered, undermined, ridiculed, or otherwise dismantled. Such descriptions of what happens, however, can only come outside or after the event. The temporal dislocation of laughter suspends thought, but locates a unique pleasure that in some sense relieves the burdens and constrictions of ethical behavior. In this sense, a community forms without an identity as the consequence of the shared event in the empty temporality of laughing.

At this level of formation, the community is clearly short-lived and unsustainable. The specific absence of duration, however, uniquely constitutes the element of laughter that is unapproachable. I realize pointing to such a duration-less event may suggest I imagine all laughter is fundamentally the same, when that is far from my intention. Indeed, a useful exercise would be to identify a taxonomy of laughter as an index of social relations. Much laughter is at least partially intentional: the polite laugh that says I know what you mean; the more polite laugh that says I won't bother to correct your ridiculous position; the chuckle that says I like you in spite of your bad joke; the dismissive laugh of being charmed, or flattered, or pleased; the derisive laugh that says you *are* ridiculous; the desperate laugh of extremity; the dry laugh of absurdity (as in Beckett); the laugh of exhaustion that approaches tears. None of these can be dismissed as irrelevant. But I have been looking more specifically for the medial territory, which is more like a vortex, between claims for some kind of universal laughter (via the world's funniest joke) and the subjective response to humor, and have had to resort to imagining an atemporal space that both employs and dissolves each of these extremities. Such an atemporality, however, is merely a break in the flow of time and perception that are radically time-bound, specific to both a unique individual and a general demographic. Like a vortex, the non-conscious element of laughter pulls in both elements and turns them into non-contradictory opposites. The temporality of laughter, and in particular the unintentional, surprised laughter, may offer something more to the understanding of time than it does to the understanding of what is or is not funny, for what is or is not funny depends fully on time and timing and it is through such timing that communities come and go, endure and dissolve, cohere and fragment. To imagine anything as time bound as humor as anything but temporal is to arrive at the classic Monty Python skit about the discovery of the world's funniest joke, which is so funny that anybody who hears, speaks, or reads it dies laughing. Many die until the war office—this happens during World War II—figures out how to have it translated, one word at a time, into German. Broadcast or shouted out to German troops by the uncomprehending British, the joke turns into a weapon of war, killing legions of the enemy without a shot fired. Such is the logic of the world's funniest joke: impossible, absurd, ridiculous, and very funny.

Notes

1. Two hunters are out in the woods when one of them collapses. He doesn't seem to be breathing and his eyes are glazed. The other guy whips out his phone and calls the emergency services. He gasps, "My friend is dead! What can I do?" The operator says, "Calm down. I can help. First, let's make

sure he's dead." There' s a silence, then a shot is heard. Back on the phone, the guy says, "OK, now what?"

According to Wiseman, "The joke is interesting because it works across many different countries, appeals to men and women, and young and old alike. Many of the jokes submitted received higher ratings from certain groups of people, but this one had real universal appeal."

2. Perhaps finding this funny identifies me as an academic. See LaughLab Fun Facts at www.richardwiseman.com.

WORKS CITED

Wiseman, Richard. "The Winning Joke." LaughLab. Web.
Wiseman, Richard, and Lewis Black. "The World's Funniest Joke." YouTube from The History Channel. Feb 19, 2008. Web.

2 Room for Comedy

Iain Mackintosh
(in conversation with Judy Batalion)

Iain Mackintosh is a UK-based theater historian, designer of theater space and former theater producer. He has designed new theaters, restored old theaters, written essays and books, and lectured all over the world. From 1973 to 2000, he served as the design director of Theatre Projects Consultants. The theater spaces which he originated or in which he was closely involved include the Tricycle, the Wilde Bracknell, the Martha Cohen Calgary, Glyndebourne, and the Royal Academy of Dramatic Art's Vanbrugh Theatre. Before that he was co-founder and producer of the drama touring company, the Prospect Theatre Company, for which he took seventy-five productions to one hundred and twenty-five theaters in twenty-one countries. In 1993, Routledge published his book, *Architecture, Actor, and Audience*.

Judy: In your writing on theater architecture, you examine the factors that influence the spread of affect through an auditorium. You stress the importance of the theater space—even above other conditions, such as whether the audience has eaten dinner—on the atmosphere of a show. For instance, you argue that the audience is an active body, helping to create each night's show, partially responsible for the "anarchy of liveness," and who are there with the intention of experiencing art, but who end up equally interacting with and looking at each other. You raise the issue of how where you sit on any given night makes it a very different theatrical experience, pointing out that the relation between performer and audience is variable as well. Indeed, you introduce a term I really enjoy—"theatrical congress"—between the audience and the actors, and you talk about how place is an intensely important factor in setting the tone for that congress, similar to the setting of a romantic dinner. I want to discuss these ideas about intra-audience interactions, theatrical congress, and the built environment, in relation to comic performance in particular.

Iain: The way to begin this discussion about comedy is actually to consider tragedy. It's easy to design theaters for *King Lear*. In tragedy, the communion between audience and actor is easier to define. The role of the designer is to make sure everybody can see and hear the performer. This is probably why a lot of modern theaters feel like lecture halls. And for *King Lear* this matters less than for *Twelfth Night*.

A theater, however, is put to the test when it hosts comedy—plays, stand-up, variety—which works on a different plane from tragedy. Why does modern architecture generally fail on comedy? Comic performance requires the creation of a particular atmosphere, for which the place is absolutely critical. But I should first mention that everything I say applies only to spaces that hold more than two hundred; small theaters can be almost any shape. The biggest theaters are for spectacles, while medium sized and smaller ones are for hearing, and atmosphere is created in a different way in each.

In spaces larger than the very small, place is critical in a number of ways: color, form, and the fundamental relationship of actor to audience in both the vertical plane and in the horizontal plane. Let's start with the horizontal. Everybody recognizes that certain theaters enwrap the audience on three sides. Wrap around spaces mean that the sightlines might be worse for some of the audience, but more of the audience is visible to the performer. People talk a little bit less about the enfolding of an audience in the vertical plane. A lot of modern theaters—and when I say modern, I refer to the past fifty to one hundred years—simply ensure that the audience can see over the heads of the people in front of them. This means the bigger the theater, the more banked-up the audience gets. The consequence for the performer in comedy is that he's being analyzed by the audience. He is pinned out, like a butterfly on a board, and the audience is criticizing him. Now in certain sorts of comedy, that's a good thing—but that sort is rare. In most comedy the performer wants to get a laugh, a reaction from the audience. Laughs, any director will tell you, start in the stalls, and a measure of whether it is a good theater is how quickly the laugh spreads upward in the vertical plane. A good theater—and I think actors recognize this often without knowing the reason why—has over half the audience below the eye-line of the actor. This means the actor is in control of the performance. If you look at pictures of any stand-up comedian in a large theater, you can see this. From this position, he is able to control the audience and to manipulate downward as well as upward.

In pantomime, vaudeville, or burlesque, there is that wonderful moment where we all sing, and there's some competition among the audience, between those in the stalls and those in each of the circles above. I was brought up in Edinburgh, where we used to refer to "the nobs in the doo'cots"—doo'cots are Scots' dove cots, places kept for pigeons for eating. The King's Theater in Edinburgh had nine boxes on each side. So the nobs in the doo'cots were encouraged to sing against the people in the stalls. This was just another way in which the different parts of the audience, both in the vertical plane and in the horizontal plane, were played one against the other.

Figure 2.1 Audience Seating Plan, Olivier, Royal National Theatre, London. Courtesy of The National Theatre.

Figure 2.2 Olivier, Royal National Theatre, London. Courtesy of The National Theatre.

I mention this to stress that theater is not a two-way communication between you the audience and me the performer. It's a three-way communication between me the performer, you the audience, and that member of the audience over there or up there. And the comic performer, addressing the audience, sets up that triangle, getting one part of the audience to conspire against the other. It reminds me of the situation when a man exits during the comic's act to go to the loo. When he comes back the performer says, "Hey you, when you were out there, could you hear us in here? Because by god, we could hear you out there!" That is a way of using a real experience to trigger the rest of the audience to have a laugh. And nobody dares leave during the rest of the act.

The use of a member of the audience by a performer is made easier when theaters have boxes that are close to the stage. And that, I think, is critical in a large theater, so that the performer can actually take the reaction of the person in the stage-box and use it in a way he can't use beyond the first few rows. Watch Barry Humphries milking the front rows when he's doing stand-up in a large theater like Drury Lane. And there are the masochists who like to sit in the front three rows, who like to be mercilessly examined by the comedian. A performer can't do that with a person in the back row, though possibly with a person in the front row of the circle. So there are vulnerable positions in the theater in the vertical and horizontal planes. And that is something that the comic performer uses that actors in *King Lear* don't employ in tragedy.

So, to get back to where I began, it's easier to design theaters for tragedy because the performer in tragedy wants a silent audience. He doesn't want to be barraged by them. Whether the theater works is a question that's difficult to measure. But if the concentration is tight between the audience and the performer, like in a concert hall when someone is playing a piano sonata, then you don't want interruption.

In comedy, on the other hand, you want reaction and interruption, and the performer wants to control it. And in the right shaped theater, he can do it. But in the wrong shaped modern theater, a vertical bank of seating facing you, the performer is acting at the bottom of a well, his chin is up in order to get the people at the back, and all he sees, the fault of modern lighting—and there is a lot we must blame modern lighting for—is the front rows. It's more difficult for the performer to see the audience, to control them.

Judy: So for comedy the house lights should be on?

Iain: Oh yes. The house lights used to be on. The idea of turning down the house lights only began in the early to mid nineteenth century when candle and oil light gave way to gas because with gas, unlike candles, you can dim the lights. In the music hall people were having drinks served to them, so the auditorium had to be lit. There the performer was competing against the clinking glasses as well, but he could see the glasses being clinked, so he could control the situation. And this is absolutely true, of course, in modern smaller stages where everybody can see everybody, which is why I get a sense that stand-up comedy is dying out in the larger spaces such as the old variety theaters in England or vaudevilles in America, despite the introduction of large screens showing the face of the comic which in themselves are alienating.

Judy: Should comedy and tragedy be performed in different spaces?

Iain: No, I'm saying that if it works for comedy it will work for tragedy. Comedy is the test. It was David Garrick who said that a good actor can play tragedy, but comedy is the test for the great actor. Any actor knows that comedy is more difficult. The actor can get to alpha-minus much easier in tragedy. True, to get to alpha-plus, you have to blow the roof off in tragedy, but up to a certain level, I think it's easier. That is not a reflection on the writing of tragedy and comedy, but on the demands of the performance and of the audience.

Judy: You've told us a bit about the space, but what about the furniture? How comfortable should the seating be?

Iain: I once made a joke, which I claimed to be original, that the future of theater lies in thigh-to-thigh contact. The bench seat is coming back—the Young Vic, the Bush, the Orange Tree, and we're probably going to put bench seating into the Cottesloe, which I'm working on at the moment. But that's probably a few years away. There are all sorts of advantages to bench seats. One is—and this is a practical one—you can squeeze people up. Sam Waters, who has run the Orange Tree for over thirty-five years, used to be on the door on certain nights, acting as the house manager and chief usher all in one. If he was on the door, he was good at going up to people sitting on a bench and saying, "Could you move up a bit?" and he would squeeze someone in at the end of the row. At the Royal Court when we put in new seating, we put folding arms in the seats in the stalls, like an old 1960s Buick; we could get more people in by folding up the arms.

The bench has the other advantage that if it's not a full house, people sprawl, and it looks full. The theater in Elizabethan times was much more densely packed. Any late Victorian or Edwardian West End theater probably held, originally, five hundred more people than it does today. They would squeeze people in at the back stalls, which was called the pit, and in the top two galleries. That jamming in of people means that the response from that audience comes as a whole, rather than separated. Today if you're separated by an arm from the person next to you, it's quite easy to maintain your composure when all those around you are laughing. But if you are sitting on a bench, you will probably be laughing sooner. Essentially, bench seating is friendly. This fullness or density makes it feel like group experience and is very important for comedy.

Judy: Benches are hard. Are seats too soft?

Iain: Many theater seats are too soft. I ask, what's the difference between a cinema seat and a theater seat? Cinema viewing is passive, and cinema seats are soft because you are in a semi-reclined position and whatever *you* do—eat popcorn or snog your partner—isn't going to alter the performance on the screen. The active seat, the ideal theater seat, is more complex in its design. It must have a vertical feel to it so that the sitter doesn't slouch. When we did the seating for the new Glyndebourne with owner George Christie, he asked us to make sure the seats were not too comfortable, as he thought the audience might go to sleep after having eaten. The supper interval, after all, lasts an hour and a half, and people come in for the last act after having eaten and drunk wine—hence sleeping in Act Two is a real danger.

The best thing that ever happened on Broadway was when people stopped eating before the show, but that's only in the last ten years. With pre-theater dinner, they went right to sleep, ten minutes into Act One. The Americans must have gone to bed much earlier than the English, who used to prefer to eat after the show. People were amazed transferring a show from the West End to Broadway: all these people had eaten first and they were always in danger of falling asleep.

But back to seating. As you go up in the vertical plane of the theater, the actual posture of the body changes, so the seats need to be an inch and a half higher than at the lower levels in the stalls because the legs are at a different angle. The seat back needs to become progressively more vertical as you go up in the space to make it more comfortable for you to look downward. Comfort isn't just floppiness, comfort is what helps the posture of the body so you don't wiggle.

Judy: So ideally one wants a seat that's comfortable, but not too comfortable.

Iain: Yes, that's the issue.

Judy: We've talked about geometry and seating, but what about color? Many theaters are black rooms. Does black work for comedy?

Iain: The great revolution in theater architecture, which started in the 1870s going up right to the present day, is founded on the fact that people misunderstood old theaters. The revolutionaries thought that all the different theater levels were for keeping the classes apart. They were, in a sense. A West End theater had three or four doors, a separate box office for each area of the auditorium. The classes were kept apart at the entrance and in the bars and lavatories, but they all met in the auditorium itself. The Modern movement looked at all these levels, and the gilding everywhere, and thought it decadent and redolent of class. They thought art was more serious, and so one should concentrate on the art. The theater should have only one entrance, fair enough, but it should also have its auditorium stripped of adornment, painted black or a single neutral color and reduced to a single level, possibly with an additional single balcony at the far end of the room rather than the two, three or even four encircling tiers of old theaters.

Also, the scene designer, right up to the present day, wants to show off what he contributes, and he prefers a black surround to the stage. Go into any school of stage design in Europe, and you will find rows upon rows of black-modeled proscenium arches. The designers then take this black frame, this thick black picture frame, and put designs behind it. Now, there's nothing worse than a thick black frame to separate what's onstage from the audience. People used to think it was the physical shape of the proscenium frame that did this, but that's absolute nonsense. The old decorated proscenium arch was just a continuation of the auditorium. The way the light hit the proscenium frame in the old days, as opposed to the cut-off you get today, meant that it actually brought the performer and the audience together. It's the blackness or darkness of the modern frame that is the problem.

I vividly remember going to a conference in Munich in 1977 and hearing a German behavioral scientist—Richard Külle—reporting on his experiment in which he measured a response that he called "crying and laughing." He took control subjects, put them in a black and concrete room for a quarter of an hour, and then exposed them to the stimuli of a performance and measured the response of the brain. He put similar control subjects in a red and a gold room, and after the same amount of time, added the same stimuli of performance, again measuring the response of the brain. Well, he found that the people who had been in the red and gold room laughed quicker and cried quicker than the people who'd been in the black and concrete room. Every actor knows that, but few architects do.

Even in re-doing old theaters, you get architects trying to paint the color dark because they're trying to make it look like a modern theater. This doesn't work.

As long ago as in 1955, Somerset Maugham said that in an old theater, you were in a comfortable state of enjoyment for the performance, but in a new theater, you felt like you'd come to undergo an ordeal. (That's why he gave his collection of eighteenth-century theater painting to the new National Theater; the collection, unfortunately, is no longer there.) Getting the audience to relax is a critical element, and was partly, and we know this in musicals of course, due to the pit orchestra. I often say that you need both music and comedy to make people laugh, because music gets people into the right mood.

As does the décor. Old theaters now are either over decorated or under decorated. They are under decorated when the architects are pressured by the designers to make them dark. They are over decorated when the historical people come in with all their paint analyses and instruct that the theater be redecorated exactly how it was in 1903. However, the amount of light hitting the stage from the front of house lighting now is ten times what it was in 1903. So, the light bounces off the stage and into the audience, picking up all that gold, and it looks like a chocolate box of the old-fashioned sort. This is a new problem because the historians won't take into account the fact that lighting has changed, and regard the change as a temporary matter. I think it's permanent, I don't think we're going back to gas or early low-level electricity. So old theaters that have modern auditorium and stage lighting pushed on them now appear over-decorated.

The old gags of the variety comedians, performed in the old theaters, like "Don't clap too loud, it's an old building," don't ring true anymore because there aren't any wonderful tattered spaces. In the 1950s and 1960s, the old theaters were shabby and gilded, so they had a tattered magnificence about them, and as such were able to blend the collection of people inside into an audience, a rare and important tool. The twilight years of variety took place in these old theaters that hadn't been repainted for forty years. I don't think it's sentimental to say they were better, in some respects, than the new or over-restored theaters. Of course, you couldn't easily get a drink, and there were not enough loos. But tattered magnificence is an elusive thing.

Judy: What about stage design? Does that affect comedy?

Iain: Oh yes. Take, for instance, a front cloth number. You know what I mean: when a stand-up comedian or a small juggling act would take place in front of the front cloth. The front cloth wasn't the curtain, it had a scene on it—but the scene was totally irrelevant to what the performer was doing.

Do you remember a show called *Sugar Babies* with Mickey Rooney and Ann Miller? It ran three years on Broadway about fifteen years ago, and then toured America for something like four years. It was written by a friend of mine, the late Ralph Allen, who had a card index (before computers) with twenty thousand jokes. He put the show together lovingly and I tried to bring it to London, but Mickey Rooney wouldn't come—I remember going to see him when he was playing in Los Angeles—and he wouldn't come because of the IRA. I had wanted to put it on at Victoria Palace with all its association to the Crazy Gang entertainers from the 1930s and 1940s. Finally someone else did bring it to London (and Rooney did come); they put it on at the Savoy, which was exactly the wrong theater. The Savoy has that smart 1930s art deco look, and it just killed the show. I remember Irving Wardle of the *Times* describing *Sugar Babies* as "a fart in a drawing room," and he was right. It was the wrong place for the show.

In that show, I remember a front cloth number: there were four people doing a barber shop quartet—I remember one of the gags—"What are you singing? / I'm singing Paganini. / That's not Paganini, that's page nine." This took place in front of a front cloth with a street scene. The cloth was totally irrelevant to the sketch, but it would never have worked in front of black curtains. Blacks came in later. The variety burlesque shows never put black curtains on the stage—they always had painted backgrounds. It takes longer to get the audience on your side in a black room.

Judy: We're back to black. Doesn't it seem that many purpose-built comedy clubs, places like the London Comedy Store, are black?
Iain: Yes, but that's partly because in a small theater, it doesn't matter. But I hate black. Black is not a neutral color. Gray, dark brown, dark blue. But black is hard, making it too hard for the performer, in my view.
Judy: You touched on the issue of the densely packed theater space. Is there an optimum density for comedy?
Iain: Density brings up the issue of legroom. People are getting bigger—that's a problem. If you put more legroom at the front, then the people at the back are separated further from the stage by the rich punters who probably laugh slower.

I remember doing alternative seating plans for the Royal Court where variations on legroom were part of the options. In some possibilities, rows were straight; in others, they were curved; in some, there was a centre gangway; and in others there were gangways at the sides and a cross-gangway—all these were elements that we went into very carefully, because of the balance. What I'm saying is that it's not just density—it's the geography of the seating. In the circle, you follow the radius of the circle, and generally, you don't provide too much legroom; otherwise the viewer cannot see all of the stage. They've got problems with the rows at the Kingston Rose because there's too much legroom in the sides of the circles and you can't see the stage properly. It's very sad. More legroom is not a good thing. It's terribly difficult to sell that to people, especially to North Americans. We did an exercise, the company I was with, Theatre Projects, for an opera house in Toronto, and they wanted an opera house, in form, like Covent Garden; however, they specified much more legroom, which meant the distance from the edge of the stage to the center of the facing tiers was twenty feet more than Covent Garden. I didn't think the singers they had in Toronto would have been superior and thus able to project their voices further than those at Covent Garden. At the other end of the scale, people always enjoy the King's Head and places like that here in London, which are uncomfortable. You can kill a theater by providing too much legroom and making it too comfortable. As I said earlier, there is no doubt a good bench-seated theater, with comfortable well designed benches, works best.

Ultimately, though, my view is that seating should not be homogenous. If you want to pay an extra fifty quid, you should get more legroom. If the super rich want to pay for extra comfort, let them: they subsidize the rest of us.

Judy: You've been discussing North American behaviors and productions. Does architecture need to be different for different national traditions, based on the kinds of comedy that are produced, and the kinds of audiences that come to see comedy? (For example, North Americans might eat, but Brits drink.) Can you even divide audiences nationally? I don't know if this is true but I heard the best seats at London's West End theaters are now mainly occupied by Americans.

Iain: Yes and those Americans often complain that they want even more legroom. That's the problem—the legroom again. In a West End theater built before the First World War, the back of the stall was the pit, which was the second cheapest ticket in the house. (The gallery was the cheapest.) So there would be three, four, or perhaps five rows of stalls, then a wooden barrier, and then the pit. Now, if you take that back section and turn it into stalls with the same legroom, you reduce the density enormously.

As for different cultures, I had an extraordinary experience in Singapore once with a lady who was a Chinese national hero—performer of the Peking Opera in the official first rank. She was the only such Chinese classical performer who had the status of a male martial performer. She sang and did extraordinary things with her body. We were talking about theaters. China is full of what I call Soviet Cinemas—they thought different levels of audience reflected a stratified society, which they were trying to get rid of, so they destroyed the old theaters. I was trying to ask this Chinese performer what she thought about the old theaters. I couldn't get through until I sketched the courtyard form of theater, the old Chinese theaters being so like Shakespeare's Globe. Then, she perked up and said "Ah! The great old theaters, we have destroyed them all; they were much better to perform in. We miss them. How do you know about them?" Communist China in the 1960s and 1970s did the exact same thing as capitalist America: destroyed all their old theaters. So, this is not so much a geographic problem, but it's something that happened at that time.

Judy: You're saying that even though national politics might influence architectural ideals, it seems that ultimately similar things occur globally. I wonder how this might fit with the idea of different nationalities having varying senses of humor, reactions, and intimacy practices. Do theaters in diverse countries represent or affect intimacies differently?

Iain: I think different forms get different priorities in different cultures, but I don't believe there's such a thing, really, as different forms for different countries.

The model for many modern European theaters was Epidauros, which was considered to have had the most wonderful acoustics. Many people advocated reproducing the form of this theater—they claimed the acoustics would be wonderful. The Olivier was the answer to that. The acoustics there are not wonderful. They spent years trying to improve the sound. Better acoustics were achieved for a recent production of *Much Ado About Nothing* by building reflective walls in the middle of the stage to reflect the downstage voices, and by the performers performing right out almost in the house. I heard laughs coming in from the circles, which I had never heard there before.

Judy: In 1993, you wrote about how TV, with its close-up to character, makes a viewer focus on the person. You wondered, then, if this trend would shift our ways of creating live performance. And I wonder now, nearly twenty years later, if television and the internet—which I would classify as extreme close-up—has had an impact on live performance and its spaces?

Iain: The people who first made comedy television work were the people who were brought up in variety. Nobody's really rivaled Morecombe and Wise, have they? That is variety taken to the screen, without any sort of alteration to the fundamental style except that we're all in a good seat. As for other sorts of comedy, lighting has corrupted a lot, almost as much as the laughter machine. But because I've never actually sat in a studio audience, I can't really comment on the latter.

Judy: My question was meant in a slightly more abstract sense. Does the contemporary viewer's experience of looking in on people's lives in a very intimate way on the screen change our experience of theater?

Iain: Yes, but much of that is in the writing. People write short scenes. To sustain a comic scene for thirty-five, forty minutes is bloody difficult. Very few people can do that today. I think the world of technology allows people to have an even quicker black out and go onto the next scene. It's laziness in the writing, really. But a good performer can cope with that.

Judy: Does all this apply to children's theater?

Iain: We have two main children's theaters in London. The more interesting Polka Theater, and The Unicorn, which I find very cold. I'm afraid the architect said to me he thought introducing color was talking down to children. I wondered if he had children himself. It's all dark blues and gray, that building, and it waits to be roughed up. In going to a big theater, I think what children enjoy is the fact that lots of other kids are there too. The last thing you want to do with children's theater is to put individual seats in. We're back to benches. But, there is also that terrible habit with mothers; they fear that little Charlie is going to behave badly, and so they interfere. But let the performers deal with it. That's what they get paid for and that's what they're good at!

Judy: My final question—ish. You had asked me to get a picture of Tony Blair. What does he have to do with comedy?

Iain: This last analogy, I'm afraid, is rather like that line from *The History Boys:* "If you want to understand Henry the Eighth, study Stalin." If you want to understand comedy, study political conferences. It's very similar, but I only saw *The History Boys* last week, so I didn't steal the idea.

There is a great difference between the modern conference hall—Brighton—and the old Winter Gardens of Blackpool. The old Winter Gardens of Blackpool were much more friendly to the right sort of politician who understood the space. Michael Heseltine was a classic example. He's spoken about performing there with the audience stacked up in front of you, mentioning that you could form a rapport with them, a physical relationship, in the vertical as well as the horizontal plane. We must compare that with the modern conference center, which has a vast unbroken bank of seating that is retractable—fortunately. So what did Blair do at Brighton? Blair retracted the front thirty rows and laid it on the flat. And then, because Blair was nothing if not a communicator, and especially to trendy young people, he moved a platform out, into the center, exactly like in a pop concert. I find great similarity between a George Michael concert and a Blair meeting.

Figure 2.3 Tony Blair at a Party Conference, *Guardian*, 28 September 2005. Courtesy of Martin Argles/Guardian News & Media Ltd. 2005.

Figure 2.4 George Michael at Wembley Stadium, *Stadium*, 9 June 2007. Associated Press.

Blair ended up on a sort of dinner plate out there, with a translucent lectern for the cue devices, and he then had the audience's heads above his knee height, because they were sitting. Of course, if he'd had that platform two feet higher, then he'd have been Hitler, because then he'd have been actually looking down on people and commanding them which would not have been good. The audiences saw Blair from the knees up, and he behaved as if he was a pop singer. This was very astute. Blair was being superficial. Bloody awful. But his people knew how to present him. Political conferences are run by very, very astute people who are being paid quite a lot of money to make the leaders, like the singers, look as well as sound better.

Judy: I was just reading about how Obama's early conferences were like rock concerts.

Iain: Yes, that is rather the same. The American people took the risk with Obama, because the charisma came out, in a way that was so much more convincing than Blair.

The Houses of Parliament are better than most of these places. You can't get away with just charisma in the House of Commons because of the way the seating is arranged. The seats are not all facing one way. When a member speaks, he or she finds people are sitting to the front, to the side, and behind, and therefore the speaker cannot just manipulate them.

Judy: Do you think that's done on purpose?

Iain: Oh, yes. There is the famous occasion with Churchill. In 1942 when the Houses of Parliament were bombed by the Germans and they had to consider alternate spaces, there was a debate in the House of Commons (then sitting temporarily in the House of Lords) about architecture and space. "We shape the buildings; after that the buildings shape us." That's Churchill. He said there should not be room in the House of Commons for all six hundred members because on great occasions they could stand. The House, said Churchill, must work so that you can have a debate with only fifty people. If there were seats for everybody, you couldn't have a debate for fifty people nor could you if you all faced a rostrum for the speaker.

All these elements—color, geometry, comfort, staging, design—influence the way atmosphere is created in a theater, and following that, whether comedy will work. However, I would like to end with a quote I enjoy because, with this, what I've said about the primacy of space is diminished: "Freud's theory was that when a joke opens a window and all those bats and bogeymen fly out, you get a marvelous feeling of relief and elation. The trouble with Freud is that he never had to play the old Glasgow Empire on a Saturday night after Rangers and Celtic had both lost." –Ken Dodd, *Guardian*, 30 April 1991.

3 The Stand-up as Stand-in: Performer-Audience Intimacy and the Emergence of the Stand-Up Comic in the United States since the 1950s

Matthew Daube

Matthew Daube is a post-doctoral fellow in the IHUM Program at Stanford University. Formerly a fellow at Stanford's Center for Comparative Studies in Race and Ethnicity, Matthew's dissertation for the Departments of Drama and Humanities centered on race and ethnicity in stand-up comedy. His article, "The Case of Rabbi Cantor vs. Roscoe W. Chandler: The Marx Brothers' Ethnic Construction of Character," was published in the collection *One Hundred Years of the Marx Brothers* (Cambridge Scholars Press, 2007). Matthew has a BA in Comparative Literature and Philosophy from the University of Massachusetts and an MFA in Playwriting from Smith College.[1]

OPENING

This article holds stand-up comedy to be a historically specific performance modality that first emerged in the United States post-World War II.[2] One could, of course, apply the label of stand-up comic to any person who stands before any audience at any time (or in any era) in order to tell jokes. Respected humor scholar Lawrence E. Mintz does just this when he declares, "standup comedy is arguably the oldest, most universal, basic, and deeply significant form of humorous expression. . . . It is the purest public comic communication, performing essentially the same social and cultural roles in practically every known society, past and present" (71). Such a broad-brushed approach may be driven by the desire to justify the significance of a neglected art form, and casting a wide net can unfold stand-up's connections to alternative modes of humor and performance. However, capacious definitions also run the risk of discounting the historical particularity of those who have been most commonly considered stand-up comics.

The term "stand-up comedy," after all, only entered the lexicon in the 1950s.[3] Its rise occurred amidst a countrywide conversation on the role of the individual in a rapidly changing society, post-World War II. David Riesman's classic 1950 tome, *The Lonely Crowd*, describes an accelerating struggle to maintain individuality in a nation increasingly dominated by large corporate and government structures. Approval from one's peers became the most pressing goal, and Riesman asserts that an escalation of conformity in the workplace sparked a greater need for leisure time pursuits. These moments of personalization could generate space, in his words, "for the would-be autonomous man to reclaim his individual character from the pervasive demands of his social character" (276). Comedy's response to these characterological concerns has been to create a site in which to probe the anxiety, in the form of stand-up.

The burgeoning fixation on individuality accompanies a decline in broader social assistance. Emily Martin's 2007 text, *Bipolar Expeditions*, describes the phenomenon in economic terms, portraying how a society increasingly ruled by neo-liberal doctrines has led the individual to "creatively pursue his or her own development with the aid of fewer supports than ever before. . . . In this environment, the individual is responsible for his or her own success or failure in a high-stakes and ever-changing set of arenas" (41). Caught between the demands to conform and the pressure to express individuality, we seek a model of being that is highly adaptable. Robert Lifton calls this individual a "protean self . . . buffeted about by unmanageable historical forces and social uncertainties," leading to a "mode of being [that] differs radically from that of the past, and enables us to engage in continuous exploration and personal experiment" (1). Lifton quite explicitly connects the protean self to comedy, stating that the "protean self lives in a realm of absurdity, embraces a tone of mockery and self-mockery along with a spirit of irony, and often bathes its projects in humor"

(94). Stand-up comedy provides a paradigm, illustrating how the solo person can operate amidst apparent entropy with the security of an ironic outlook.

As might be expected, stand-up comedy reflects not just the specific zeitgeist but also the particular audiences, who help fashion the comedian's narrative identity via feedback mechanisms such as laughter, applause, attendance, and occasional heckling. Given that the material tends toward the autobiographical, the collaborative relationship between comic and crowd is quite intimate. This symbiotic relationship is marked by a constant fluctuation between the affirmation and negation of identity, with the comedian alternately acting as the audience's antagonist or their chosen protagonist. From Mort Sahl to Margaret Cho, stand-up comics vie to represent the audience and gain its acceptance, articulating individualism even as the public give-and-take reinforces the underlying social reality of self-authorship. The process reflects our contemporary interest in self-created individuality and helps explain why stand-up comedy has become such a popular performance movement.

The comedians to whom I refer in this essay are those I believe best illustrate the evolution of this turbulent relationship with the audience over the second half of the twentieth century. Mort Sahl was the first on the national scene to cast aside the established convention of the polished professional stage comedian so thoroughly, presenting his off-stage self as the principal fodder for his on-stage persona and pronouncing a new-fashioned ironic attitude with which to face the art of living. Lenny Bruce established the stand-up stage as a free speech battle zone for taboo expressions and the performance of ethnicity, which allows the individual comic to claim group affiliation through their articulations of identity. Richard Pryor's unprecedented work in front of multiracial audiences revealed that race had always been a backdrop of American comedy and audience relationships in performance. Roseanne Barr punctured stand-up comedy's glass curtain by directly addressing misogyny, briefly hinting at possibilities of a gender revolution in the form before exiting the stage for the greener pastures of the television sitcom. Margaret Cho attempted the same transition but—possibly due to the triple pressure of race, gender, and sexuality—found herself spurned by the mass market and compelled to return to the more intimate audiences of stand-up comedy. Considered together, these comics demonstrate that stand-up comedy is centered on the joint narration and identity created in the space between performer and audience, a focus that emerged in the 1950s but has been in a constant state of evolution.

Out of the Audience: Mort Sahl

More than any other comic, Mort Sahl (b. 1927) pioneered stand-up comedy as a platform for the individuated everyman. Before the latter half of the twentieth century, the United States lacked specialized venues for the performance of comic monologues. Rather, there was an assortment of forums, from vaudeville to burlesque, and solo joke telling appeared onstage alongside songs, skits, dancing, juggling, magic, animal acts, and more. Jokesmiths tended to ply multiple show business trades—e.g., Jack Benny played the violin, Fanny Brice sang, and Sammy Davis, Jr., a prime example of a Chitlin' Circuit veteran, could sing, dance, play music, tell jokes, and do comic impressions. Some comedians toyed with a façade of the personal—think of the married couple George Burns and Gracie Allen playing a married couple—but their jokes remained generic and professional, lacking stand-up's affectation of non-professionalism and seeming dependence upon the specifics of performers' daily lives off stage.

Stand-up distinguishes itself from previous structures of comic monologues largely through this focus on the non-performer as performer—or, alternatively, on the performer as non-performer, engaged in the public construction of the private self.[4] When Sahl premiered in December of 1953 at the San Francisco nightclub the hungry i, his casual dress and conversational style signaled a sharp break from the traditional tuxedoed nightclub comedian. Donning a sweater, Sahl consciously evoked the guise of a graduate student from neighboring Berkeley. The conspicuous newspaper tucked under his arm indicated an intent to occupy the audience with news of the day, and he embraced a colloquial tone more suited to that of a family seated around the kitchen table than that of a professional entertainer and his middle class audience. Sahl substituted jokes about current events and ostensibly private experiences for the then standard target of mothers-in-law.

This allowed for a closer relationship with the audience, predicated on a conversation in the present, and topical enough to include events of the moment. His first album, *The Future Lies Ahead* (1958), opens with references to the low ratings received by the press conference held by President Eisenhower just a day before the performance. Teasing both the President and the taste of the nation, Sahl tells his audience: "and, uh, he made a speech last night, which got a '7' on NBC, that says . . . right? And uh . . . and *Zorro* got an '18'?" Public sentiment (as measured by market share) had become more important than either Eisenhower or *Zorro*, and an era that measures opinions so meticulously conjures comedians who do the same.

Sahl engages the audience as silent partners in a comic conversation. This leads a shift away from the transposable joke telling of vaudevillian comics, whose material could be delivered by any comedian with the requisite technical skill, to humor contingent on the revelations of the comic's stream of thought. As can be seen in the extended opening from side two of *The Future Lies Ahead*, Sahl simulates the concatenation of free association:

> I'm kind of nervous in general about the army, anyway, having been in the National Guard, and I think that you'll find, uh, college kids have really gotten off the army thing because, uh, during World War II everybody was really hot for the program, you know. And there, you know, I wanted wings, everybody was out of their minds. Or everyone was out of *his* mind. Gotta watch that. And uh—That's a sort of kind of sloppy habits, collective noun, isn't it? Well, even though the Russians are ahead up there, we may lose the battle for language here. So, anyway. Right, that's for you English majors, because they have nothing else in life. I know, so, I, I did that, too. Anyway, a little later, if there are enough college people here, I do all the jokes about statistics. I have a lot of offbeat non-commercial jokes about a course I took at Cal once called Statistical Analysis. And there was a guy in the course who used to make up all his computations and he never used sigma. He used to use his own initials, be—right, cause he was a standard deviation, that's all I was going to say. Alright, so, anyway, I, so, it's . . .

Within a few scant minutes, Sahl's stream-of-consciousness approach accommodates the Cold War, leading political figures, his own service in the National Guard, his time at college, and a meta-commentary on the use of English. The closest Sahl gets to a traditional joke is the pun on standard deviation, after which he goes on to discuss his radio show, his apartment, touring with jazz pianist Dave Brubeck, the NAACP, the AMA, a recent bank robbery committed by veterans, and more. More than an anonymous jokester, Sahl shares his interior monologue with all onlookers. By adopting colloquial speech and mimicking the mannerisms of an audience member, his speech full of hems and haws and stuttered repeating phrases, Sahl both plays the part of a man on the street speaking his mind and *is* that man.

With the possible exception of the trick rope artist, star satirist, and Hollywood actor Will Rogers (1879–1935), no American comic monologist had cut such an intimate figure onstage. Both men spoke as outsiders, closer to the crowd than high society. However, Rogers, while undoubtedly an influence, did not weave his personal life into public material to the degree done by Sahl, who includes anecdotes from his actual dating life alongside opinions on Vice President Nixon's foreign travels. This is a bold move for an era when, as Gerard Nachman attests, "the mere idea of a stand-up comic talking about the real world was in itself revolutionary" (51). Even more radical and influential is that Sahl situates himself front and center, calling into question whether the so-called real world ends at the stage's edge. With Sahl, the comedian becomes an everyman, not in the abstract, but as an actual next-door neighbor. As Joan Rivers puts it, "Audiences nowadays want to *know* their comedian. Can you please tell me one thing about Bob Hope? If you only listened to his material, would you *know* the man? His comedy is another America, an America that is not coming back" (qtd. in Nachman 22). The content of specifically held beliefs are less important than the basic act of announcing opinions, so Sahl's stories are simultaneously unique and representative. Sahl's attempt to be both performer and audience member has been adopted by the entire medium, as stand-up comics continue to highlight the contiguity between their on and off stage personas, deliberately and consciously projecting an aura of casual non-performance, building onstage characters that purport to coincide with the persons behind the personas.

OFFENDING THE AUDIENCE: LENNY BRUCE

Lenny Bruce (1925–1966) ventured beyond addressing his audience as friends invited into the sitting room, broadening the jurisdiction of stand-up with routines built around sensitive subjects such as race, sexuality, and addiction. No US comedian has fought more vigorously to protect the comic's relationship with the audience and to establish a free speech zone within the world of entertainment. Bruce pushed comic intimacy from the realm of the polite into the impolitic, speaking as if the public stage were his private bedroom or bathroom, helping to build an atmosphere of frankness about personal issues that still pervades contemporary comedy clubs.

With great significance for the course of the field, Bruce emphasized his Jewish ethnicity. Working backward, we can see that stand-up is the descendant of comedy forums such as the African American Chitlin' Circuit[5] and the Jewish Borscht Belt resorts,[6] both of which offered their audiences greater interaction with the performers than one could expect at more conventional theatrical settings along the lines of Broadway or the opera. On the Chitlin' Circuit, black comedians grabbed the opportunity to present black audiences with characterizations of greater depth and nuance, receiving abundant feedback via boos or applause. Sonia Brock, reminiscing about Chitlin' comics such as Redd Foxx and Pigmeat Markham, states point-blank that "[a]udience participation was a given."[7] Nevertheless, the status of black entertainers remained tenuous enough for them to shy away from monologues or direct eye contact with the audience, a position Michael Miklos suggests was done so as not to rile white bookers (1171). In the Borscht Belt, stand-up progenitors such as Danny Kaye, Sid Caesar, and Buddy Hackett served as social directors or *tummlers*. These "all purpose entertainers" (Kanfer 6), as comedian Joey Adams recalls, "had to sing, dance, tell stories, arrange parlor games, plan hikes, organize the community sings at the campfire, kibitz with the fat old women and entertain in the dining room during meals" (43). There was proximity between entertainers and clientele, but the comic monologue remained one of multiple options in their entertainment arsenal. By interjecting his ethnic background into the performance foreground, Bruce deepened the ability of stand-up comedy to serve as a site of shared stories of social experiences.

Bruce highlighted his ethnicity in front of mixed audiences, testing the public acceptance of private identities in an era that rewarded assimilation. While Sahl denied being Jewish impacted his performance, Bruce peppered his act with Yiddish and developed bits such as "Jews vs. Goys" in which every item and idea in the world can be placed into one of the two categories: "Kool-Aid is *goyish*. All Drake's Cakes are *goyish*. Pumpernickel is Jewish, and, as you know, white bread is very *goyish*. Instant potatoes *goyish*." In Bruce's comedy, ethnicity signifies authenticity. The more artificial an object, the more likely it is to fit the label of *goyish*, which becomes a synonym for generic. Writer and cartoonist Jules Feiffer remarked that this display "frightened me, because when I grew up, you didn't wear your Jewishness on your sleeve, because you were essentially among enemies" (qtd. in Nachman 397). Bruce's aggressiveness was electric, but made even sympathetic audiences uncertain of whether to accept his pronouncements as dictums or fantasies. With Bruce, we see the aggression accompanying the comic's closeness to the crowd as if, on some level, the two are joined together forcibly.

The most resistant audiences were quite literally foreign, encountered on Bruce's international tours. During appearances at the London cabaret, The Establishment, in 1962, there were walkouts, fistfights, and objects thrown onstage. One evening, Bruce tape recorded the audience and played their insults back the next night, implicitly accusing the British of the sin of rudeness. Later that year, Australian newspapers expressed shock and accused Bruce of obscenity and blasphemy for a series of performances that included his infamous announcement to a Sydney audience, "I'm going to do something that's never been done before in a nightclub—I'm going to piss on you!" (qtd. in Goldman 430). John Limon questions whether this was a standard bit (15), although Bruce does not seem to have been the only comic making such threats.[8] I believe Bruce's shock value came from the way he personalized his obscenity, delivering the line as a private individual and not just as a public performer. The episode in Australia is also representative of what can occur when a stand-up ventures beyond the home front.

Bruce clearly established stand-up comedy as a site of rebellion and taboo, where the avant-garde could signal their opposition to society's structure. American audiences tended to thrill at Bruce's daring, reacting as if the comic's accusations bestowed hipness. Playing Carnegie Hall in 1961, Bruce claimed males are carnal beings who will adapt their sexuality no matter the circumstances, and announced to the audience that, as a result, "I assume that you're all faggots." The reaction indicated on the audio recording is of half-laughter. The crowd first appears to grapple with how seriously to consider this comic allegation, but laughs boisterously when Bruce reshapes the joke into a variation of the well-known men-are-pigs shtick, declaring, "You put a guy in the joint for fifteen years he'll schtup anything—*mud*." The audience finds refuge within ambiguity: "mud" can be understood as "other men" or "women," or could even signify "mud." This multiplicity of meanings works to reinforce Bruce's argument that sexual preferences are contextual, not just for him, but for everyone. That is, through stand-up, Bruce not only reformulates his own personal attributes but also those of his audience members, so that by narrating his own identity he also infers theirs.

Bruce's exploration of the forbidden cast him in the role of a free speech crusader, with audiences seeking to bask in his outlaw aura as he rebels on their behalf. At a 1962 gig at a Hollywood coffeehouse, ticket holders entreated him to repeat the routines for which he had been previously arrested. Bruce, sensing enemies in the midst, called out two middle-aged men whose staid appearance clashed with the surrounding bohemians and intellectuals. The potential police officers were booed by the crowd, but Bruce turned the tables, proclaiming: "Don't boo them . . . It's *your* fault I'm being busted. Until you change the law, they have to do what the law requires them to do" (qtd. in Collins and Skover 115). Bruce then proceeded to walk out the backstage door and onto Sunset Boulevard. Owner Herb Cohen had provided Bruce with the forty-foot microphone cord in anticipation of just such an occasion. Cohen recounts, "There he was, out on the street . . . and he was repeating 'motherfucker, motherfucker, motherfucker, motherfucker!'" (Ibid). Yes, Bruce was arrested again, but not before he showed himself to be, quite literally, a man of the streets. The audience, on the other hand, remained safely in their seats as Bruce was escorted by vice cops to the West Hollywood police station. One danger of speaking on behalf of the audience is that such representation can alleviate their inclination to speak and act for themselves. We see nowadays comedy club chains sometimes serve as sanctioned societal steam valves, where grievances are aired and thereby assuaged, only to allow the customers to resume their principal roles as workers once the work week begins again.

Bruce can be specifically credited with—or condemned for—introducing four letter words to a profession that is now nearly impossible to imagine without such expletives. However, his daring stemmed at least as much from his motifs as they did from any particular choice of words. His very first obscenity arrest, for use of the word cocksucker while playing San Francisco's Jazz Workshop in October 1961, served to warn against the public exposure of homosexuality and homophobia. Ironically, Bruce had been referencing a time he was hired to clean up the nearby Ann's 440 and replace an act the booker derisively called "not a show. They're a bunch of cocksuckers, that's all. A damned fag show." [9] Bruce later mocked the rampant anxiety over impropriety, stating onstage, "Now it's weird how they manifested that word as homosexual, 'cause I don't. That relates to any contemporary chick I know or would know or would love or would marry, you know." [10] Bruce's averment of heterosexuality was dangerous in itself for suggesting homosexuality cannot be defined (and thereby contained) by a unique set of sexual acts. The word cocksucker was Bruce's overt offense, but it was his covert exposure of a dubious sexuality that frightened his prosecutors and raised the possibility that comedy nightclubs would host a repertoire of taboo topics.

This comic mode of frank communication was viewed as a threat, and local municipalities from San Francisco and Los Angeles to Chicago and New York took it upon themselves to protect their citizens. While Bruce fought successfully to overturn all convictions,[11] the legal woes effectively ended his entertainment career and are considered to have contributed to his escalating drug use and subsequent death. The battles also begged the question of who constitutes the stand-up's audience. None of the legal complaints against Bruce originated from patrons, suggesting Bruce's speech acts threatened state control and a hypothetical society-at-large rather than actual ticketholders. The state abstracted Bruce's stand-up from its live comedy setting, substituting the sterility of the courtroom for the intimacy of the nightclub. Worse yet, Bruce was forced to argue through lawyers, who disallowed him from presenting his own material. He was convinced that, allowed the chance to speak directly, he could have successfully wooed each judge and jury.

Obsessed with legalities, Bruce read trial transcripts aloud at his increasingly infrequent public performances, and in private he spent countless hours addressing lawyers, either writing letters or talking with them on the phone. Once the law became Bruce's primary audience, his personal and professional lives declined precipitously. Out of shape and drug-addled, Bruce overdosed on morphine. He was discovered lying prone on his bathroom floor, alone and absent any audience, the inverse of the stand-up comic in full bloom. His influence, however, persisted. Bruce's rampant propagation of taboo words and concepts set a precedent in favor of stand-up comics' power to challenge audiences and the wider community using their own language.

Crossover Artist: Richard Pryor

While Mort Sahl's stand-up brought the personal into the public and Bruce established the centrality of social circumstances to that endeavor, the comedy of Richard Pryor (1940–2005) called out audiences, making it apparent that the public is the personal and that, at least in the US, each individual is formed in part by their relation to race. Prior to Pryor, there were two chief strategies for African American stand-ups playing to integrated audiences. The first was to educate white patrons, utilizing humor to temper the criticism. Dick Gregory (b. 1935) was first on the national scene and employed this tack before abandoning his career as a joke teller in favor of life as a political activist. The second option was to consciously sidestep the topic of race, as practiced by the ultra-successful Bill Cosby (b. 1937), whose superstardom inspired Pryor. Aided by arriving after Gregory and Cosby, Pryor's use of personal raced experiences in front of a multiracial audience was unprecedented. As Mel Watkins puts it, his "disclosure of previously closely guarded comic referents, racially based attitudes, and cultural eccentricities that were often 'embarrassments to the black middle class and stereotypes in the minds of most whites' was untried on the mainstream stage" (544). The public encounter with this previously private racially charged material also served as the source of his electric relationship with the audience, a paradigm that remains a crowd-pleaser in contemporary clubs.

Pryor came to this modus of operation after first utilizing a middlebrow approach heavily inspired by Cosby's genial precedent. His two act career exemplifies the necessary consonance between the stand-up's personal and professional life personas, as the lack thereof led to a famous flameout at the Las Vegas Aladdin Club in 1967. In his own account, Pryor looks out into the audience, noting Dean Martin in particular, but otherwise observing an unsettling sea of people staring back at him. This rattles him, as he is unable to tell what the audience is looking at. Pryor writes in his autobiography, "I couldn't say, They're looking at you, Richard, because I didn't know who Richard Pryor was. And in that flash of introspection when I was unable to find an answer, I crashed. I had a nervous breakdown" (94). Pryor, his comedic guise, and the evening's entertainment all fell apart, simultaneously. It was a prime example of how the protean self posited by Lifton can collapse in on itself, centerless.

For Pryor, the key to rebuilding his personal and private selves involved stepping away from his white audience. Shortly after the Las Vegas incident, friend and frequent collaborator Paul Mooney introduced Pryor to Redd Foxx's Los Angeles comedy club, and it was there that he "saw black people laughing—and not just at cute shit. They laughed at the people I knew. The people they knew. It was enlightening" (98). Afterward, his humor more openly acknowledged the particulars of his upbringing as a black man. If stand-up comedy requires the performer to mine the intersection between their stage material and their personal life, it is understandable that these experiences before black audiences helped Pryor develop an onstage character that felt, to use his own term, "more natural" (98). Even so, Pryor's goal remained to get back to integrated audiences, if only for the sake of the big money.

Pryor's third album, 1974's *That Nigger's Crazy*, marked his return to the multiracial national stage and turned him into an icon. The album is remembered today as a "crossover" success, a term that followed Pryor for the next decade, including Universal Pictures executive Thom Mount's proclamation that Pryor was "the most significant crossover artist in the history of the movies" (qtd. in Williams and Williams 10). But Pryor's example begs the question of whether it is necessarily the artist who crosses over in such cases. Given that this recording was made by Laff Records, with a primarily black audience in mind, we should consider that it might have been the white audience members who entered into Pryor's world, with his individuation of race allowing for a cross-cultural meeting point.

It is remarkable how clearly the dynamism of Pryor's audience relationship comes across on his albums, considering that comedy records cannot recreate the live event, and only serve as documents of performances. Pryor begins *That Nigger's Crazy* by voicing audience thoughts before they have a chance to settle themselves: "Thank you. Good evening. Hope I'm funny. Yeah, cause I know niggers ready to kick ass. [Mimicking an audience member:] 'Um, you'd better be funny, motherfucker.'" Greeting specific audience members, he establishes personal connections with rapidity:

> [Addressing specific audience members:] How you doing? Good, good. Did, did you want a drink? Uh, waitress? Waitress? No, let's see, the waitresses are working as fast as they can, but see, you niggers have funny orders. [Mimicking audience members:] Uh, give me a 'cardi and orange juice, and, uh, coke on the side. No, wait, change that! Give me two—what you want, baby? Bring my old lady a champagne cocktail, with a cherry twist. Piece a lemon. Piece a lemon? Wait, bitch, I wasn't through! Piece a lemon, and some turtle soup.

Pryor does not invite us into his world so much as he makes himself at home in ours, an uninhibited visitor entering the commons, commenting on the habits of those he visits even while revealing his own idiosyncrasies.

The start of the landmark 1979 concert film, *Richard Pryor: Live in Concert*, exemplifies how Pryor continues to call out audiences even after becoming a comedy superstar. The show begins with him taking the crowd by surprise—an intermission had followed singer Patti LaBelle's opening act, and a number of concertgoers have not yet returned to their seats by the time he strolls onstage. Pryor acknowledges this, telling those already present that he intends to "wait for the people to get from the bathroom. People in there pissing now." He mimics an audience member complaining while at a urinal, "Wait, the shit done started. Damn." Pryor then addresses an individual walking by the lip of the stage, before looking at the incoming audience and declaring: "[w]hite people. This is the fun part for me, when the white people come back from intermission, and find out that niggers done stole their seats. [Imitating a stolid white person:] Weren't we sitting here, dear?" It is a mark of his supreme technical prowess that he can create the intimacy of a club while playing a concert hall. By marking his audiences racially, Pryor reverses the tradition in which the performer plays the object, forcing audiences to identify themselves as audiences, making them self-aware of their subjecthood. He takes Bruce's model of challenging the audience and expands it to incorporate onlookers for whom the particular comic would traditionally be considered an outsider.

Rage Reversal: Roseanne Barr

Sahl, Bruce, and Pryor are exemplars of comics for whom the stand-up formula functions, but the notion of the stand-up comic as audience representative falters when we recognize that male comics dominate the main stage to an extraordinary extent. This raises the question of to whom this intimate exchange between comic and audience is available—which comics are allowed to present their selves, and what role do audiences and critics play in this determination? Given stand-up's capacity to tackle social issues that are both national and personal, one might have expected a gender breakthrough similar to Pryor's precedent-setting confrontation of race, but when it comes to female performers, stand-up has been a let-down. Visit a typical comedy club on a weekend night and one tends to see both men and women in the audience, but odds are high the performers will be primarily men. The relative dearth of major women stand-up comics is particularly startling when one considers the amount of stand-up material that revolves around gender stereotypes. In contrast, the fields of music, movies, and television all boast a greater number of female stars. The most successful female stand-ups have left their strongest mark in other media, including Joan Rivers guest-hosting *The Tonight Show* in the 1980s, Roseanne Barr's groundbreaking sitcom in the 1980s and 1990s, and Ellen DeGeneres's sitcom and talk show in the 1990s and 2000s.

The most common explanation for stand-up's fraternal cast has been its concurrence of aggression and power. Philip Auslander wryly assesses, "a performance genre that apparently depends on the dominance of the audience by the performer through phallic assertion does not seem a promising candidate as a medium for women's expression" (318). Many practitioners agree with critics and theorists on the subject. New York comedy club owner Cary Hoffman expresses views widespread in the industry that "[s]tand-up comedy has a lot to do with control and power. And most men seem to exercise it more easily than women" (qtd. in Horowitz 4). This precept suggests a sufficiently aggressive female comic could achieve superstardom on the stage, but this has yet to happen.

Resistance to female comics comes from multiple fronts, from club owners to network executives, and from agents to audiences. Eddie Brill, who books comics and serves as the warm-up act for *The Late Show with David Letterman*, speculates that it is the audience in general and the male audience in particular who spurn potent women, stating, "My gut tells me that society doesn't like to see a woman in power, and standing on a stage [telling jokes] is a powerful position . . .

Some of the best comedians on the planet are female. But a lot of men are afraid to laugh at a woman. It sometimes can turn insecure men into even more insecure people" (qtd. in Farhi C01). Accordingly, the tight-knit feedback loop between audience and performer that powers stand-up also provides the former with veto power over the comedic transaction, with female comics at a palpably greater risk of rejection. Studies of laughter suggest that while men are particularly resistant to laughing at female jokers, "neither males nor females laughed as much at female as male speakers" (28).

A number of female comics seek audience acceptance by propagating the humor of conventional gender stereotypes, which typically entails a heightened use of profanity and a steady dose of misogyny, frequently self-directed. A representative joke from the trailblazing Phyllis Diller reads as follows: "Most people get an appointment at a beauty parlor. I was committed. I spent seven hours there, and that was just for the estimate. The receptionist told me, 'Lady, we do repairs, not reclamations.' That ugly, insulting broad. She's had so many face-lifts, there's nothing left in her shoes!" (43). The pressure to adopt a male-centered approach comes from the wings as well as from the floor; when discussing her decision to "play on the boys' side and tell more R-rated jokes," aspiring comic Diane Cupps cites her male colleagues' disparagement of women-centered comedy topics (qtd. in Rhodes). Bruce underscored the underlying antagonism between comics and their audiences, but in order to create a friction that is generative rather than static, the comic must have reign to tap into an acerbity that is endemic to their personal and social selves, rather than emulating the anger of others. When adopting the preferences of male comics, female comedians run the risk of losing the rich specificity made possible when fashioning material from one's own life.

Of all the female comics who have attempted to storm stand-up's main stage, Roseanne Barr (b. 1952) is the most financially successful and the only to have cracked the top ten of Comedy Central's "100 Greatest Stand-ups of All Time," where she occupies position number nine.[12] Barr continues the tradition of female self-deprecation, particularly when it comes to body image,[13] but does so with a defiant twist. Her HBO special, *On Location: the Roseanne Barr Show*, contains jokes such as: "I go in this dress shop, I ask this brat, you got anything to make me look thinner? She says yeah, howsabout a month in Bangladesh? Rude, you know. I hate them types anyways, so I tell her, you know, hey, I eat the same amount of food that you eat, I just don't puke when I'm done." Barr reiterates prevailing cultural attitudes concerning women and weight, but also points to the negative repercussions of these pressures, and verbalizes resistance.

Barr's special includes a faux commercial advertising FemRage: "for that one time of the month when you're allowed to be yourself. It's pure encapsulated estrogen which enhances the natural female hormone and counteracts that learned feminine social response." For Auslander, FemRage becomes the central symbol of how Barr's "distinctive hybridization of the situation comedy and stand-up comedy genres and her explicit designation of anger as the source of her humor enable her to thematize, and thus to resist, recuperation in a way that [Gracie] Allen and [Lucille] Ball could not" (326). Moreover, Barr's expressions of rage reverberate with increased vitality because she reverses the traditional trajectory of stand-up's aggression pertaining to women. She attacks men for their physical failings, mocking men who comb hair over their bald spots and belittling the power of the phallus, announcing men can do two things better than women: "They are good at that map-reading, ain't they? Cause only the male mind could conceive of one inch equaling a hundred miles. Right? And then the other thing they do better, the other thing they do better is, like, peeing out a camp fire." Much as Pryor did with race, Barr confronts and exposes an institutionalized hostility, and spins it one hundred and eighty degrees.

Barr's meteoric rise to fame began with appearances on *The Tonight Show with Johnny Carson* and continued with her ABC sitcom. Unlike Sahl, Bruce, and Pryor, she had most of her greatest success on television and not via stand-up. Even her HBO special belongs to the lineage of television variety shows as much as it does to documentaries of stand-up such as Pryor's *Live in Concert,* given that it mixes footage of live stand-up alongside scripted video clips of Barr and two "stage" families. On television, her person and personality could be edited by a production team and diluted with the presence of other characters, particularly the ubiquitous nuclear family. This meant relinquishing some of the personal details that fuel stand-up. Most tellingly, the series omits her background of growing up Jewish in Salt Lake City.[14] We cannot know how Barr would have developed as a more fully developed stand-up persona because she found her audience support in the Nielson ratings, and not in the comedy clubs. Her story suggests stand-up success is not reliant solely on the performer; even the most aggressive comics need audiences that are open, and up to the task. It could also be that the unfulfilled opportunity for gender awareness to dominate stand-up comedy has been impeded by two trends begun in the 1980s: the cooption of comics by television before they have a chance to develop more fully on the road, and the leveling effect of chain comedy clubs.

STAND-UP IN THE MARGINS: MARGARET CHO

Margaret Cho (b. 1968) is a prime example of the protean self unable to harness its fragmentation and achieve audience acceptance on a mass-market level. In contrast to Barr, Cho has maintained an extended stand-up career, returning to the stage after a failed 1994 sitcom. In her breakthrough concert film, *I'm the One That I Want,* Cho relates her struggles against television's tendency to simplify its comedians. She tells of a writer named Gary [Jacobs] who:

> took five minutes of my stand-up comedy and stretched it out into a half hour pilot about a rebellious daughter growing up in a conservative Korean household, when the real story was that I had moved back home after a brief stab at independence, and I couldn't even live in the house, I had to live in the basement, because my father didn't want to watch me come down off crystal meth. [*Audience laughter.*] Now that would have been a great sitcom. [*Audience laughter and applause.*]

Cho and her stand-up audience share the implicit joke that the generalizing power of sitcoms waters down complicated and troubling life stories, which are better-suited for the particularity of stand-up. Like Barr, Cho was obliged to excise key elements of her performative self when transitioning from stand-up to the small screen and its economy of scale. On the stage, she manifests her individuality through narratives expounding on life in America as experienced by women, non-heterosexuals, and people of color. In the mass market, her narrative identity continues to be perceived as overly provincial, preventing her from standing in as an everywoman.

At the core of the film is the subject of the female body and Cho's tale of breaking down on the set of her television show after being asked to lose weight in order to play herself. Cho lost thirty pounds in two weeks before being rushed to the hospital when her kidneys shut down. Cho speaks candidly about what happens to her genitalia, from the moment she starts urinating blood, to the nurse who announces: "Hello-o-o, my name's Gwen, I'm here to wa-a-ash your vagina." Cho announces, "I don't ever want to hear that, ever. That is like the worst thing you can hear," but proceeds to utter the lines repeatedly, with growing energy and intensity. It is a remarkable episode for a medium replete with so-called "dick jokes." Indeed, the entire concert finds Cho facing fears and reclaiming space, both as a female, and as an Asian American who "has to deal with something racial every day"—whether it is a television host asking her to make an announcement in her "native language" or a man walking down the street and accosting Cho with the phrase "Me so horny" (Cho). The latter appellation points to the conjunction of gender and race, and the greater obstacles encountered by racialized women.

Some exponents of women comics protest that gender difference shouldn't factor into matters of humor. Journalist Paul Farhi writes of Allyson Jaffe (part owner and manager of the D.C. Improv) who, although "acknowledging that female comics do have to combat audience expectations that they will present predictable 'female' material . . . says the best performers—male or female—have a universal appeal. Jaffe cites a comedy-club veteran such as Kathleen Madigan: 'A man or a woman could say what she does and it would be funny. It doesn't matter what sex she is. It's just funny." Leaving aside the questionable existence of universal appeal, this well-intended inclusiveness contains flaws similar to the embracement of predominantly sexist humor, in that both run contrary to stand-up's dependence on the personal. To adopt the predilections of a group to which one does not belong, or to speak in an all-embracing universal voice, is to abdicate the unique puissance of stand-up. The reality is that women are often asked to laugh at male-centered humor and frequently do, even while female-centered stand-up remains the exception.

I suspect the same personalization of the artist that drove the development of stand-up can actually work against the affirmation of female comics, which is why performers such as Cho still find themselves standing in the margins, playing to smaller audiences. The contradiction comes into focus when comparing criticism of Barr and Cho with that of Sahl, Bruce, and Pryor. Sahl was attacked for venturing away from the jokes and demeanor of the traditional nightclub comedian, with an early *Time* magazine review grumbling that he "freewheels through a labyrinth of rambling asides to his punch lines," with "too much smugness and too little showmanship";[15] Bruce was attacked for his use of profanity and his portrayals of religion; and Pryor was attacked for his use of the N-word, which he himself disavowed in his 1982 concert film, *Richard Pryor Live on the Sunset Strip*. However, despite their use of personal material to make public humor, the men tend to be assailed for their actions and utterances, rather than their person or body. That is why, when Bruce was jailed for drug use or prosecuted for obscenity, it was done in the guise of combating a societal ill. In contrast, Barr and Cho undergo vilification of what would commonly be considered their person. For example, after Barr's controversial rendition of the national anthem at a Padres baseball game, the front page headline of the *San Diego Union* read "The Fat Lady Sings (Poorly)" (Wolf), while hate mail directed against Cho for her 2004 benefit work on behalf of the political action group Moveon.Org "involved people calling her a 'chink whore,' telling her to go back to North Korea, [and] making fun of her 'slanty eyes.'"[16]

The supremely personal performance medium of stand-up comedy is supposed to proffer stand-ups as stand-ins for us all. However, the double bind of the female stand-up comic is to work within a medium built on performers using their private lives to craft highly individual public personas in a culture reluctant to accept this individualization in women playing themselves. Excluded from the media mobility acquired by male stand-ups from Pryor to Seinfeld, the exclusion itself becomes fuel for Cho's comedy. Thus far rejected by the vast white television audience, Cho finds empowerment in the margins of stand-up. Interestingly, she regularly posits her audience as gay men, situating herself as a heterosexual woman in their midst, proclaiming: "I am a fag hag. Fag hags are the backbone of the gay community. Without us, you're nothing." Cho's affiliation with disempowered groups helps explain the fervor of her audience, which has fewer public individuals representing its collective voice. However, the urge to obtain the widest possible audience remains. Before debuting her short-lived reality show *The Cho Show* on VH1, Cho told *The New York Times*: "I want mainstream acceptance, I want huge success, I want to play huge stadiums . . . I just do."[17] The precedents of Sahl, Bruce, Pryor, Barr, and Cho suggest new bonds between mainstream audiences and previously unaccepted minority subjects will continue to emerge. That the field has yet to produce a female comic playing huge stadiums on the level of Pryor—or, for that matter, Steve Martin—indicates stand-up comedy continues to be in flux, with plenty of opportunity for further development on the side of both performer and audience.

Closing

It is against and with the audience that the stand-up comic stands up, simultaneously one of the crowd and yet distinct from it. The intimacy of the relationship is literal as well as metaphoric, affecting the very shape of comedy clubs, where comics frequently reach the stage by making their way through the house.[18] This movement echoes the passage of the personal into the public, accentuating the impression of comics appearing onstage as if rising from amongst the ranks of the audience; on a 2004 visit to the Punch Line in Sacramento, my companion expressed surprise when an audience member walked next to our table, headed to the stage, and turned to face the crowd, only to transform into Margaret Cho. A number of clubs seat ticket holders at tables that press flush against the main stage; during a 2007 show at Rooster T Feathers in Sunnyvale, California, comedian Dana Carvey stowed his water bottle on one such occupied table, motivated by the practical need for space, but playfully acknowledging he was taking advantage of stand-up comedy's license to breach the proscenium and address the audience directly. The closeness of comedy clubs allows nascent comedians to develop their performance persona in public, in relation to live audiences.

The twenty-first century question is how possible it remains to retain this intimacy as electronic entertainment continues to feed upon comedians and flatten their product in order to make it more palatable to mass, non-live audiences. It's instructive that Dave Chappelle, having achieved his greatest acclaim on television, nonetheless abandoned that very lucrative endeavor in order to return to the intimacy of the live, precisely because it grants him a closer connection with the audience and correspondingly greater control over the reception of his performances of identity and stereotype. The larger identity concerns that inspired the emergence of stand-up comedy continue today, and the form has proved flexible enough to adjust to the anxieties of the present year or decade. Note, for example, the rise of self-identified Arabic and Muslim stand-up comedians following the events of September 11, 2001. Some, such as Muslim Indian American Azhar Usman, turned to stand-up expressly due to its capacity to create community and forge understanding between comedians and audiences.

From the 1950s to the present, the comic dialogue between the speaking comedian and the laughing audience continues to be a major forum for the performance of self, with a series of personal confessions and accusations all focused on a single body. Sahl, Bruce, Pryor, Barr, and Cho have established divergent paradigms for collaboration with their spectators, and yet such audience dependency is common to all who have worked in the genre. Standing in front of the crowd, proclaiming their sins and opinions, stand-up comics serve as primers on how to mark oneself as an individual through opinions and quirks, even while their action provides an excuse for the majority of the crowd to remain seated and silent. For their part, the stand-up audience sits, representing society-at-large, gathered to pass judgment on the comic individual. Of course, the process is circular, for to judge one's representation is to judge oneself, if only in comparison. The crowd is cast in the role of shameless voyeur, openly spying on the willing exhibitionists, and the resultant intimacy is two-sided. With the advent of stand-up, the comic has become the audience's representative—the stand-up as stand-in—although stand-up comedy's power ultimately stems neither from the stage nor out of the audience, but from the constantly evolving tension between the two, performed in the intimate immediacy of the live.

NOTES

1. My thanks to Daniel Sack and Professor Alice Rayner of the Stanford University Department of Drama, and to my editor, Judy Batalion, for their generous and productive feedback on this work.

2. Betsy Borns provides a valuable chronicle of stand-up, starting with the birth of showcase clubs in the 1960s, in her *Comic Lives* (New York: Simon & Schuster, 1987). The most notable academic precedent for locating stand-up in this post-war era is John Limon's impressive *Stand-up Comedy in Theory, or, Abjection in America*. Limon employs a psychoanalytic framework to examine stand-up's role as a force operating in the margins, focusing on abjection and the account of Jewish integration into mainstream white middle class America. He is less concerned with the historical development of stand-up than with providing a psychoanalytic geometry for the form. We

both deal with the towering figures of Lenny Bruce and Richard Pryor, but Limon omits the crucial Mort Sahl, admitting that he is not "trying to locate and analyze the most influential post-World War II American stand-up comedians . . . or the funniest ones" (3). I am quite specifically attempting the former.

Limon also defines stand-up more broadly than I, venturing beyond the live solo figure into comedy teams (such as Nichols & May and Reiner and Brooks); television hosts (David Letterman); and performers who could be considered comic actors rather than practitioners of a genre in which one performs one's self (again, Nichols & May and Reiner and Brooks). While many stand-up comics have had great success and impact performing in alternate media, my primary concern is with stand-ups performing stand-up per se—that is, with individual performers facing live audiences. Of course, my focus on the interrelationship between specific performers and their audiences does not necessarily clash with a genealogical or psychoanalytic perspective, and I do consider alternative media when addressing the paucity of prominent female comics on stand-up's main stage. Their absence necessitates references to adjacent sites that have provided greater access to women.

3. I found use of the term "stand-up" in *The New York Times* as early as 1954. See: Lohman, Sidney. "News and Notes from the Television and Radio Studios." *The New York Times* 18 April 1954: X9. The earliest *Oxford English Dictionary* listing stems from the 11 August 1966 edition of *The Listener*, a weekly magazine published by the British Broadcasting Corporation from 1929 until 1991: "stand-up, *a*. and *n*." *The Oxford English Dictionary*. 2nd ed. *OED Online*. Oxford: Oxford University Press, 1989. Web. 2 November 2006.

4. The blend of public and private is familiar to comedy, which has long had a tradition of scrutinizing the workaday world gone wrong. As early as Aristophanes, comic drama tended to pass over mythic legends (such as the myriad tales of the House of Atreus) and alight on contemporary subjects (such as Lysistrata's campaign against the Peloponnesian War), with actual citizens both named and portrayed onstage. From the clever slaves of Plautus to the bourgeois buffoons of Georges Feydeau, comedy has explored the topical travails of the domestic realm. In the 1950s, 1960s, and 1970s, comic monologists pushed the everyday emphasis of traditional stage comedy one step further, perforating the fourth wall by addressing audiences directly, and blending offstage personas with onstage characters.

5. The Chitlin' Circuit refers to "a network of predominantly white-owned theaters in black areas of towns in the South and the Midwest . . . where black entertainers performed before exclusively black audiences." See Miklos, Michael. "Theater Owners' Booking Association." Cary D. Wintz and Paul Finkelman, eds. *Encyclopedia of the Harlem Renaissance*. New York: Taylor & Francis Books, 2004. 1170–71.

6. The Borscht Belt was a collection of Jewish summer resorts located in the Catskill Mountains of New York State, and flourished primarily in the 1940s, 1950s, and 1960s.

7. Brock, Sonia Fricker. "The Chitlin Circuit." 23 April 2007. Web. 12 May 2007.

8. For one, Lawrence J. Epstein's *The Haunted Smile: The Story of Jewish Comedians in America* notes, "B.S. Pully was famous for threatening to urinate on audience members." Epstein, Lawrence J. *The Haunted Smile: The Story of Jewish Comedians in America*. New York: Public Affairs, 2001. 173.

9. *Trials* CD track 9.

10. Ibid. track 15.

11. At the time of his death in 1964, Bruce was still appealing an obscenity conviction handed down in New York. In 2003, Governor George Pataki granted Bruce a posthumous pardon.

12. Sahl ranks fortieth, Bruce third, and Pryor first. There are nine women on the list.

13. The three most famous practitioners of this tactic were probably Phyllis Diller (b. 1917), Totie Fields (1930–78), and Joan Rivers (b. 1933).

14. Such a striking past would traditionally be considered ripe comedy material, and Barr touches on it in her special, stating, "I come from about the worst place on earth, Salt Lake City, Utah. And I'm Jewish, so that's why I'm like this and everything, in case you wondered. It was really bad, being Jewish there, okay, cause like, for our synagogue we had to sublet space out of a PhotoMat Booth and everything." How is it her eponymous sitcom missed her explanation of "why I'm like this"? Anti-Semitism may have played a part; it was only two years later that NBC executive Brandon Tartikoff almost passed on the subsequent mega-hit *Seinfeld* because he deemed it "too Jewish." Tapper, Jake. "Too Jewish?" *Salon*. 9 August 2000. Web. 6 June 2011. In addition, the erasure of Barr's Jewishness probably stems from the fact that she was already pushing against boundaries of class and gender, while the suburban male, Jerry Seinfeld, was eventually given rein to address his ethnicity in prime time.

15. *Time,* 21 April 1958.

16. "When Comedy and Activism Violently Collide: Margaret Cho Sounds Off." UCLA International Institute. 11 November 2005. Web. 6 June 2011.

17. *The New York Times,* 8 August 2008.

18. Budd and Silver Friedman began the trend in 1963 with the first showcase comedy club, the New York Improv; Mitzi and Sammy Shore, along with Rudy DeLuca, founded the Comedy Store in Los Angeles in 1972, the same year that Rick Newman opened Catch A Rising Star in New York City; in 1976, Richard Tienken, John McGowan, and Robert Wachs started New York's Comic Strip Live; the boom of stand-up comedy chains arrived in the

1980s, with the Funny Bone and the Punch Line franchises both launched in 1982. Stand-up's standing as an independent branch of comedy performance is possible largely due to these establishments. For information regarding the establishment of stand-up clubs, see Borns, Betsy. *Comic Lives*. New York: Simon & Schuster, 1987.

WORKS CITED

Adams, Joey with Henry Tobias. *The Borscht Belt*. Indianapolis, IN: Bobbs-Merrill Company, 1959. Print.

Auslander, Philip. "'Brought to You by Fem-Rage:' Stand-up Comedy and the Politics of Gender." *Acting Out: Feminist Performances*. Ed. Lynda Hart and Peggy Phelan. Ann Arbor: University of Michigan Press, 1993. 108–126. Print.

Bruce, Lenny. *The Carnegie Hall Concert*. Blue Note Records, 1961. LP.

---. *The Essential Lenny Bruce*. New York: Ballantine Books, 1967. Print.

Collins, Ronald K. L. and David M. Skover. *The Trials Of Lenny Bruce: the Rise and Fall of an American Icon*. Naperville, IL: Sourcebooks, 2002. Print.

Diller, Phyllis. *Like a Lampshade in a Whorehouse*. New York: Penguin, 2005. Print.

Farhi, Paul. "Beaten to the Punch Line: The Odds Against Female Stand-Up Comedians Are No Laughing Matter." *Washington Post* 31 March 2007: C01. Print.

Goldman, Albert. *Ladies and Gentlemen—Lenny Bruce!!* New York: Penguin Books, 1974. Print.

Horowitz, Susan. *Queens of Comedy: Lucille Ball, Phyllis Diller, Carol Burnett, Joan Rivers, and the New Generation of Funny Women*. Amsterdam: Gordan and Breach Science Publishers, 1997. Print.

I'm the One That I Want: Margaret Cho Filmed Live in Concert. Writ. Margaret Cho. Dir. Lionel Coleman. Perf. Margaret Cho. Cho Taussig Productions, 2000.

Kanfer, Stefan. *A Summer World*. New York: Farrar Straus Giroux, 1989. Print.

Lifton, Robert Jay. *The Protean Self: Human Resilience in an Age of Fragmentation*. Chicago: University of Chicago Press, 1993. Print.

Limon, John. *Stand-up Comedy in Theory, or, Abjection in America*. Durham, NC: Duke University Press, 2000. Print.

Martin, Emily. *Bipolar Expeditions: Mania and Depression in American Culture*. Princeton, NJ: Princeton University Press: 2007. Print.

Miklos, Michael. "Theater Owners' Booking Association." Ed. Cary D. Wintz and Paul Finkelman. *Encyclopedia of the Harlem Renaissance*. New York: Taylor & Francis Books, 2004. 1170–71. Print.

Mintz, Lawrence E. "Standup Comedy as Social and Cultural Mediation." *American Quarterly* 37.1 (1985): 71. Print.

Nachman, Gerald. *Seriously Funny: The Rebel Comedians of the 1950s and 1960s.* New York: Pantheon Books, 2003. Print.

On Location: the Roseanne Barr Show. Writ. Bill Pentland and Rocco Urbisci. Dir. Rocco Urbisci. Perf. Roseanne Barr. Home Box Office, 1987.

Provine, Robert R. *Laughter: A Scientific Investigation.* New York: Viking Penguin, 2000. Print.

Pryor, Richard. *That Nigger's Crazy.* Partee, 1974. LP.

---. *Pryor Convictions.* Revolver Books, 2005. Print.

---. *Richard Pryor: Live in Concert.* Writ. Richard Pryor. Dir. Jeff Margolis. Perf. Richard Pryor. Special Event Entertainment, 1979.

Rhodes, Dusti. "Funny Business: Playing with Boys." *Houston Press* 24 May 24 2007. Web. 3 June 2011.

Riesman, David. *The Lonely Crowd: A Study of the Changing American Character.* New Haven, CT: Yale University Press: 1961. Print.

Sahl, Mort. *The Future Lies Ahead.* Verve Records, 1958. LP.

Watkins, Mel. *On the Real Side: A History of African American Comedy.* New York: Simon & Schuster, 1994. Print.

Williams, John A. and Dennis A. Williams. *If I Stop I'll Die: the Comedy and Tragedy of Richard Pryor.* New York: Thunder's Mouth Press, 1991. Print.

Wolf, Buck. "Oh Say, Can't You Sing: Celebs Who Tortured the National Anthem." ABC News/Entertainment. 2 May 2006. Web. 6 June 2011.

4 A Comedic Tour de Monde

Shazia Mirza
(in conversation with Judy Batalion)

Shazia Mirza is a UK stand-up whose act revolves around her Muslim faith, alongside other observational material. She began performing in 2000, and since then, has traveled the world as a comedian headlining at clubs and performing one-woman shows. She has also worked as a writer, winning Columnist of the Year (Consumer Magazines) in the PPA Magazines 2008 Awards for editorial and publishing excellence for her column in *The New Statesman*. She has appeared on CBS's *60 Minutes*, NBC's *Last Comic Standing*, and BBC's *Have I Got News for You*.

Shazia Mirza's stand-up material is based around her personal experiences and identity as a British-Asian-Muslim-woman, often addressing her feelings of outsiderness. Mirza has performed widely—in different types of comedy clubs and in different countries and cultures, from San Francisco to Kosovo, Muslims to Buddhists, and commercial clubs to alternative gay events. I was curious about how her kind of act was received in varying environments, and here, I talk to her about the intimate connection between performer and audience in different surrounds, addressing notions of comfort, love, gender, and the development of the relationship between a comedian and their audience over time.

Judy: The personal nature of your act interests me because you perform in so many different contexts—at Highlight, and on the lesbian circuit, on Brick Lane, at urban political nights, and at Glastonbury. You perform in different countries—India, San Francisco, America, the Middle East. Do you adapt for these varied audiences? Do you show them different sides of yourself? Or is there just one you and that's what they get?

Shazia: Sometimes I change the material. Occasionally, there are certain terms the audience won't get. But I don't prejudge audiences anymore. The first time I go anywhere, I keep my original set. I'm doing a tour of the Middle East—Beirut, Cairo, Abu Dabi, Saudi, Dubai—and I'll do what I do and be myself. If you do what you normally do, you can always see what works and what doesn't. The next time you go there, you can make changes based on that first experience. You try to figure out why certain jokes didn't work: Was it the language? Were the references too local? Did I speak too fast? If you change things the very first time, then you'll never know what will work, or what might have worked.

Judy: What sorts of changes have you had to make for different audiences?

Shazia: Word changes. In San Francisco, I had to change the word "shag" to "sex."

Judy: Right, so it's little changes to colloquial terms, that kind of stuff.

Shazia: Sometimes I also have to speak slower, even in America. Because if you talk really fast in a British accent they stop following. And you know, I do have a bit of a Birmingham accent. I've seen great Manchester comedians die because audiences couldn't understand what they were saying.

Judy: Yeah, I can never understand what people from Manchester are saying. But you were saying, your material is based on your real life experience. In fact, in your gigs, you sometimes even discuss your other gigs, you tell one audience about another. I saw you perform recently and you told us a story about a gig you did in India, where the producers were particularly worried that you would offend the crowd.

Shazia: The audiences were great in India, they really loved my act, but the people running the gigs were difficult. They had never had a British comedian perform live in India before, and they didn't know how people would react to British humor, worrying that I would offend. Even though the first gig was great, the organizers of the tour—the British Council in India—were considering canceling the second night because the venue was concerned about losing its license. I challenged them, saying the audience had loved it, and it was ridiculous to cancel. We negotiated, and they agreed to go on, but asked me to cut out parts of my material—the bits about sex. Plus, they wanted me to say a disclaimer before I did the show, apologizing to the audience, telling them if they are offended, it's not the venue's fault, but the fault of my material; this is my comedy and these are my opinions.

Judy: Did you do it?

Shazia: Yes, I had to. I understood their concern. They'd never seen British stand-up comedy live, and also, they'd never seen a woman doing it. This was a big thing for them and they had no idea what to expect. They'd heard a lot about me; I was in all the press, the papers, and all the Bollywood stars and Indian glitterati came to watch me. It went very well, but I must say, that first night, the men were not that interested in some of my material.

Judy: Like what?

Shazia: Like, I mentioned the word vagina onstage.

Judy: And?

Shazia: And the men didn't laugh. Not at all. But the women did! All the women thought it was hilarious. I didn't mention it gratuitously; I was talking about *The Vagina Monologues*, actually.

Judy: So in Indian audiences, the women were more receptive?

Shazia: That was the first time anyone ever asked them to laugh at these things—things they weren't normally allowed to laugh at. In India, men just aren't used to women talking about sex. I mean, I know that in India sex is a thing. Everybody in India is doing it—it's the most overpopulated place in the world! They don't have this population because of immaculate conception, they're fucking like no one. But the minute you talk about it in public, it's a complete taboo. I just mentioned the word vagina and they thought I was crazy. But the women, they loved it.

Judy: So among all your controversial material, it seems in India, sex was the shocker. You've mentioned to me before that New York audiences want to be shocked. I assume a different type of shock? Do you change your set when you perform in New York?

Shazia: In New York, you have to get straight to the point. It's set-up punch, set-up punch, set-up punch. You have to make people laugh immediately and continuously. Otherwise you're in trouble. You're not funny.

All my New York comedian friends are very forward, brash women. They're all like Joan Rivers: loud and in your face. Particularly as a woman, that's how you have to be. In a way, you have to be that anywhere as a woman, even here in the UK. Some women comedians here use their sexuality onstage, but it doesn't get you very far. It may in the short run, but the female comedians who have made it big in the long run have all been people like Joan Rivers, Ellen Degeneres, Rhona Cameron, Donna McPhail, Jo Brand—all ballsy, brash women who don't use their sexuality. They come on and do material. Using your sexuality doesn't work as a comic, because half the men in the audience are thinking, "Do I fancy her? Do I want to sleep with her?" And then a huge part of your audience is not taking your comedy seriously, they are not listening and laughing at your material: they're not *really* laughing. In order to really make an audience laugh, a woman has to hide her sexuality, to make herself non-sexual.

A lot of times, people think I'm a lesbian because I'm very forthright, I don't use my sexuality, and I even dress like one. Not on purpose, but I don't like my clothes to overtake my act. My act has to overtake everything, otherwise there's no act. Onstage, it has to be about the jokes, and nothing must get in the way. I've got great legs, but if I went onstage in a mini skirt, people would look at my legs. No one would say I have good jokes, but good legs. No one would listen to my comedy. Why *would* they be listening to my jokes when I have great legs?

Judy: Ah, the British male audience. But let's get back to the different audiences you've performed for in different places. In New York, you say audiences are like: I want jokes, now, fast. And in India sex is taboo. What else has come out of your travels?

Shazia: I've performed in Sweden several times, doing three or four sellout tours. That's where I really developed as a comedian. Their English is very good, and I don't have to change a word. And they do understand the humor, which translates very well. They are a repressed people, and hearing me say the things I say is freeing and funny for them. I mean, I went to some villages in the outback of Sweden, and they'd never even seen a brown woman before! And yet, they understood the humor, and because they were never allowed to laugh at the things I make jokes about, they were really laughing.

Judy: So their suppression benefited you?

Shazia: It's a very warm place. Sweden is a very reserved nation, less so than Denmark, but still very reserved. The first few times I performed there I thought, oh my god, they are so quiet. But that's just the Swedish way of laughing, a laid back laugh. Not screaming out loud, the opposite to the Americans in every way. Once you give Swedish audiences that permission to laugh, they just love it. As a reserved nation, they've been told, don't do that, don't express that, it's rude. They love actually hearing it. If I have new material, I take it there. Or San Francisco.

Judy: Is San Francisco different than New York?

Shazia: San Francisco is like a mini-England.

Judy: (laughing) I never heard it described quite that way.

Shazia: It's a part of America that's not America. It's liberal, open-minded, forward-thinking, progressive. They're accepting of things, ideas, people; it's not that prejudiced. How can it be prejudiced when most of the city is gay? The city has a hoard of gay people, and also a hoard of intelligent people who are progressive groundbreakers, movers and shakers really, who are often based where there are a lot of gay people. They all like to break the mold. They like to open people's minds, and they like mind-opening material.

I recently did a charity gig for the Buddhist Centre in London—they were raising money for poor kids in India. Because it was a Buddhist fair, there were a lot of gay Buddhists in the audience. I didn't even know it was possible. I did an hour's show, and afterward this gay guy came up to me and said, "I love it when you make people feel uncomfortable." I explained that I don't set out to make people feel uncomfortable deliberately. Some comics purposefully go out to make the audience feel uncomfortable. I don't aim for that but sometimes I get uncomfortable laughter—it's like the audience wants to laugh, but they don't know if they should. So you get that uncomfortable response, but it is still laughter, the kind of laughter that indicates that they'll go home and tell somebody, "I heard the most hilarious thing . . . " When they're in there, though, they don't laugh that much. I want people to laugh, and to leave the show happy. But I realize that because some of my material breaks barriers, it will make people uncomfortable, even though my only intention is to talk about myself and my life. There is only one of me in comedy, and I talk about things not everybody has talked about before me. We've all heard jokes about fat people, and what it's like to be fat, about being depressed or splitting up with boyfriends or getting pissed. But maybe most audiences haven't heard jokes about the things I'm talking about, and because it's new, it makes them uncomfortable.

Judy: What exactly do you mean when you say you "break barriers?" Can you give me some examples?

Shazia: I mean I talk about my life from a point of view they wouldn't have heard before—and certainly not on a comedy stage. Audiences are used to men talking about smoking and drinking. But when I first started, I would talk about how my parents were desperate for me to get married off, the guys they would introduce me to, and how none of them wanted a Muslim wife who was a comedian. Audiences were surprised, and genuinely thinking: is she joking or not? Now, people in England, they know me, I've been doing this for a while so they're not as surprised as they were at first. But when I first started off, audiences just looked at me like [her jaw drops]: Why are you doing this? Why are you doing comedy? A brown woman? You don't see many women onstage. It's always unusual. And I'm a dark British woman. It's not what most audiences associate with comedy. It's still like this in many places, like Sweden, which is very white. I'm the last person they expect to see onstage.

Judy: So you broke barriers in England, and continue to in Scandinavia, but you claim you don't want to make people feel uncomfortable. Do you also try to make the audience comfortable? How?

Shazia: Yes, I urge them to feel comfortable. I smile and laugh, and even tell them it's a joke. Once you give an audience that permission, there's no stopping them. But sometimes they don't know what that permission is, or how to read it. And sometimes they're so PC, they'll go, "I can't laugh at this," even though they might find it funny.

Judy: Shazia, you've only been performing for about ten years, and yet you've done all this touring and have such a large audience listening to your personal life. I wonder, as time goes on, as you develop, as people begin to know who you are *before* the show and come to see you specifically, like at the gig I saw you perform at recently, where the whole audience was there for you . . .

Shazia: Really? All six of them?

Judy: Yes, all six were fervently there for you from the start. How does that change your relationship with your audience, compared to when you started out and no one knew who you were? Do you adapt more to them at first, and then you . . .

Shazia: No, no, no. You're the thing that is unique. Why would you go see someone? Because you think they're funny, and you're interested in what they have to say. You like the things they talk about. Or you're interested in their life.

Judy: But do you feel that over the past few years, your relationship with audiences has changed since they know you? Or do you not think about that at all? Are you the same, just writing your material based on your life?

Shazia: You never play to an audience. They don't want you to play to them. If I'm performing at Comedy Camp for a gay audience, they don't want me to deal with gay material because I'm not gay. They want to see me do comedy about me. That's why they like me, because they're interested in what I have to say. Obviously, they like it when it's something they can relate to, or something that challenges them. They want something unexpected—it's comedy. You don't want to give them what they expect, or they'll get bored. If they get what they expect all the time, you'll lose your audience. You always have to generate new material and keep them on their toes.

Judy: So then, even in London, when you're playing Comedy Camp or Highlight, do you modify what you're doing for each of those?

Shazia: Yes, because Highlight is like the McDonald's of comedy. They don't want you to be clever, they want you to be funny. At Highlight, say whatever you like. Just make sure it gets a laugh, even if it's the cheapest thing. Do it. That's the job. Take your trousers off, take your top off, swear, insult, be rude. Just be a comedian. But, there's a difference between a comedian and an artist. Making audiences laugh is what qualifies you as a comedian, but with art, well, you don't quite know.

Judy: But art or not, it is hard to make people laugh.

Shazia: Yes, that's right. These comedians have got craft. But art is much deeper. It's still funny, but might include something that you have to think about. At Highlight, every line has got to be a laugh.

Judy: Sounds like how you describe New York.

Shazia: Yes, what happens at Highlight happens in loads of New York clubs every night. Commercial comedy.

Judy: Have you ever performed in a culture that might be thought to be the opposite of brazen, for instance in Japan, or an East Asian country? I'm interested in the idea that social repression in a culture, and thus in its audiences, affects the show.

Shazia: It changes the vibe. I've never performed in Japan, but a few years ago, I did a couple of gigs in Kosovo. That was a difficult environment. Everything was bombed out, but actually the Kosovan people were very grateful—they said if it hadn't been for the Americans, they wouldn't be alive. The people were liberated, but the place was hard; it was extremely cold, power supplies were awful and unreliable, there was no heating, and at the hotel I had to sleep in my jumper and clothes—and shoes. In the morning, there were icicles hanging from the ceiling. I landed at the airport and thought, this is like going back seventy years, like *War and Peace* Berlin. It was like nothing I had ever seen before.

The shows were difficult, too. The first one, in the capital Pristina, was in an old bombed out building. There were loads of people there, and it was freezing—I had to do the gig in my coat. They had all these electric heaters trying to heat the building, but it was so cold.

Judy: What were the audiences like?

Shazia: They were really supportive. They managed to get some lights on. I went onstage and started very slowly. There were translators next to me, translating my material for them. And then, in the middle of the gig, all the electricity went. There was a blackout, and I had to carry on doing the gig in the dark. There was no seating, people were standing, and it was completely dark.

Judy: Frightening.

Shazia: But they were laughing.

Judy: They were? They were happy to be there, nonetheless?

Shazia: I couldn't really understand why they were laughing. They didn't necessarily understand the show. And with a translator, some of the jokes became a bit labored. But the people were warm and had a great time; I got many emails afterward saying they hadn't seen entertainment for years.

    Sometimes comedy can travel even if the language and humor can't be translated. Because if you go onstage, being yourself, and you have a bit of personality, and are a bit of a performer, your performance itself can translate—the audience can see the humor in it. They pick up on jokes that are based on the performer; they may not necessarily understand the entire joke, but they laugh at the mannerisms, at expressions. You can pick up communication in that way, which must have been what happened in Kosovo, because I know they didn't understand much of the material, and it was an hour's show, and they were still laughing. I did a second gig in Prizen, a harsh town in the north of Kosovo, and there, they just couldn't understand what I was saying. I couldn't get them to. There was a real language barrier—it didn't work.

Judy: That sounds extremely difficult. More difficult than the gig with the six people.

Shazia: I love those gigs. There's something raw about them.

Judy: You have to be funny at those gigs.

Shazia: You have to be funny at all gigs, but at some gigs it's harder to get away with not being funny. Though, I've seen so many comedians get away with not being funny. You must have seen it?

Judy: How do they get away with it? Because audiences let them? Why do they laugh?

Shazia: In the case of a male comedian, maybe they fancy him. In the case of a female comedian, it might be that they think, aw, she's cute. They're laughing because she's cute, but it's not necessarily ha-ha laughter. As an audience member, you know real laughter, and you know when a comedian is really fucking funny. You go, *that's funny*. Like, Jo Brand—she's funny. No sexuality, no looks, no props. Like all truly funny acts, she just stands up there and makes people laugh with what she's saying. It's so strong that everyone is laughing, and everyone knows that it's working. People that are really, really funny are timeless. You can watch them in 1972 and you can watch them in 2007 and they still seem funny. Dave Allen, Richard Pryor, Lenny

Bruce—though a lot of Lenny Bruce has just become funny, it wasn't even funny at the time.

Judy: And *now* audiences like it? *Now* it is funny?

Shazia: Now it is. Some of the stuff wasn't funny then, and is still not now. But some of the stuff he did about blacks, gays, and Jews, and that thing about the teacher fucking a kid—he was the first guy to do that kind of stuff. It was hilarious then, and it's hilarious now. And every other comedian has a version of it.

I'm a huge fan of Richard Pryor. I watch his stuff all the time. It is so personal, and still so funny. It's really good the way they filmed *Live at Sunset Strip* because they shot bits of the audience, and it's fascinating. The audience was black, white, men, women, young kids, everyone. In his act, there isn't a black bit, a white bit—his material is intelligent, insightful; he talks not just about being black but about everything. Pryor's work transcended time, but also, generations, races, religions, genders and sexualities. He's really a great comedian.

Sometimes you think you don't want the audience to know a certain part of you because then they'll know too much and there will be no mystery. But Richard Pryor opened up about everything. He even talked about fame. He said, "The reason I wanted to become famous was because I thought there are two things I can get out of fame. One is money. And one is pussy. And so I thought, my god, if I can get fame, fucking hell, I can get pussy for the rest of my life. I am really looking forward to this." He was so honest. It's funny, about fame. I've heard many comedians say that once they got onto television, the girls came running. On a day I'm on telly, I get more offers from men. Television makes you famous. People think they know you.

Judy: I guess it might seem more intimate because you appear to people in their own homes, you enter their private spaces.

Shazia: It makes an audience think they know you. So now, when I go onstage, my audience thinks they know me, but they don't. But then, at the end of the show, they probably know me a bit better, because I give of myself. But I wouldn't go as far as Richard Pryor, talking about his own fame. Pryor never held back; that's why he was so funny. The audience appreciated that. Even if I wasn't sober, I wouldn't get onstage and say the reason I want to do television. I wouldn't have the guts. Even if I wrote it. There's always something I hold back.

Judy: When you're writing material, do you think of an audience in your head?

Shazia: No. Never. No one. Just me. You have to be totally free when you're writing. If you have someone in mind, you're not totally free. You'll never say what you truly think. Therefore you'll never be truly honest; therefore you'll never get the biggest laughs. If you're honest—if you think it's funny, and that's what you really think, you have to go for it. And also, comedy is about saying the unsayable. You want to say something that your audience is thinking, but that they would never say.

Judy: Do you ever perform for Muslim audiences?

Shazia: Yes.

Judy: Are these gigs different?

Shazia: Hmm. Yes. The audiences look at me like, "you better not cross the line here." Basically, they're not into comedy, it's not part of our culture. They're very reserved. They want me to behave onstage as if I was sitting with my mom and dad in the living room.

    I think Muslim audiences are not listening to the material as a primary thing. Like my family, they're judging me first: how I look, how I'm speaking, how I'm dressed, am I swearing, am I being rude . . . The material is secondary. Muslims in America, by the way, are different audiences than in the UK because they are more liberal. Americans are more Americanized, more open. To them, being Muslim is more of a cultural thing. They all eat non-halal, they drink, they wear miniskirts, they go out. Here, they're all much more religious and conservative because they're influenced by the culture in which they live.

Judy: How do you handle that? Do you tone yourself down?

Shazia: Yeah.

Judy: So in that sense, would you say you're playing to your audience?

Shazia: That's the way I'm gonna *survive* with that audience.

Judy: But aren't you contradicting yourself? You are adamant about writing for no one and being yourself onstage, but here you're telling me you work around an audience.

Shazia: I say I try to be the same at every gig. I am the constant. I like to do the same material all over the world. There are certain things that might not work all over the world—words, phrases, meanings—but not the material, and not what I'm trying to say. Comedy is not an academic thing. It's a creative thing. It's an art. It's the way you feel and how you think. You can't say, today I'm gonna give them this side of me, and tomorrow I'll keep that back and give them this. That's ridiculous.

Judy: Your intention is one thing, but what about the audience's effect on you? Does the Muslim audience, or any particular audience, bring out a different side of you? A different element of your personality, identity, and demeanor?

Shazia: I'm just myself, wherever I go, which is probably why some people find me offensive. They don't get it. But still, I just try to be myself in front of every audience. You can't pick and choose who you're gonna be based on the audience: in this audience I'll be more of this, in that audience I'll be more of that. Then, you'd never be yourself. You have to be who you are in the moment with those people, but I try to be the same in every single gig, even if it comes out differently.

Judy: So the moment when you get onstage, for Muslim or any audiences, do you generally know what material you're going to use and go with that, or do you look to see what kind of audience it is—not based on demographics, but on their vibe—and then decide what jokes to do?

Shazia: Sometimes. I like to be free. That's why I like doing the smaller gigs, because I feel liberated. At a huge gig like Glastonbury, I have to have a fixed set. It's a big audience, you can't banter. You have to get on and say, look, this is who I am. I have fifteen minutes to show you who I am. But if I'm doing my own show at a theater, I like to get to know the audience and then decide what to tell them.

Judy: Is it because at your own show, you feel in control? You're really developing a relationship with them?

Shazia: Yes. And whatever I say, it's me. They've come to watch me.

Judy: What sorts of characteristics might you notice about an audience as you're trying to get to know them?

Shazia: They're very quiet, or very reserved, and jokes that normally get a big laugh are getting a quieter response. The way to test the audience is to do your old standards that are almost guaranteed to work anywhere and everywhere.

Judy: Why are some audiences reserved?

Shazia: Because I'm a brown woman, and they're used to seeing me as a housewife. But I'm a comedian, and they're not used to seeing me in that role. You have to make them feel comfortable.

Judy: Can you give me an example of an audience that you loved, and why? Why were they comfortable? Why did it work?

Shazia: When I started stand-up I never thought the audience that would love me the most would be gay men. They're my core audience who support me.

Judy: Do you have a lot of gay male friends?

Shazia: Yeah. I always have, since I was fifteen. I don't know what it is that attracted them to me. I suppose it's that I challenge things. Gay audiences like Madonna, Cher, Liza Minelli—women who broke a few barriers. Think of Joan Rivers: she's nearly eighty, and young and good-looking gay men come out to watch her. That's because she was a groundbreaking, ball-busting woman, and they like that. I guess it's also that thing about being an outsider. They understand what it's like to be an outsider. I talk about being an outsider, and I think they relate to that in some way. I do relate to gay men, I feel a connection to them, as I do with women. And I also feel a connection with good looking young men... Madonna's audience is gay men—that's what made her. Kylie, too. Any woman that has a gay audience is on her way.

But gay audiences certainly don't like everyone. If a gay audience hates you, my god, they hate you. I've seen it. They've been horrible to people. Sometimes there are bands, music people, and they go seek the gay audience, they know they're gonna be loyal and stand by them. You can seek them, but they won't necessarily like you.

Judy: My friend, an L.A. entertainment lawyer, always says, first the gays, then the women, then the world. In fact, I think there was a *Sex and the City* episode about it.

Shazia: Have you seen Margaret Cho? She's really fucking fantastic. Her comedy is brilliant: witty, poignant, funny, and personal. She talks about being an outsider, being a Korean, in America. And it's not just gay men with her. It's gay women as well. Same with me. I have a lot of gay women who support me. Actually, they don't support me, they try to convert me.

Judy: What was your worst audience?

Shazia: My worst audience is any audience that doesn't love me. Because if they love you, they will put up with you no matter what. If you're doing badly, they'll stand by you, even while you try new stuff, even if it's not working.

Judy: Is this love something that you, as a professional performer, can make happen? If they don't love you, can you make them love you?

Shazia: I didn't make the gay audience love me. They just love me. To be really loved, you have to be yourself.

Judy: You've mentioned "love" several times—what does it mean to you in this context? Are there different loves from and in different cultures and places?

Shazia: Yeah. In England, people know me. They've probably seen me loads of times before. And they love me because no matter what I do they will support me, and they laugh and encourage me.

Judy: Because you're part of them? Is that it?

Shazia: No, because I'm not gay, and the gay audiences love me. They're supportive. I can try out new material and they will laugh and applaud. Even if it's not ok, they'll be supportive. You can't do that in every audience, because most audiences will get pissed off after a couple of minutes if you're not making them laugh. They'll want you to get on with it.

Judy: Are there cultural differences in how audiences love? Do audiences love you in different ways, or do they demonstrate it in different ways?

Shazia: Here, if I'm doing a gay club, I get two or three encores. Screaming, shouting, whooping, cheering. They come up to me after to tell me, "we love you, I came specifically to see you." In Sweden, they don't show their feelings that much. They will applaud a lot, they'll smile. If it's not going well in Sweden, they'll still be quiet, listen to you, and give you a huge applause at the end. They will appreciate you. And the way they write about you in the papers is very intelligent.

Judy: Could you say, then, that you "know" your audiences?

Shazia: No, you don't know your audience at all. They think they know you because they may have seen you loads of times. But if there's a thousand people sitting there, you're not gonna know and remember them. Sometimes after a show I am bewildered. I think, god that audience was nice. That joke was shit and they gave me a lot of laughter for it. Sometimes, you feel real warmth onstage.

5 Audienceship and (Non)Laughter in the Stand-up Comedy of Steve Martin

Lesley Harbidge

Lesley Harbidge is a Senior Lecturer in the Division of Film, Photography and New Media at the University of Glamorgan in Cardiff. Her broad research interests lie in contemporary American Cinema, British and American Television, and Stand-up Comedy, and she has published work on film comedy, contemporary comedian comedy, rom-com and sitcom.[1]

The existing criticism on stand-up comedy is united in recognizing the unique sense of bonding and interaction it promotes (see especially Borns; Carter; Rutter; and Stone). Certainly, the live and informal nature of the performance, as well as the venue itself, can facilitate a performer-audience relationship unlike that found in most conventional theatre: personalized address and candid geniality intended to strike up a rapport with the audience combined with a relaxed, democratic viewing experience to generate a distinctly organic art form. Commonly perceived by the criticism as part of the creative process, the stand-up audience's consolidated presence, its vital responses and actions, are seen to help feed a performance that is "as reactive as it is active" (Borns 16).

What is perhaps less pronounced in the existing commentary, however, is a sustained focus on intra-audience bonding, or what I am calling "audienceship." Indeed, the (secondary) collective relationship with the comic performer depends, first and foremost, upon the (primary) relationships between individual audience members. So variable are these intra-audience relations that any attempts to analyze them are necessarily tentative. Yet, I would argue, to omit to offer them up for closer examination, to fail to sufficiently unpack them, would seem to undervalue the role of the audience, and, consequently, to oversimplify the overarching relationship with the performer. A wholly social experience, the stand-up gig not only promotes but also positively thrives on a complex nexus of intra-audience relations—relations, it will become clear, that are significant precisely *because* they are so intricate and multifaceted.

In an attempt to tease out the dynamics of the more often discussed performer-audience relationship in live stand-up; to explore the conditions of the audience's agency; and, further, and most significantly, to explore the pleasures of the medium,[2] it is appropriate to turn to the point of *laughter*, that physical and most gratifying manifestation of both intra-audience and performer-audience relations. A phenomenon distinguished, as Robert Provine suggests, by its "awesome sociality;"[3] a truly concrete marker of the crucial bonds or contracts promoted and exploited in stand-up, laughter is a most fruitful focal point for analysis. In fact, since it facilitates such a tangible and immediate relationship between comic performance and laughter, the medium of stand-up may well provide one of the most fertile environments for laughter study: with the likelihood of instant vocal appreciation from the audience, the comic performance feeds off the laughter, becoming at once its cause and effect. As comedian Mike Nichols puts it:

> . . . [stand-up is] the only kind of creative life in which the work and the reward come at exactly the same moment. In every other kind of work, even the theatre, the reward comes at least an act later. Mostly, it comes months, or even years, later or not at all. (qtd. in Gopnik 102)

Given its fundamental place within stand-up, it is my intention here to examine moments of laughter and, more importantly, (non)laughter in the live comedy of Steve Martin, whose unique status as the first "rock 'n' roll stand-up comedian"[4] (playing to audiences of 25,000, and attracting the kind of "cult"[5] following more akin to that of rock bands)[6] surely renders his work ripe for discussion of audience response. Though nowadays better known for increasingly mature roles in films such as *Parenthood* (1989), *The Spanish Prisoner* (1997), and *Shopgirl* (2005), Martin was *the* stand-up comedian of the 1970s, famous for an eclectic mix of banjo-playing, balloon animals, and silly prop gags.

Specifically, here I look to certain types of gags that recur across Martin's work, from the intimate gigs relatively early on in his career to the huge stadium gigs at the height of his fame, and I illustrate how an intriguing range of moments of (non)laughter—spanning stunned silence through to resounding cheering—may reveal the audience's crucial role in the creative process. Despite, and later, *because of* increasing fluency in his unconventional comedy, the early and later cult audiences actually respond to Martin with (non)laughter, but in quite different capacities. The intra-audience response to Martin's early comedy comprises an array of (non)laughter responses and as such is heterogeneous at the surface; however, this heterogeneity belies an underlying crucial audience bonding in the face of the unknown and unexpected. This early surface heterogeneity becomes, later, a discernable and overwhelming homogeneous intra-audience response, both at surface and more profoundly, signaling persistent audience bonding in the face of the expected.[7] Examining the subtleties of the hetero- and homogeneous responses, and the shift in these intra-audience dynamics, helps clarify the shift in the performer-audience relationship for Martin, and also serves to underline that which is so acute across Martin's career—a most pleasurable sense of belonging to the group.

Approaching Stand-Up

It is clear that any attempt to evaluate stand-up comedy ought to make recourse to the physicality of the venue itself, for it is first and foremost the physical space of the stand-up venue and what is permitted in and by that space that has important ramifications for performer-audience relations and audienceship. While the dedicated comedy club is nowadays a fixture of most cities, it remains that many stand-up gigs, certainly on the amateur circuit, take place in modest and makeshift spaces where performer and audience are necessarily physically close to one another.[8] As Jason Rutter observes, "the amount of space that is marked out as the performer's in stand-up venues is minimal" (71). Moreover, and unlike in much theater where the usually distant stage is more prominently lit and the audience is in darkness, stand-up lighting tends to be characterized by less contrast, with the performer able to make out his audience and audience members able to see one another. From the very outset, then, the stand-up venue can provide for physical proximity conducive to performer-audience interaction, as well as crucial intra-audience activity. Further factors such as the presence of alcohol, as well as the seating in the venue, fuel the notion of a distinctly collective, informal experience: likeminded audience members buy drinks in rounds and are often seated together around tables, able to share their responses as the performance unfolds.[9]

The stand-up venue, then, is a vital determining factor in the creation of a truly social experience, an experience that is fully exploited once the gig gets underway and the comedian assumes his distinctly informal stance toward the gathered crowd. So, the audience is referred to collectively as "you," the second person plural; the comedian urges them to sympathize with him using phrases like "isn't that right?" and "don't you think?;" and the frequent requirement for vocal participation feeds the notion of an integrated and participative audience. As such, the consolidated audience becomes partner to the comedian. And this is a relationship, it seems, dependant upon that audience's very unity. As Rutter explains:

> Stand-up consolidates individuals in the audience into adopting a single role within the communication process. The audience expect, and are expected, to act and react as a single body as much as possible and discourage individual actions or deviations. (118)

Likewise, David Marc describes how "anonymous members of the assembly . . . spontaneously merge into a single emotional organism capable of reacting uniformly to the metaphor, wisdom, and worldview of one appointed personality" (14).

For all the apparent recognition of activity, of unity and bonding within the performer-audience partnership, there is a troubling hierarchy of power, here, and this is one that seems to dismiss crucial intra-audience activity. With its use of religious terminology likening the gig to a sermon, accounts such as Marc's seem, somewhat simplistically, to pit the elevated and superior performer against an inevitably passive and submissive audience. Certainly, issues of authority and control are a common concern across the criticism; and, in a discussion that is entirely relevant to Martin's work, Laurie Stone usefully observes how power relations in stand-up are actually flexible and changing, more intricate and complex than much of the criticism suggests. As I explain here, the audience does not necessarily respond to or identify with Martin in any straightforward manner that might signal a clear hierarchy between them, nor is the audience always the straightforwardly homogenous entity envisioned by many analysts. It is never Martin's intention that his audience comes together to vicariously experience life through his performance; his comedy is not a "cleansing" one, as Betsy Borns suggests, an opportunity for audience members to "relinquish [their] frustrated ids" (17). Rather, Martin's is *anti-comedy*: comedy of disconnection and disavowal that would seem to challenge perceptions about the roles of the comedian and his audience in stand-up, to defy any clear-cut hierarchy of power relations, and most crucially, to lay bare the very special pleasures facilitated by the medium.

"Can you believe this guy?!": Connecting in the Face of Absurdity

Some rare footage featured in a 1974 special for Canadian television (though actually recorded in the Ice House in California) reveals Martin in a small and intimate venue where he and the audience are close to one another. Though it would seem to provide all the facilitators for bonding and identification we might expect from the stand-up gig, significantly, this is not the case. Now, in many recordings of stand-up gigs, the use of the camera tends to be minimal: it functions as a means of preserving and occasionally highlighting, and rarely registers more than an omniscient viewpoint of the performance. In this instance, however, the camera is a revealing one: for the most part, Martin, dressed smartly in a black suit and white shirt with a black bow-tie, is framed in medium or long-shot on screen left, allowing the audience, seated around about him, to occupy more than two-thirds of the frame. Further, and by means of some quite probing intermittent mid-shots and close-ups of the crowd, we are given privileged insight into the actual live audience and individual reactions. In fact, what makes this such a valuable document in terms of stand-up reception is that it reveals a whole range of physical and audible audience reactions, and, most fascinating, lots of silence. Thus, we see audience members alternately look puzzled, remain silent, clap, shoot darting looks at one another, and gaze on at Martin in wide-eyed bewilderment.

One of the most simplistic gags performed here, and, for that reason, one of the most notable, involves Martin donning a novelty arrow-through-the-head. He begins:

> You know, when I, I first started out I realized I should put a little comedy into the act. You know, I was just playing the old banjo [motions playing the banjo], and, well, I don't really have a sense of humor so I hired some Hollywood comedy writers, and I paid 'em three thousand dollars and they wrote a fantastic piece of material for me, and, well, I'd like to do it for you right now. It's pretty funny. I think you're going to enjoy it. (*The Funnier Side of Eastern Canada*)

At this, he turns away from the audience, slowly reaches for and pulls on the arrow-though-the-head, and then turns back to face the group expectantly. Tellingly, what ensues is a very noticeable and lingering silence: it is only belatedly and hesitantly that individuals laugh or exchange brief and unbelieving looks and commentary with one another. Although an isolated laugh or two punctuates the beginning of his monologue (primarily as Martin mimes playing his banjo), for the most part the audience is silent, listening and watching on intently. The conversational, confessional discourse he initiates with "you know" seems to draw the group in, only to leave them stumped, left out on a limb, when Martin comes to produce the ridiculous prop. In a similar notable example he begins by ostentatiously holding out a paper napkin in front of the audience. In the manner of a magician he waves his hands and looks intently at the napkin as if summoning his magic powers. After a climactic pause and with a dramatic flourish, he places the napkin over his face; then, after another conspicuous pause, sticks his tongue through it. Once again, silence predominates before a smattering of laughter ensues.

What is apparent with these examples is that laughter is delayed because the build-up to the gag is exaggerated—too big and too inappropriate for the weak culmination that occurs. Ironic showmanship bearing only an excuse for a cheap gag, eventual, self-enforced laughter permits a sense of relief from the audience's astonishment. Clearly this is comedy of incongruity, and the audience is responding accordingly: that is to say, audience members laugh as they recognize the ironic juxtaposition of Martin's ridiculous actions and conventional speech. Yet, crucially, the strangeness, the inappropriateness of Martin's comedy seems to be realized *slowly*, if at all. While laughter here certainly conforms to the popularly held belief of tension release, it is the audience's *belated* response that is so intriguing: the lapse in performance before the onset of laughter underlines that it is through the audience, on the surface, at least, that the all-important tension is broken. Contrast this with the conventional comedian's delivery of the punch line, which acts as a cue for the audience to laugh, and we may begin to grasp the transgressive nature of Martin's comedy and of his relationship with the audience. Thus, after donning the arrow-through-the-head, it is in part Martin's relative *in*action that stuns the audience into momentary silence. So he waits silently, simply looking from one side of the room to the other before he motions somewhat arrogantly with his hands and asks, "So, you think it was worth three grand?" In a sense, this question *is* a punch line and it is certainly greeted with the most immediate laughter so far. Yet, in serving merely to reinforce what I would argue is the central incongruity and crux of the gag (Martin's *visual* donning of a cheap prop that clearly wasn't worth the money), such verbal reiteration may simply remind us that the audience's recognition of Martin's absurdity is a slow-burning one.

While we ought to bear in mind that Martin must surely have had some standing on the comedy circuit for this gig to be recorded for television in the first place, evidence here suggests that his persona is still very much an unknown quantity. When this audience *does* laugh, it seems to be neither laughter of complete recognition nor entirely collective laughter, but frequently a smattering of individualized and somewhat self-conscious laughs. Apparently quite new to his absurd brand of humor, these particular audience members seem unsure how to react to Martin.[10] Of course, familiarity or unfamiliarity with the performer is a vital determining factor in analyzing reception, and such instances of disconnection, both from Martin and amongst the audience, abound across his early career. In the segment of the TV special that sees Martin take to the streets of Toronto and busk with his banjo, the crowd, clearly having been rounded up with some trepidation for the occasion, convey bewilderment and even suspicion in the face of this rambling guy who tells them he is playing for money to get him to Montreal. Despite the impromptu nature of this particular performance, familiar intra-audience dynamics are at work: once again, a sense of conventional group identity is, on the surface, lacking, with uninitiated audience members reacting divergently and at their own pace to Martin's incongruities. Completely unaware of who he is (though this is doubtful in the case of the formalized performance at the Ice House), or, more likely, not yet fully "in" on his act, these audience members, though clearly to varying degrees, somewhat miss the incongruity of a self-conscious and savvy entertainer who is merely *playing* naïve. Crucially, and as I explain in due course, it is a contradictory familiarity with this central incongruity, a greater knowingness of the separation between Martin (or, more accurately, Martin-as-performer) and his stage persona, *Steve*, that promotes an entirely different set of responses from the later audience.

The divergent and individualized reactions we are privy to in these early gigs seem to sit problematically with the commonly held belief of laughter as contagious.[11] In fact, when one individual does laugh, that laugh is more likely to be met with bemused silence from other members of the audience, rather than further laughter. In instances such as these suspicion and bewilderment may be directed not only at Martin but at fellow audience members ("Why on earth is that guy laughing?! I don't get it!"). Yet, if we extend analysis of response, as I am doing, to account for such examples of (non)laughter, and, thus, to look beyond the superficial heterogeneity of the audience, what becomes apparent is precisely the shared nature of its response. For what envelops this particular group is certainly not collective laughter but a much more generalized sense of pleasure and belonging. Perhaps most significant about these performances, and over and above individual moments of laughter or silence, is that the majority of audience members wear broad smiles throughout. Such is the distance manufactured by Martin's surreal comedy that they may not necessarily fully "get" Martin at this point, nor may they even always "get" the responses of those around them; yet, significantly, they appear to be having a great time trying. If there *is* a sense of collective identity here, it is not one of communal identification with the performer.

It may be precisely Martin's disconnection from and alienation of this early audience that serves to unite the group and thus to strengthen intra-audience relations and promote audienceship. Indeed, it is this audience's seeming heterogeneity in the face of the performer's bizarre and unfamiliar antics that denotes crucial bonding: though they certainly convey the individualized and "deviant" responses Marc claims the stand-up performance actively discourages, this group may nevertheless be a more integrated force, and more complicit with one another than any simplistic or superficial analysis of their role might suggest. In fact, and with increasing familiarization with Martin's comedy, and of the complex mechanics of his performance, this sense of compliant interaction becomes more extensive, arguably strengthening intra-audience relations and facilitating an additional layer of performer-audience relation.

Getting in on the Act: Martin and the Cult Audience

If we fast forward a few years, audience response to precisely the same types of gags takes an entirely different form: here, in Martin's huge concert performances, the likes of which had only previously been afforded to rock 'n' roll performers, the audience responds, rarely with actual laughter, but with loud and resounding cheering. Comedian Steve Allen has commented usefully on audience response to Martin's act, detailing a most "unusual psychological response." He writes:

> The sort of laughter that greets Martin's witticisms, funny faces, and bits of physical business is markedly different from the simple hearty laughter most comedians evoke. It is more like the noise one hears at rock concerts, consisting of a mixture of screaming, hooting, and that particular falsetto "Whooo," which seems to have been introduced into the language of mob psychology in the mid-1960s by girls in their early teens attending rock concerts. (174)

Now, this "noise" Allen refers to as quite "unique in the history of American comedy" (174) may be seen as problematic. Constant, unyielding and non-discerning, it seems to occur no matter what, *if anything*, Martin does. Indeed, laughter, screams, and applause may erupt simply because the performance is marked as one of a hugely successful comedian: audience members, faced with their idol, and, further, caught up in the excitement of the gig, may find themselves unable to control their responses or, even, in the case of the uninitiated audience member (though there could not have been many of these), they may feel they *should* laugh, scream, or whoop. As John Limon cautions in a discussion that has resonance for the cult audience: "Perhaps, say, a comedian has been so successful (in his routine, in his career) that your laughter is indiscriminate" (12).

When looking to these performances at the peak of Martin's career, we must be careful to recognize that this is a period where he can do no wrong. These are audience members so enamored with Martin that they even try to copy his act and appearance. Thus, footage of fans outside one of these huge concert venues sees them dressed in familiar white suits and sporting amateur arrows-through-the-head, and is fascinating testimony to the cult status of Martin.[12] In the BBC's documentary *Steve Martin: Seriously Funny*, Martin's sister, Melinda Dobbs, describes how she truly knew her brother had "arrived" when she would see kids "wrapped around the building," many wearing the familiar comedy glasses, rabbit ears, and arrows-through-the-head: "They knew his routine, forward and backward," she says. And, as Richard Corliss notes, his catchphrases, the famous "well, excuuuuuse me!" and "naaaah!," had became "schoolyard mantras." While Martin's props and gags originally alienate his audience, over time, then, and into these huge concert-sized gigs with a much more knowing and complicit audience, precisely the same surreal comedy becomes the expected norm, and familiar material is received with resounding cheering. By this point in his career, the audience recognizes, adores, and even emulates the material, and is entirely familiar with the comic character that delivers it. Audience response by this time serves overwhelmingly to signal membership in Martin's cult.

There is clearly an issue of safety in numbers here, of conduct appropriate to and facilitated by the specific stand-up space. Of course, ascertaining what individual venues provide for and permit is very much part of my project; just as important is to consider Martin's cult following, and the much more blatantly uniformed audience responses this brings.[13] Yet to deduce that a larger stadium crowd responds more homogeneously to a performer may be too simplistic. Despite the pervasiveness of the performer-audience and intra-audience connections I outline below, we should not dismiss the fluctuating notions of dis/connection that persist in Martin's comedy, and even become more complex within this cult context. In fact, of vital significance is that the separation between Martin and *Steve*, his stage persona, is much more pronounced in these later gigs, giving rise to more layered performer-audience relations than we have seen thus far, and, further, that make analysis of Martin's comedy so intriguing. In short, the early audience is arguably responding to *Steve*, the third-rate comedian, and it is shared bewilderment at his antics that serve largely to unite the group, but to distance them from Martin. What becomes increasingly apparent, however, is that the later audience is responding to cult comedian Martin as *Steve*. This is to say that it is precisely the audience's awareness of this split, as well as, crucially, Martin's fetishization of that very knowledge, that serves both to unite the group with Martin and with each other. As I explain below, those intra-audience dynamics that were originally predicated on shared confusion come to be informed by knowingness and inclusivity; further, such audienceship may facilitate a closer, though by no means complete or conventional, audience-performer connection.[14]

A celebrated 1979 gig at the Universal Amphitheatre in Los Angeles (featured on *Steve Martin Live!*) sees Martin—now dressed in the immaculate white suit and carrying the banjo, attire that quickly became synonymous with his act—descend onstage to boisterous applause and cheering. Saying nothing, but moving ostentatiously across the stage, arms outstretched in mock recognition of his rock star status, he allows the raucous reception to build. Brief shots of the sizeable crowd standing and clapping are our first visual indication that this is a truly rapturous reception that shows little sign of abating. Finally, making a dismissive movement with his arms and urging, "go away, go away!" Martin reaches for a camera and takes a snap of the audience. It is only at this point that something resembling actual laughter can be heard, audience members responding to what is essentially the first comedic bit of the gig: the absurdity of Martin, a huge comic superstar, taking a photo of *them*. As laughter gives way to a few distinct shouts and cheers, Martin gives a purposeful "thank you" and raises his hands above his head, palms forward, as if indicating, "that's enough, on with the show." The briefest of interludes follows, punctuated only by isolated shouts from single audience members hopeful that their voice will be heard by Martin and, of course, be forever documented on videotape. (You can imagine the cries of "That's *me* you can hear!!" as those attention seekers later view the gig with their friends.) For the first time Martin stands still, claps his hands together as if on the cusp of something, and, in a low voice, begins with that confessional phrase, "You know. . . . " What then follows is the beginning of a barely audible monologue, one that, within seconds, is drowned out by increasingly loud and collective shouts and whooping sounds. Gesturing more wildly as the audience cheers, we realize that Martin is now saying nothing, only miming words we can only guess at. We recall that the monologue preceding the arrow-through-the-head gag in the earlier gig similarly began with "You know," only for audience members to respond with silence because they, in fact, *didn't* know, *didn't* identify with what he was saying or doing. Here, however, the much more complicit audience is responding instantaneously and riotously so, and to absolutely nothing. This is clearly Martin at play: at this point standing back from the microphone, he knows that nothing he says will be heard over the noise of the crowd. The crucial point is that he could be saying or doing anything, yet the audience simply cheers him on regardless.

Moments of apparently isolated clapping are heard on a few occasions throughout the first few minutes of the act, most noticeably when Martin turns to take a sip of water from a nearby glass, only to vulgarly spit it back out again. So pervasive are the shouts and screams that these claps are often indiscernible. However, the volume of the clapping momentarily comes to match that of the shouts and screams at a most significant moment. Here Martin begins by asking the audience, "Are tickets, were tickets, nine, nine seventy-five during the week? . . . That's not bad, really, to see a big show like this [gestures towards the practically empty stage around about him]. Um, well, with all the, eh . . . [reaches out to a table on his left] *props* an' everything." With this, and a self-satisfied smile, he produces the arrow-through-the head. Now, while his pause as he moves to pick up the prop attracts brief silence, as soon as it is placed on his head the audience explodes with a combination of loud cheering and clapping. (We can only assume that the audience is now clapping more quickly and vigorously for the claps to be more audible amongst the cheering.) This seems to be the audience at its most ecstatic and appreciative so far. And members are responding, not to Martin being conventionally clever or funny, nor merely to that absurdity the early audience only belatedly detects, but to the fact that they have seen, with their very own eyes, one of Martin's most iconic props and, further, been the honored butt of a cheap Martin gag. While such recognition and identification are completely at odds with the earlier bewildered response to the same prop, once again audienceship is solidified in the face of Martin's now wholly familiar antics; the group is bound together by shared and, this time, arguably more knowing, pleasures.

What is further significant with this gag is the more pronounced transition between Martin and *Steve*. Now, while the kind of conversational air Martin initially adopts here (and that recalls the similar dialogue he utilizes before donning the prop in the earlier gig) seems clearly to align him with those more traditional comedians who attempt to strike up a rapport with the audience, we are reminded that such familiarity is a performance, and that any attempt to appeal to the audience's common experience, particularly given the extreme self-consciousness of Martin's comedy, is necessarily tongue-in-cheek. That said, however, there is a definite change in tone here, and a more noticeable separation between the voice and posturing of Martin and that of *Steve* who, now wearing the prop, steps back from the microphone, arms outstretched and grins inanely at the audience. In fact, the separation between Martin and *Steve* becomes even more pronounced later in the gig when Martin, as *Steve*, breaks into his happy feet gag where his body, beginning with his feet, becomes comically possessed, and he dances erratically across the stage. As *Steve*, Martin's voice and mannerisms invariably become childlike, a marked contrast to his otherwise more adult and savvy musings. Thus, though no comedian is entirely himself onstage, and, further, though the transitions between Martin and *Steve* are fast and furious, and clearly more internalized within the overarching and thoroughly self-conscious Martin as cult performer persona than I am making out here, it is arguably Martin who converses with the audience about ticket prices, but *Steve* who surfaces once the arrow-through-the-head prop has been adorned. Charged, as cult performer, with pleasing his audience, Martin marks the appearance of *Steve* with appropriate aplomb—and the expectant audience responds instantaneously and riotously to the transition. Conversely, the separation between Martin and *Steve* is much more understated in the earlier gig, and the tone of Martin's voice more consistent. The shift in comedic discourse is thus comparatively both underplayed and undetected in the early gig, a combination of a more subtle mode of comedy and the audience's unfamiliarity with Martin accounting for delayed and hesitant response.

Martin continues to wear the prop throughout the next few gags, and is still wearing it when an initially (deliberately) faltering piece on the banjo breaks into a most accomplished performance. Familiar cheering and clapping erupt momentarily, yet we hear it gradually subside as he plays, the camera coming to fix upon a remarkably serious-faced Martin.[15] Relative silence ensues, the audience seemingly mesmerized by his playing, and, upon his finishing, hearty cheers erupt. While it is extremely difficult to discern the precise nature of any of these responses, this particular bout of cheering seems to express a kind of fascinated awe. The audience knows, of course, that Martin is a talented banjo player, and that the previous ineptitude he displays is all part of the act; yet the group seem to be responding to *how* good he actually is. Though the talents are incomparable, there is perhaps a similar dynamic at work, a similar pleasurable surprise, when Martin creates his balloon animals in the early gig and later, in this gig, when he expertly juggles oranges. Here, with the banjo playing, a return to normality, to Martin's feigned stupidity through the performance of *Steve*, and to the audience's complicit recognition of *Steve's* stupidity, is marked by a mixture of cheers and laughter as Martin, apparently only just noticing the prop still on his head, asks of the audience, "Did I have this on the whole time? . . . Well, I must have looked like an idiot up here. [Becoming serious]. I'm sorry. I've degraded myself. And I will never, ever, wear something like this again." As he moves to return the prop to the table, isolated boos can be heard. Yet, after a brief pause, and in response to him reaching for the infamous rabbit ears, surely another "degrading" prop, the audience erupts with loud and appreciative cheering and clapping. Though he pauses, apparently considering whether or not to put them on, this only triggers a more raucous reaction when he finally deigns to place them on his head. Once again, the transition between Martin and *Steve* is laid bare, the surreal nature of his comedy both apparent and anticipated, allowing the audience that crucial overarching connection with Martin.

What is essential for my argument, however, is that this is not to say laughter or cheering, shouting, clapping, or silence, for that matter, is entirely indiscriminate or otherwise negative, as Limon might have us believe. Rather, this wide range of responses serves to stress the enjoyable sense of belonging to the group that is so acute across Martin's career. Borns perhaps gets closer to recognizing the distinctive pleasures of the medium when she notes, "many comedians see themselves as adventure surrogates for those in the audience" (16). She writes:

> Like a group of children playing "house," we become a single entity playing "life," responding together to exaggerated problems that are close enough to the real thing to make the game interesting, yet abstract enough to keep it fun. We draw strength from the sense of community and comfort from the group feeling of "me, too." (17)

United, either by shared bewilderment ("Like *you*, I can't believe this guy!") or adulation ("Like *you*, I can't believe I'm here watching this guy!"), Martin's audiences certainly experience what Borns describes as the "me, too" syndrome; yet understanding and compliancy are overwhelmingly symptoms of audience members' relationships *with one another*. And, with the later gigs, the buffer of *Steve* permits another discourse of compliancy. In short, Martin and his audience are now all in on the joke while *Steve* goofs around, blissfully unaware. Thus, audience members are united with one another, and with Martin, by their privileged and shared knowledge of *Steve's* inadequacy. By now, the (of course, only superficial and highly self-conscious) collective relationship with the comic performer becomes just as significant in facilitating the pleasures of stand-up as those relationships between individual audience members. Despite, or, more appropriately, *because* of the larger, more impersonal space of stadium stand-up, a much closer performer-audience relationship is permitted.

Further, issues of power have become almost inextricably intertwined, both performer and audience arguably displaying ownership of Martin's comedy. In these later gigs, Martin very much orchestrates his audience's responses: "It was like playing an instrument. The audience was an instrument. I can do this and they'll do *this*" (Fong-Torres). That said, however, it is clear that comedy, as well as Martin, may actually be playing second fiddle here. Thus, and though I would argue his comedy still harbors an intelligence, a philosophical stance that is much more than just being "wild and crazy," the nuances of Martin's comedy are now overwhelmed, displaced by the thoroughly active and compelling input brought about by cult audienceship. Martin himself has said, "My original act came out of a philosophical point of view. A new point of view. I was just a guy up on stage acting like a comedian" (qtd. in Millner). Indeed, and in possibly the most telling incongruity of his comedy, Martin's very success comes to demand that he act "like Martin."[16]

Performing Relations: Martin and Hyper Self-Consciousness

Even at its most manipulative, and with increasing compliancy amongst individual audience members, the fact of Martin's comedy's pervasive knowingness still serves to deconstruct and destabilize traditional notions of audienceship. Part of Martin's individuality, in fact, is that he consciously parodies such loftiness and wisdom so often attributed to the comedian, and it is this, rather inadvertently, that renders him so intriguing a case study for analysis of performer-audience relations. Martin's comedy of disconnection may actually facilitate a most knowing and complicated performer-audience partnership that belies its apparent inaccessibility. By the height of his career, Martin has created a comedy that is hyper-aware, both of its audience, and of itself. As Adam Gopnik writes:

> Steve's audience was so wired in to the clichés, including the clichés of hipness and reference, that Steve could get a new kind of laughter by treating that knowledge at a higher remove, parodying the whole mechanism that produced show-business clichés in the first place–parodying the fact of entertainment itself. (102)

Aware that this is *Steve*, aware that they are an *audience*, and aware that they are being "played," the group nevertheless relish their vital role. With the free abandon of the excitable throngs who subject themselves to the pleasures of the thrill ride, the audience places itself in someone else's hands, but willingly so. This remains an audience on edge, dependant upon Martin for its "fix." Yet the cult audience is now very much "in" on the incongruity of his act. Responses certainly still serve to convey a pleasurable and active release of tension; yet this is not a release of tension from the occurrence of the unexpected (as we saw with the early audience where delayed laughter greets Martin's bizarre and incomprehensible antics), but often a release of tension from the occurrence of the gloriously expected.

The real distinctiveness of surreal Martin's comedy, it seems, arises from entirely complex, yet utterly pleasurable, performer-audience relations; (secondary) relations, it is clear, that may only be properly explained with recourse to the intricacies of audienceship by unpacking those (primary) intra-audience relations. While, and as I began this chapter by saying, audience compliancy with the performer is not unusual in stand-up gigs, the complexity of audience awareness and identification and, moreover, the kind of unspoken knowingness we find at the peak of his career, is testimony, I think, to the uniqueness of Martin's comedy. At a time when his contemporaries were delivering much more patently relatable material (from Murphy and Pryor's race-driven observations to Cosby's tales of being a father), Martin, adorned with an arrow-through-his head, arguably spoke louder and more compellingly to a generation weary of relevance and import.

Notes

1. A version of this essay also appears in *Participations: Journal of Audience & Reception Studies* 8, Issue 2.

2. In its attempt to elevate the status of stand-up, to take it as seriously as other art forms, much of the criticism may actually dismiss the very special pleasures it promotes. Further, and as I outline later with respect to Philip Auslander's reading of Andy Kaufman, some stand-up performance seems actively to resist the kinds of pleasures that Martin's comedy delights in.

3. Provine explains the useful term "sociality" as "[referring] to the ratio of social to solitary performance of a behavior" (45).

4. In the BBC's 1999 documentary, *Steve Martin: Seriously Funny*, fellow comedian and friend of Martin, Billy Connolly, deems him the "comedy Led Zeppelin."

5. In much the same vein as writers on cult cinema, I take "cult" to refer to a specific instance of performance defined in terms of a quirky, oppositional style and content, and a mode of reception marked by an active, loyal, and inclusive fan base. See especially Jancovich.

6. The rock and stand-ups gigs have much in common, not least because of the large, raucous, and dynamic constitution of their audiences (see Steve Allen's comment later in this chapter); but, further, and as Auslander illuminates across a body of work that encompasses both rock music and the stand-up comedy of Kaufman and Sandra Bernhard, because of the complex attributes of "liveness" they share (*Liveness*). Invoking a wholly postmodern, intertextual notion of performance that has particular resonance for Martin's later work, Auslander draws upon examples such as the recreation of music video imagery in live rock concerts and the restaging of familiar routines from television shows into live stand-up performances of the 1980s in order to challenge the conventional distinction between the primacy of the live event and the secondary nature of the "mediatized," dominantly televisual performance. (Borrowing from Baudrillard, Auslander defines "mediatized performance" as "performance that is circulated on television, as audio or video recordings, and in other forms based in technologies of reproduction" [*Liveness* 5]). In the specific case of stand-up, he writes that "the traditional privileging of the 'original,' live performance over its elaborations and adaptations is undermined and reversed. . . . the mediatized performance has become the referent of the live one" (*Liveness* 31).

7. Indeed, at the peak of his career, the live Martin gig functions as a wholly intertextual experience; an interactive simulacrum of his, by then

familiar, *mediatized* performances, thus giving rise to quite distinct conditions of reception. Yet, rather than mere negative response, I argue, these consistent moments of (non)laughter are extremely telling signifiers of intra-audience dynamics: affirmative components of the performance itself.

    8. One biography of Martin details how he was once made to work the stage lights himself with a foot pedal, and even, in one particularly undignified (but perhaps appropriately absurd?) instance, deliver his performance standing next to a salad bar (Lenburg, et al. 42–43).

    9. Contrast this with the more formal viewing experience of theater or cinema where the audience must necessarily wait until the end of the performance to discuss it with peers.

    10. For fascinating documentation of a truly dumfounded and, further, clearly uncomfortable audience, see footage of early Pryor gigs.

    11. See especially Provine's work.

    12. In the L.A. stadium gig, Martin draws humorous attention to the copy-cat props worn by his audience. After donning his, he remarks, "It's kind of fun for me to see the people in the audience with the amateur model arrow-through-the-heads."

    13. The 1978 comedy album, *A Wild and Crazy Guy*, is useful testimony to the changing nature of audience response to Martin's work, as well as the significance of venue. The first half of the album captures part of a gig performed in front of a small audience at The Boardinghouse in San Francisco, while the second half features material from a later stadium gig at the Red Rocks Amphitheatre near Denver (a venue whose current website invites: "See the biggest stars, under the stars. Rock is better on the rocks"). Plain to hear is the switch between the enclosed intimacy of the first venue, and, with this, the occurrence of many individualized and often-hesitant audience responses, and the rapturous collective cheering of the large open air gig.

    14. In this respect, Auslander's insistence upon the separation between Kaufman-as-performer and Kaufman-as-character in his chapter, "Comedy, Mediatization, Resistance: Andy Kaufman and Sandra Bernhard," is illuminating (*Presence* 139–176). I would argue that Martin's performance is similarly "resistant" in that it works to eschew any conventional notions of identification. Indeed, although the later audience feels itself more connected with Martin, and, in fact, there are moments in Martin's act (usually marked by his long pauses and knowing facial expressions) whereby he lets his audience know that *he* knows his character's absurdities are all part of the act, Martin exists, ultimately, at (at least) one remove from his performance. Arguably, Martin is always, and never less than, Martin-as-performer-as-performer. Now, Auslander himself sees Martin's comedy as less resistant, less effectual, less critically resonant, than that of Kaufman and Bernhard. Evoking a distinction between Martin's "blank and cynical" practices of

"pastiche" (*Presence* 137) and the "*critical* impetus" (*Presence* 139, emphasis added) of Kaufman and Bernhard, he writes: "[the work of Kaufman and Bernhard] . . . draws on the self-reflexivity of postmodernist comedy like Martin's but goes beyond that point to mount an implicit critique of postmodern culture" (*Presence* 138). Martin may, indeed, not put himself "radically at risk" (*Presence* 140), as Auslander suggests of Kaufman; nor may he illicit the "fuller gamut" of audience emotional involvement that Allen describes for Kaufman: "He wants you to feel uncomfortable, uneasy, unhappy, ecstatic, deeply moved, derisive, bored" (165). Yet, I would argue for a not dissimilar reactive, provocative refusal to assert authority and identity in Martin's comedy. If Kaufman "[insisted] that his unconventional work be read conventionally, by which standard it could only be seen as *bad*" (*Presence* 142), thereby alienating much of his audience, then Martin's insistence in his later gigs that his audience members don their rabbit ears and join in with the tacky gags, thereby implicating *them* as willing and knowing participants, may be tantamount to the wholly subversive, yet ultimately pleasurable, nature of his particular critique.

15. If the *real* Martin—the art-collecting, New Yorker-writing, philosophizing Martin—makes his presence felt at all onstage, it is at this very point.

16. The inability to practice the kind of comedy he wished was, in part, the reason for Martin giving up live comedy and moving into film: "comedy. . . . actually is too sensitive to be shouted and yelled at," he says, somewhat disparagingly (qtd. in Allen 176).

WORKS CITED

Allen, Steve. *Funny People*. New York: Stein and Day, 1981. Print.
Auslander, Philip. *Liveness: Performance in a Mediatized Culture*. London: Routledge, 1999. Print.
---. *Presence and Resistance: Postmodernism and Cultural Politics in Contemporary American Performance*. Ann Arbor: University of Michigan Press, 1994. Print.
Borns, Betsy. *Comic Lives: Inside the World of American Stand-Up Comedy*. New York: Simon and Schuster, 1987. Print.
Carter, Judy. *Stand-Up Comedy: The Book*. New York: Dell Publishing, 1989. Print.
Corliss, Richard. "Sensational Steve." *Time* 24 August 1987. Rpt. at SteveMartin.com. Web. 25 August 2007.
Fong-Torres, Ben. "Steve Martin Sings: The Rolling Stone Interview." *Rolling Stone* 18 February 1982. Web. 25 August 2007.

The Funnier Side of Eastern Canada. Dir. Bruce Campbell, Stanley Z. Cherry, and Donald Wilder. Perf. Steve Martin, Pat McCormick, and Neil Lundy. Independent United Distributors, 1974. Videocassette.

Gopnik, Adam. "Steve Martin: The Late Period." *The New Yorker* 20 November 1993: 98–113. Print.

Jancovich, Mark, ed. *Defining Cult Movies: The Cultural Politics of Oppositional Taste.* Manchester: Manchester University Press, 2003. Print.

Lenburg, Greg, Jeff Lenburg, and Randy Skretvedt. *Steve Martin: The Unauthorized Biography.* New York: St. Martin's Press, 1980. Print.

Limon, John. *Stand-up Comedy in Theory, or, Abjection in America.* London: Duke University Press, 2000. Print.

Marc, David. *Comic Visions: Television Comedy and American Culture.* Boston, MA: Unwin Hyman, 1980. Print.

Millner, Cork. "Steve Martin: Wild and Serious Guy." *Saturday Evening Post* 21 November 1989. Rpt. at sharingsteve.blogspot.com. Web. 15 July 2011.

Parenthood. Dir. Ron Howard. Perf. Steve Martin, Mary Steenburgen, and Dianne Weist. Imagine Entertainment, Universal Picture, 1989. Film.

Provine, Robert. *Laughter: A Scientific Investigation.* London: Faber and Faber, 2000. Print.

Rutter, Jason. *Stand-up as Interaction: Performance and Audience in Comedy Venues.* Diss. University of Salford, 1997. Print.

Shopgirl. Dir. Anand Tucker. Perf. Steve Martin, Claire Danes, and Jason Schwartzman. Touchstone Pictures, 2005. Film.

The Spanish Prisoner. Dir. David Mamet. Perf. Steve Martin, Ben Gazzara, and Campbell Scott. Jasmine Productions, Inc., 1997. Film.

Steve Martin Live!. Dir. Henry Winkler. Perf. Steve Martin, and Henry Winkler. Lions Gate, 1986. Videocassette.

Steve Martin: Seriously Funny. Dir. Adrian Sibley. Perf. John Cleese and Nora Ephron. BBC, 1999. Documentary.

Stone, Laurie. *Laughing in the Dark: A Decade of Subversive Comedy.* New Jersey: Ecco Press, 1997. Print.

6 Hoyle's Humility

Gavin Butt

Gavin Butt is Reader in the Department of Visual Cultures at Goldsmiths, University of London. He writes about live art and club performance, and queer cultures and their histories. His book on gossip and homosexuality in US art, *Between You and Me: Queer Disclosures in the New York Art World 1948–1963*, was published by Duke University Press in 2005. He is editor of *After Criticism: New Responses to Art and Performance*, Blackwell, 2004. He is co-director, with Adrian Heathfield and Lois Keidan of Performance Matters, a three-year creative research project on the cultural value of performance. See www.thisisperformancematters.co.uk.

British alternative performance artist, actor and comedian David Hoyle, also previously known as the Divine David, talks to Gavin Butt about his public spat with transsexual media personality Lauren Harries, the risks of self-exposure in his live queer cult show *Magazine*, and the importance of not taking yourself too seriously. The piece addresses the live comedy audience in a tangible way, commenting on audience-performer boundaries. In the interview, Butt and Hoyle touch upon several facets of the live comedy audience, including: the relationship between two performers onstage—how they are an audience for each other (in particular, in the case of the talk show, where one is meant to be the listener); therapy and the role of the live audience in the therapeutic process (compared to an analyst, even); the queer audience's relationship(s) to non-PC material; experimental comedy and the particular demands that the unconventional places on a live audience; honesty and expectation in the performer-audience contract—does a different truth emerge in the live realm?; and, the ways in which a performer-audience relationship develops over time, including phases of conflict.[1]

I meet with David Hoyle the week after his fractious exchange with Lauren Harries at his weekly show, *Magazine*.[2] Already something of a cult hit for the unpredictability of its live encounters between Hoyle and his guests, *Magazine* frequently showcases discursive interactions for which neither the words "discussion" nor "interview" are particularly appropriate. This is because Hoyle tends to favor something more like a "heated debate" (to quote Mrs. Merton) rather than the polite etiquette of liberal intellectual discussion or the staid respectful conversation of, say, a celebrity media interview. This was particularly evident in the fiery exchange of views between Hoyle and Harries—which stayed very rarely on the "right" side of insult—and in the boisterous interventions of audience members at the Royal Vauxhall Tavern in London. Some people simply shouted expletives, at both host and guest, whilst others made impassioned and angry political points. Tempers ran so high that at one point security was forced to eject someone from the building to prevent a fight breaking out. Hoyle tells me he'd never felt more "vulnerable to physical assault" than on this occasion. "The energy was unbelievable," he says. And it didn't stop there. Virtual exchanges continued on websites between variously affronted spectators long after the show had ended. Some bloggers claimed Hoyle had "bullied" his guest, whilst others counter-claimed it was Harries who was guilty of impoliteness and of being ill informed (i.e., of not knowing what she was talking about).[3] In short, the show generated much talk about both what, and how, things had been said. In many ways, this is Hoyle's metier: to use the medium of performance to make controversial spectacle out of such ethically troublesome exchanges. And the point? According to Hoyle, the point is to keep it *real*. To embrace, not airbrush, the uglier side of *Magazine*'s participants—of guests, audience members, and host—and to demonstrate that when we *really* engage with people and their differences, the results might not be pretty.

Harries is the latest among a long motley lineup of guests who have graced Hoyle's stage since *Magazine* began its three season run in 2006, including an octogenarian recovering alcoholic called Peter, the artist Maggi Hambling, sex worker Sleazy Michael, and human rights campaigner Peter Tatchell. Such people have been invited to discuss various subjects, from God, debt, and the Trade Union Movement, to gender dysphoria, America, and the internet. They take their place alongside the show's other regular features including videos, live painting, the performance of so-called "abstract shapes," and Hoyle's own particular brand of warm, yet simultaneously sneering stand-up comedy. Hoyle appears particularly keen on maintaining a stage for rather humble and popular human performances, upon which people avow their necessarily partial and limited views alongside their moral inconsistencies and impurities. Arrogance, bombast, and superiority are qualities clearly frowned upon at *Magazine*. "I'm interested in questioning and betraying my own ignorance and prejudice rather than sounding learned and PC-ed up to the eyeballs. I think it's more interesting to say (adopts modest, unassuming tone), 'Oh, well, I thought it was like this. . . .'" Such a performance ethics may, at least in part, be rooted in Hoyle's newly found faith in a more reparative, therapeutic approach to life. This results from his stint in the performance wilderness between 2000 and 2006 when he took time out to deal with his personal demons and depression. Since his return to the performance circuit he has been noticeably mellower, and has embraced the healing and empowering effects of avowing one's fears and vulnerabilities. This mellowing is evident, perhaps, in Hoyle's personal demeanor, which is warm, courteous and respectful when we meet over a pair of posh chip butties at the BFI Southbank. But this is not to suggest he's completely lost the edginess—either on- or off-stage—that brought him a certain notoriety on the 1990s queer performance circuit as the manically charged Divine David. He still can be brought to the limits of his tolerance, and be publicly scathing, even provocatively offensive, to those with whom he disagrees—to which the recent encounter with Lauren Harries was testament.

Harries—formerly *James* Harries—was a precocious child TV star and antiques expert in the 1980s. Now, after having had gender reassignment surgery in 2001, Harries is a struggling transsexual media personality. Hoyle tells me, "I have lots of admiration and understanding for people who seek gender realignment because I know it's a massive decision and it's not an easy process to go through." This sympathy had led Hoyle to invite Harries back onto the stage at *Magazine* to give her another chance to put herself across to an audience after a previous gin-soaked appearance ended up with the transsexual star too drunk and insensible to take part in any engaging exchange. But the return appearance—though less fuelled by booze—was just as unruly a meeting between the two, if not more so, than the first time around. The views (or insults, depending upon your point of view) that were exchanged are perhaps too much to print here. Suffice to say, Hoyle variously accused Harries of being a "right wing cunt," and of transitioning into a stereotypically glamorized embodiment of respectable womanhood, while Harries counter-accused Hoyle of being mean, and of being too afraid to own up to his own transsexuality.

Away from the melee of the evening, and after having had some time for reflection on what took place, I find Hoyle in an unforgiving mood:

> When someone has gone through that journey, and has had gender realignment surgery, you'd think the process would instill a little bit of humility. But I detected none, which got my back up. My natural sympathies just went out the window, really. I just thought, this person is very reactionary and, god love her, not a particularly well informed person. I know it sounds very schoolyard to say she started it . . . but she did.

In fact, it was Harries having the temerity to venture that she was "disgusted" by a previous performance at *Magazine* that made Hoyle see red. He stills rails at what he sees as her superiority: "Lauren's very into herself, presenting herself as a character, a caricature, a sweet little dairy maid or something." Indeed, she appeared onstage dressed very much, as Dawn Right Nasty has suggested, like Heidi or something right out of *The Sound of Music*.[4] "Was that a trans manifestation or does she sincerely think she was dressing as a woman? You can detect chauvinism in a lot of drag and transsexuality because the way people choose to manifest is very often at the more glamorous, bimbo end of the market. Very few are, say, modeling themselves on Andrea Dworkin."

Of course, Hoyle does have a (feminist) point here. There *is* a conservative strand in trans culture that places great value upon a gender transitioning that assimilates the trans-person into hetero-normative society. But to reduce all transsexuality to this reading, I suggest, is unfair. I mention, by way of example, the Los Angeles-based actress Calpernia Adams who recently described herself as a "*radical* assimilationist" (emphasis added) to signal her paradoxical desire to *both* pass as a normative woman *and* be visible as a trans MTF. I wonder if the same could be said of Lauren, especially as she made much on Hoyle's stage of wanting to be visible as a transsexual media figure? Hoyle is having none of it. "Aspects of her personality were just like a coarse

Liverpudlian drag queen. I said to her, transsexuality is not the same as being an uncouth drag queen, and yet there you are representing yourself in exactly that way." Hoyle seems so resolute in his position I wonder if he learned anything new about trans issues that night, to which he replies, "What it taught me was even though transsexuals have a shared experience it doesn't mean they're going to come out of it the same. You know they've all got different personalities, different levels of education, different levels of interest in contemporary politics or the avant-garde. And some are completely uninterested in art." He gives me a knowing grin.

We go on to talk a little about how we both *felt* that evening. I say—without wanting to sound like the usual liberal—that I'd left with split loyalties, that I'd felt both sympathetic to, and affronted by, both Hoyle and Harries in more or less equal regard. But perhaps my response wasn't typical of that night as many more rooted vociferously for Harries. "I felt like the pantomime villain," Hoyle tells me. Being vilified by his own audience was, he says, a "horrific feeling," but "I also knew there was an integrity to it. If I wanted to maintain where I was coming from it wasn't going to be an easy ride for anybody, me included, because I was bringing elements of northern stand-up, and northern brusque, and being very direct with the questions. But I did find it difficult." He impresses upon me the importance of taking such risks, of even being prepared to lose his audience. "I think it makes it livelier. When we're grown up and mature we realize that not everybody is going to like us. And that's ok. I think some people might have thought I was heavy handed, but best to be that rather than be patronizing or condescending."

Talk of a northern, brusque directness (Hoyle has more recently referred to Harries as "that cock-hacked-off cunt") raises interesting questions about *Magazine*'s indebtedness to traditional working-class pub entertainment. Hoyle is "proud" to hail from Blackpool, and calls the north of England "his bedrock." There's more than a whiff of regional belonging and class consciousness here, which makes sense of his broadly trailed socialist politics. But it's the *cultural* differences Hoyle seems to hang onto here perhaps more than anything else, especially in the midst of cosmopolitan, politically correct London. He relishes telling me that, in his view, "Bernard Manning is the ultimate avant-garde artist." This I take to be only partly ironic, and partly genuine, and provocative, a clue to the vernacular derivation of Hoyle's own brand of avant-garde performance. But in many ways, *Magazine* is perhaps less like Manning and rather more like the contemporary forms of working-class entertainment that have replaced such 1970s pub and club entertainers: namely, chav-baiting reality TV shows like Jeremy Kyle's. What's the difference, I wonder, between the kind of bust-ups we regularly see on these kinds of programs and the bear-pit scenarios, such as between Hoyle and Harries, at the Royal Vauxhall Tavern?

> Maybe there's not a lot of difference. We're all putting people in the spotlight and asking questions, trying to get to the bottom of things. But I think I'm more inclined to be aware of socioeconomic reasons for why people are like they are, which they never go into on *Jeremy Kyle*. They don't analyze why people behave the way they do due to chronic poverty and under-education. Judge Judy I find the most disgusting person on earth. If you had a bit of kindness, humility, and a sense of responsibility to wider humanity, you wouldn't be so condemnatory and punitive. You'd be a bit more understanding. But I think there are elements (in *Magazine*) that are played for spectacle and for laughs.

And this, lest us not forget, is what makes Hoyle such a successful performer: that he is so funny and able to make *laughter* out of it all. In conversation, Hoyle is quite philosophical about the role of humor in his shows.

> I look at a lot of the things we do, either singularly or collectively, as a constant displacement activity as we wait to die. To me life is all very comedic. The things we concern ourselves with and get ourselves in a lather about. So what? You're not meant to laugh at certain things because they're serious. But they're not. Humor is wonderful. It is my balm. I go from the perspective that we've all been hurt and that we're all pretty damaged. I see humor as the salve that will take away some of the pain, for some of the time.

This tragic-comic view of life is evident in Hoyle's particular take on camp humor, which is often laden with darkness in his shows. "We all love a camp laugh, don't we?" is a near catchphrase of his at *Magazine*, usually delivered after reminding his guffawing punters at whose expense such queer joviality is bought. On the children in Iraq he has been know to quip, "Surely they could make more of an effort for the cameras?" Hoyle quite reasonably tells me during the course of the interview, "You can give camp a weight or a lightness." Sure, he's right. But this either/or understanding of camp (*either* weighty *or* light) seems to me to miss what makes Hoyle's camping so remarkably funny: namely, that it solicits laughter that is *both* grave *and* flippant at the same time.

I say that camp seems to be under attack at the moment in contemporary academic queer studies as a privileged white gay male thing. Hoyle, I am happy to say, disagrees.

> I think it's open to everybody. A lot of people could camp it up. I mean, members of gangs could camp it up. In Los Angeles there's the phenomenon of the "crumping" community. When they manifest with the clown makeup they look sensational. It would be nice to think the old reality of being a man, of "You've got to look like a man, and hate art and have no imagination, and have five pounds of potatoes between your legs, and be really serious, etc." is on the way out. I hope people like that do lighten up and start wearing Pucci prints and enjoying life. No wonder a lot of people are stabbing themselves to death otherwise. A lot of heterosexual men should be thoroughly ashamed of themselves. They're not suitable role models.

And, smiling conspiratorially, he adds: "In fact, it would be nice if some of them were publicly executed."

Finally, I turn to ask him about the importance of collaboration, not only to his performance practice but also to his moral view of the world more broadly. This was thematized at *Magazine* by, amongst other things, the campy recycling of a 1960s civil rights anthem, "We Shall Overcome," by Joan Baez. Played each week by the resident DJ Father Cloth, Hoyle knowingly resurrected it as a hymn for today's apathetic times. Its perverse appeal, I take it, residing precisely in how the song's collectivist spirit jars so obviously with our individualist and consumerist present.

> We've got to be very aware of divide and rule. When as human beings we keep going on about how different we are. . . . You know you're really not that different. You're just a human

being. Like we all are. And neither better nor worse than anybody else. So get over yourself and work together for the common good. If we can't get on, if we refuse to collaborate and work with each other, then we're making ourselves into these tiny satellite states that really don't mean anything. Yes everyone wants to be seen as an individual, but it's not really going to change the situation, say, of migrant workers, or people who make our clothes for next to nothing. It's whether or not you put yourself before being part of a more massive organic form.

Of course, he could have Lauren Harries in his sights again here: his credo of the importance of collective political agency trumping the vanities of any narrow personal ambition. But, he adds, if we *can't* get on with one another then perhaps "we should all be armed, all be as selfish as possible, and just go round killing each other." So watch out, Lauren. David Hoyle is nothing if not a glorious and unpredictable performance of contradictions.

Notes

1. Reprinted with the permission of the author and *Dance Theatre Journal*. This article originally appeared in *Dance Theatre Journal*, Vol. 23, No. 1, pp. 30-34.

2. *Magazine* had three runs at the Royal Vauxhall Tavern in London between winter 2006 and spring 2008 and was produced in association with the London-based performance group Duckie. For full details see the Duckie archive http://duckie.co.uk/generic.php?id=63&submenu=david.

3. See Dawn Right Nasty's blog at http://redhairedqueer.blogspot.com/. You can find numerous posts here by Lauren Harries fans, responding to Dawn's defense of Hoyle. See "Lauren—Round Two" and "Shout, Shout, Let it all Out." Thanks to Kate Pelling for alerting me to Dawn's site.

4. Ibid.

7 George Lillo's *The London Merchant* and the Laughing Audience

Diana Solomon

Diana Solomon is Assistant Professor in the Department of English at Simon Fraser University. A specialist in Restoration and Eighteenth-Century theater, she combines performance theory and print culture studies to ask what we can know about eighteenth-century theater from the texts it has left us. Her book project on female prologues and epilogues in Restoration theater studies how these paratexts enabled actresses to critique contemporary issues and social attitudes toward women.[1]

One does not normally attend a contemporary performance of *Macbeth* expecting a laugh a minute. The drunken porter scene offers fleeting comic relief, but most of what follows is despairing and violent. A performance of *Macbeth* in 1664, or 1730, or 1799, however, possessed more comic potential. During the earlier dates, Sir William Davenant's operatic adaptation of the play emphasized not compulsive hand washing but the new "flying machine" that propelled the three witches through the air. As the century progressed, Shakespeare's version returned to the stage, but as part of the same show audiences might have also watched dances, acrobatics, or pony races. And throughout this time, comic prologues and epilogues flanked performances and publications of *Macbeth*. Eighteenth-century theater patrons arrived to see tragedies prepared to cry *and* laugh. In this article I examine how one aspect of eighteenth-century theater—the comic, often bawdy, epilogue concluding a tragedy—demonstrates how the audiences delighted in comic incongruities. Their taste is all the more remarkable because retrofitting tragedy for comedy violated the neoclassical idealization of the tragic form as elegantly symmetrical and morally corrective. Ignoring such patrons and their demand for direct and self-conscious audience asides thus means misinterpreting eighteenth-century theater. A 1747 prologue by Samuel Johnson captured the power audiences had over the players: "The Drama's Laws the Drama's Patrons give, / For we that live to please, must please to live" (Johnson 185).[2]

Figure 7.1 William Hogarth, *The Laughing Audience*, 1773. Courtesy of Dartmouth College, Hanover, New Hampshire; Gift of Hamilton Gibson, Class of 1897.

A study of the performance and publication histories of George Lillo's 1731 tragedy, *The London Merchant*, and its bawdy epilogue illustrates the insistence of the eighteenth-century audience on taking comedy with their tragedy. The most enduring eighteenth-century English tragedy, George Lillo's *The London Merchant, or, The History of George Barnwell*, represents the greatest implications for ignoring the comic epilogue, yet this has been the approach of nearly every critic to date. Whereas most other eighteenth-century tragedies with comic epilogues rarely receive critical attention, Lillo's canonical text is frequently credited as founding the genre of domestic tragedy.[3] Inspired by the "Ballad of George Barnwell," Lillo's play was the one tragedy between 1715 and the end of the century that has remained popular today to study, if not to perform. We know of 243 recorded performances in eighteenth-century London alone, and the play also traveled.[4] *The London Merchant* was also novelized twice by 1810, with one version abridged and reissued in 1820 (Hudson 122). The epilogue, moreover, continues to appear in most editions. All of the twenty-six total editions and issues currently available on the *Eighteenth-Century Collections Online* database print the epilogue, and nineteen also include the name of its original speaker.[5] A 1731 Dublin broadside reprints the original prologue and epilogue but lists their speakers as Mr. Elrington and Mrs. Sterling, indicating a performance at the Smock Alley Theatre. Given the play's extensive performance and publication history, not to mention its frequent presence on college syllabi, critical neglect of the epilogue must be remedied, and the epilogue's appearance following a tragedy suggests a need to study affect and the eighteenth-century audience.

Poetic bids for spectators' good opinions, dramatic prologues and epilogues originated in Hellenic times and reappeared in Medieval English plays to welcome audiences to the theater and bid them return, preferably with their friends. Shakespeare and his peers recognized comic potential in the form, and their inventiveness increased the percentage of plays that had prologue, epilogue, or both.[6] Rosalind, the epilogue's speaker in *As You Like It*, even declares that "good plays prove the better by the help of good epilogues" (434). Coinciding with the rise of the English actress, prologues and epilogues then became *de rigueur* in the Restoration and eighteenth century, appearing in ninety percent of all plays (Wiley xxvii). Customarily assigned to the most popular players, prologues and epilogues also helped introduce new actresses.

Audiences adored prologues and epilogues in general and especially favored comic epilogues to tragedies. Sometimes playgoers treated a prologue or epilogue as the main event—theatrical practice in the eighteenth century permitted them to show up for the two "curtain tunes" and the prologue, and then exit the theater with a refund. Audiences alternatively could pay "after-money" for admission to Acts Four and Five, the epilogue, and subsequent entertainment. They also could enrich their authors; John Dryden made a tidy profit writing prologues on commission. Their printing history also conveys their popularity. Some prologues and epilogues circulated on broadside sheets as play advertisements; most were reprinted in quarto form alongside their plays; and some were printed in newspapers or miscellanies. The later eighteenth century saw several collections of prologues and epilogues published.

What accounts for their popularity? While there are no definitive answers, prologues and epilogues pioneered several persuasive devices. One attraction was their customization to specific performances. A play's opening night featured a prologue and epilogue commemorating that event, and new prologues and epilogues accompanied revivals. By the late seventeenth century, prologues and epilogues, like today's advertisements, had developed many techniques for selling their product. Featuring onstage donkeys and cross-dressing actresses, bawdy language and characters rising from the dead, they were customized to specific performances and implied that *tonight's* audience was worth such efforts. We also see that specificity in publication; beginning in the 1660s many of them featured the speaker's name and sometimes specifics of the performance. Epilogues also appealed to audiences by allowing them to witness what Richard Schechner calls "transportational" performances, where performers transition from role-playing back to their offstage existence (91). This process enabled metacommentary, where the speaker remained in costume yet satirized the just-concluded main piece. Yet another reason is their sheer perversity. When discussing an epilogue by Pope, eighteenth-century critic Joseph Warton suggests this attraction: "It is written with the air of gallantry and raillery, which, by a strange perversion of taste, the audience expects in all epilogues to the most serious and pathetic pieces. To recommend cuckoldom, and palliate adultery, is their usual intent" (270). Warton's scold ironically captures the gleeful degeneracy of many comic epilogues.

In favoring prologues and epilogues, eighteenth-century audiences preferred a comedy similar to contemporary stand-up. A stand-up comedian delivers mini-narratives, customized to the audience, with no necessary connection to one another save that they develop and trade on the comedian's persona. Successful comedians also create a persona the audience can imagine in a variety of circumstances; it is easy to imagine, for example, Rodney Dangerfield's perennial loser not getting any respect in many situations. Shows vary nightly; performance theorists remind us of the lack of fixedness between any text and performance, but the degree of vacillation is especially wide due to the emphasis on eliciting audience response (Parker and Sedgwick 13). Philip Auslander implies this when he describes stand-up as "a fundamentally old-fashioned, labor-intensive, low-tech performance mode" that depends upon the "human presence" of performers and audience (199).

For prologue and epilogue speakers, persona similarly dominated. The comic content and delivery style had to appear either consistent or recognizably deviant from the persona. The speaker targeted belief systems of present individuals, groups, or absent third parties. Always present for audiences was the potential—some might say threat—to become involved in the act. Prologues and epilogues also used little of the Restoration and eighteenth-century theater technology prevalent elsewhere in the performance. Especially for prologue speakers, who performed before the curtain rose, there was no need for a complex background scene; in order to connect with the audience, performers mostly used the forestage. For these reasons, prologues and epilogues, like stand-up, depended for their comedy on the persona and the word.

While both modes cater to their audiences, the eighteenth-century audience possessed more agency to reshape the performance. Many of us delight in re-experiencing our favorite jokes, but enraptured eighteenth-century audiences sometimes demanded prologues or epilogues be repeated on the spot. In one example, actor Thomas King delivered a prologue to an afterpiece (a short, usually comic play) by Elizabeth Craven that the audience insisted on hearing again even after the afterpiece and its epilogue were performed. King had already left the theater, so another actor had to deliver it (*Town* 230). Audiences demanded star actress Anne Oldfield perform epilogue encores to Ambrose Philips's *The Distrest Mother* during each of the first three nights; it was subsequently called for during each successive performance of this wildly popular tragedy, outliving Oldfield herself by sixty-six years.[7]

The stratification of the theater auditorium indicates spaces where audiences could exert control over the performance. Upper classes generally sat in the box seats, where their view of the stage was rather poor but others' view of them was rich. Like those in the boxes, spectators watching from the pit—the area directly in front of the stage—could create spectacles, whether due to their loud critiques or fruit-throwing, or their distracting conversations and procuring of prostitutes. Many audience members, moreover, watched the play while onstage themselves. A common practice until 1762, audiences usually either stood or sat on benches or stools; this semi-fixed space, to use Edward Hall's term, enabled a high rate of exchange between actor and spectator (Hall 101–104; Bennett 132). It meant that the actor had to negotiate pathways to and from the stage; to watch those actors, audiences seated in the box, pit or gallery necessarily had to also watch their audience counterparts on stage. This scenario could provoke onstage audiences to return the gaze, diverting their attention away from the actors. Observing that proximity can enable comedy, Judith Fisher describes how during various performances of tragedies onstage, audience members interfered with performers, generating laughter instead (63). And so rather than futilely attempting to keep audience attention from veering, theater personnel used devices like epilogues to harness humor, directing audiences back to the play even if doing so resulted in a change of tone. The interplay between performers and audiences thus stands as another example of how audiences introduced and amplified the comic, even during the performance of tragedies.

Nor was the power of eighteenth-century audiences relegated to the stage. Male admirers of actresses often occupied the backstage area; Samuel Pepys logs many diary entries on cavorting with Nell Gwyn and other female performers in their "tiring" rooms. Theater patrons could visit backstage during as well as before and after the performance. The fact that we have records of dates when the public was prevented from visiting the tiring rooms indicates, as Tita Chico points out, that access was the status quo (48). On the night of what was probably the most violent backstage event of the Restoration, one Charles Dering approached the great actress Elizabeth Barry backstage and later returned there to murder her lover (Milhous and Hume 149–74). While the vast majority of audience members did not go backstage to assault their romantic rivals, this event exemplifies how audiences encroached on theatrical spaces that are now customarily off-limits.

Given the audience's predilection for comedy and control of the theater, we must study the development of domestic tragedy in the eighteenth century alongside the development of what it ironically sustained: the comic epilogue. The first example of a Restoration tragedy with a comic epilogue was spoken by actor John Lacy to Sir Robert Howard's *The Vestal Virgins* (1664). His opening couplet, "After a sad and dismal Tragedy / I do suppose that few expected me," indicates both the intended generic interruption and Lacy's public persona as clown (Danchin, *Restoration* 203–06). It was the next example, however, that set the tone for all that followed: the epilogue John Dryden wrote for Nell Gwyn to conclude his tragedy, *Tyrannick Love* (1669). Her heroine has committed suicide from unrequited love, but following Act Five, when carried out on a stretcher, she suddenly sits up and declares, "Hold, are you mad? you damn'd confounded Dog, / I am to rise, and speak the Epilogue" (192–93). All subsequent tragedies in this vein take a prominent, suffering female character and reconceive her as a comic, usually bawdy figure within the epilogue. The popularity of this form—through 1731 there are sixteen of these so-called "revived" epilogues alone, a subset of the number of tragedies with comic epilogues—indicates a difference in affect between audiences then and now. Then, tragedies with comic epilogues were not just tolerated but demanded.

One in demand was the epilogue to Lillo's *The London Merchant*. Performed by Jane Cibber, daughter-in-law of the prominent actor/playwright/theater manager Colley Cibber, the epilogue features the character "transporting" back to the persona of the actress, employing brash sexual innuendo and challenging the audience. Acts One through Five of *The London Merchant* feature sweeping emotional scenes. A woman hurt by other men, Millwood exacts revenge by seducing the London merchant's apprentice, George Barnwell, and persuading him to steal from his friend and murder his uncle for profit. Millwood then hands over the repentant Barnwell to the authorities, and his eponymous employer, Thorowgood, pleads for mercy. The pair is found guilty and sentenced to hang. The play concludes with the pair in contrasting emotional states: Barnwell grieves that he neglected to consider Thorowgood's daughter, the beautiful, moral Maria, as a lover until now, just before he is executed, while Millwood remains unrepentant. It is implied that Maria is wracked with grief over Barnwell's death, a pain of inopportune love.

Although largely considered a tragedy, some interpretations of the plot then and now have veered toward either sentimental comedy or comic incongruity. This is one of the first times in which the London audience is prompted to sympathize with the merchant class, with the apprentice George Barnwell and the merchant Thorowgood tapping the tear ducts more readily than Shylock. Several critics have argued that the play extends tragic sympathy to the merchant class; in his trace of continental adaptations of the play, Lawrence Marsden Price locates three such instances in the 1760s (134–35). Such readings, however, miss the risible element of the dominant woman-passive man combination. Other plot elements also suggest the plausibility of a comic reading. Lincoln B. Faller identifies a scene where Millwood breaks off with Barnwell expecting him to protest, but instead Barnwell agrees (99–101). Although classified as a tragedy, the play does contain moments of comedy.

Such comic elements, however, are of a different nature than those present in the epilogue. The epilogue's liminality, an extended transportational shift between the character Maria and the persona of actress Jane Cibber, necessitates that we reconceptualize the play. Elsewhere I have termed the epilogue's amalgamation of character and persona "betweenness," where this figure creates comedy by alternating between the two, thus creating a guessing game for the audience as they determine which words evoke which entity (Solomon 156). Maria's ability to overcome the loss of her beloved shifts the end of Act Five from moralizing about loyalty to family and employer, to demonstrating a recovery from hardship. The actress, a respected Drury Lane company member who had a history of stretching mediocre plays into successful multi-night runs, completes the rounding of this character. Among the records of Jane Cibber's talent is an "act-off" where she beat Elizabeth Younger in a contest of whose performance of the role of Margery Pinchwife in William Wycherley's *The Country Wife* received greater audience approval. Having married into the famous theatrical family of the Cibbers, Jane supplemented their fortunes. Best known for being the subject of Pope's revised and scathing satire, *The*

Dunciad, the family patriarch Colley Cibber was a talented actor and playwright in his own right, and a continuous source of controversy. Cibber's biographer, Helene Koon, credits his daughter-in-law with saving his son Theophilus's play, *The Lover*. With the play debuting in 1730 when Colley was facing harsh attacks, Jane Cibber not only diffused a near-riot on opening night but also performed her part so well that the play enjoyed an eight-night run—by eighteenth-century standards, a success. Had she not died in childbirth shortly thereafter, Jane Cibber would be better known.[8]

Rather than concentrating on the tragic demise of the would-be couple, the epilogue combines character and actress to showcase Maria's independent comic survival. She spends one mere couplet grieving for her dead lover, and then promptly begins a new manhunt:

> Since fate has robb'd me of the hapless youth
> For whom my heart had hoarded up its truth,
> By all the laws of love and honour, now
> I'm free again to choose–and one of you. (Steffensen 209)

This statement shifts the audience's attention away from the tragic end of the play, and alters its sense of Maria's character from one who did not pursue Barnwell at all during the play to one who now takes charge of her love life by suggesting that something "real" could happen between her and an audience member. In doing so it changes the focus of the audience. We know audience members grieved when Barnwell died; such responses, in fact, seemed to have been compulsory. Quoting Lady Mary Wortley Montagu, who proclaimed, "whoever did not cry at *George Barnwell* must deserve to be hanged," David Mazella establishes that the play evokes this kind of moral trumpeting because tearless audience members are made to feel akin to Millwood (795). Montagu's statement implies an appropriate emotional response. As Lawrence Price has identified, moreover, Sarah Fielding's *The Adventures of David Simple* features two ladies arguing over which play was more moving, Joseph Addison's *Cato* (1713) or *George Barnwell* (151). And in a prologue to Lillo's *Elmerick; or, Justice Triumphant* (1740), written while Lillo was dying, actor James Quin says, "*Barnwell* . . . from each Eye still draws the natural Tear" (Danchin, *Eighteenth Century* 5–6). Functioning like an audience aside, Maria's epilogue thus followed a strongly evidenced cathartic end to Act Five.

By blurring the divide between character and actress, the epilogue casts *The London Merchant* audience in a new role. It playfully reverses the scenario created when the first woman stepped on the London public stage in 1660: that men in the audience voyeuristically enjoyed actresses and seduced, pursued, and sometimes married them. Here Maria/Cibber suggests she can survey and choose one of the spectators: both a comic gender role reversal and a kinky bit of theater given that Cibber's husband played Barnwell and her father-in-law wrote the epilogue. The sexual charge also changes because of a new consciousness of the expanded stage. During the play, Maria and Barnwell never exchange direct confirmation of each other's love; instead, Barnwell's friend Trueman functions as an intermediary. By not having Maria and Barnwell exchange poignant expressions of love before he dies, Lillo avoids a moment of high drama. But by enlarging the performance space to include box, pit, and gallery, the epilogue reimagines the theatrical apparatus as enabling sexual connections. The epilogue also uses to the speaker's advantage the fact that the theater lighting illuminated the audience more brightly than the figures onstage. Maria/Cibber's sexually acquisitive gaze thus broadens the scope of the epilogue's comic charge.

The epilogue also disrupts what many critics have suggested was the function of the play: providing a moral education for the many apprentices in the audience. According to Jones DeRitter, the final three years of an apprentice's indenture were economically favorable to the master and detrimental to the apprentice, often inspiring the latter to rebel (378). Wishing to stress the theme of apprentices' loyalty to their masters, Freemasons sponsored many revivals of the play, and masters compelled their apprentices to attend. Although records are insufficient to support William Henry Hudson's claim that until 1819 the play was performed every Christmas and Easter week, in many of these years there are multiple performances in the days just after Christmas (121). When considered with its epilogue intact, it is hard to reconcile the play's cultural manipulation for moral instruction. Instead, Maria/Cibber flirts with the audience when she pretends to identify various audience members as "the cit, the wit, and the tawny Jew" and refuses to search the "sober gallery" for lovers because it contains "prentices—and cuckolds all a-row" (Steffensen 8–11). By mock-classifying male audience members into unfavorable categories, she distracts from moral messages.

Although most original prologues and epilogues were not revived along with their plays, audiences demanded certain epilogues be repeated, including this one. Sometimes audiences called for epilogue encores on the spot; while there are no records of whether this happened to Jane Cibber's epilogue, there is evidence the epilogue was performed past its usual expiry date. Scholars disagree whether prologues and epilogues were normally performed only on the first night, on the first three nights, or during the play's entire first run, and eighteenth-century theater practices and record keeping is inconsistent. It is unusual, however, for the original epilogue to be performed during a play revival's first run, but such is the case with *The London Merchant* epilogue. Besides the premiere on 22 June 1731, the epilogue was performed at least six more times in the 1730s by Cibber and Miss Anne Brett, and on 9 November 1741 by a Miss Carter.[9] The epilogue was also likely performed on a minimum of seven additional occasions, including the Irish staging mentioned above. In performance, then, the epilogue enjoyed at least a ten-year afterlife.

The original epilogue, moreover, continued to be published with the play and remains so to this day. In the thirty-one English-language editions between 1731 and 1814 that have been available to examine, all publish the epilogue, and twenty name Jane Cibber as the speaker.[10] Most recent English-language publications either include it or, like the *Broadview Anthology of Restoration and Early Eighteenth-Century Drama* of 2001, omit nearly all prologues and epilogues on policy (Canfield and von Sneidern xix). The editor of the Regents Restoration Drama edition, William McBurney, points out that performances of the play were normally followed by comic afterpieces (Lillo xx). These shorter pieces bore no obvious relationship to the main plays; they involved an entirely different cast of characters and plot, and featured different actors. Were the audience unaware of the performance to come, they would have found the tone of the afterpiece jarring. Since printers did not publish afterpieces along with the plays they accompanied, we need to consider what they *did* publish; but afterpieces also make clear the importance of studying theater in performance since they followed comedy and tragedy alike.

Whereas members of eighteenth-century society designated Acts One through Five to demonstrate moral lessons to apprentices, the epilogue addresses all classes of males in attendance and threatens to disrupt the moral lessons previously imparted. Maria then warns men in satisfying marriages that they too can be cuckolded, further attesting to her power as a sexual agent. In this unusual situation, a woman has the power to rebound from a lost love, announce she is again available, survey all the suddenly eligible men, reject large swathes of them in insulting generalizations, and remind them that even those who might consider themselves off-limits because they trust their wives are still in danger of being cuckolded, and therefore might consider having an affair with her.

Maria's last words extend beyond character and problematize the audience's response. In her final couplet, "In short, my heart to this conclusion draws: / I yield it to the hand that's loudest in applause," she revisits the intended purpose of the epilogue: to win audience support for the play. It is a neat reification and it diffuses the intense sexual joke she has created. But the applause at this point would seem to be mixed—is one still applauding the tragic catharsis that existed before Maria's epilogue, or is one rewarding her virtuosity as a comedian? Or are men trying to clap the loudest and play along with the game of winning Maria/Cibber? Susan Bennett points out that typically, applause is the tool the audience uses instantly and collectively to judge the merit of the performance (163). But the epilogue's reconceptualization of the applause function complicates the issue of judgment; in meting out claps, the audience judges Maria/Cibber for judging them. Maria's game, moreover, transforms applause from a collective act to an individual and potentially antagonistic one. Claps might mean either "I loved the play" or "Pick me!" *The London Merchant* audience has now entered its own state of betweenness, vacillating between observing and acting.

A consideration of the epilogue casts light on the critical question of *The London Merchant*'s genre. The play contains markers of both tragedy (the deaths, the dissolutions of love) and sentimentalism (the implication that Barnwell is to be mourned despite his crimes). In an often-cited exchange, Raymond D. Havens and George Bush Rodman debate which quality predominates in the play (Havens; Rodman). Rodman claims that because Lillo's attitude toward human nature was distrustful rather than benevolent, the play should be considered a tragedy rather than an example of sentimentalism. Havens counters by saying that since Barnwell generates audience tears for feeling remorse for his sins both before and after he commits them, there is no evidence that, if he had been spared the gallows, he would not repeat his crimes. To Havens the play is sentimental, therefore, because Barnwell's feelings are judged more important than his actions. Yet in their debate over genre, they neglect to consider a third option: that given its epilogue, the play mixes tragic, sentimental, and comic elements. In focusing exclusively on Lillo's opinions of humanity, and Barnwell's actions and feelings, Rodman and Havens neglect to consider both the play as performance and the remainder of the characters. Lisa A. Freeman's recent consideration of the play's genre treats the play more completely; her omission of its epilogue is thus the more prominent. In defending her compelling argument that eighteenth-century tragedy failed because it portrayed a domestic middle class that did not yet exist in English society, Freeman points to *The London Merchant* as a shaper of public virtue (539–61). To make this claim, she cites the play's dedication and prologue, but avoids the less-than-virtuous epilogue. In considering the play's genre, therefore, Freeman, Havens, and Rodman neglect to consider the role of the comic epilogue, which satirizes many of the play's emotional outbursts and coincidences.

Lady Mary Wortley Montagu's command to "cry at George Barnwell" thus expires at the epilogue. The sentimental comedic concept of "laughing through one's tears" could be relevant here, but its application would seem to make tragedies with comic epilogues especially perverse at this moment, because the laughter they generate would erase, rather than complement, the audience's tears. An analysis of the play as a moralizing tear-jerker, therefore, is challenged when the play is considered in performance, since the epilogue's pragmatic comedy, its reshaping of Maria as capable of surviving and progressing to her next romantic relationship, promotes a laughter not through one's tears, but at the expense of them.

The tragedy with a comic epilogue appealed to a demanding audience accustomed to influencing the course of theater. Like modern-day comedy club audiences, they enjoyed the proximity to and direct address of the performer, and the opportunity to direct the performance. William Hogarth's *The Laughing Audience* might therefore reflect a moment from *any* evening, regardless of the play's genre, at the eighteenth-century theater.

Notes

1. Thanks to Fiona Ritchie and Betsy Verhoeven for their comments on this essay.

2. Johnson wrote this prologue for David Garrick's reopening of the Drury Lane theater.

3. Richard Helgerson's study of English domestic drama challenges this classification because he locates an earlier domestic tragedy in *Arden of Faversham* (1592). One can claim, however, that *The London Merchant* rebirths the tradition after two centuries of dormancy. See *Adulterous Alliances: Home, State, and History in Early Modern European Drama and Painting*, Chicago, IL: Chicago University Press, 2000.

4. This number represents performances listed in *The London Stage*, which, although not error-free, remains the most comprehensive eighteenth-century theater calendar. See William Van Lennep, et. al. Thanks to Amy Russell-Coutts for her assistance.

5. Of these, sixteen self-designate as editions, even though bibliographers would consider some of them issues.

6. Autrey Nell Wiley has calculated that between 1558 and 1642, approximately forty-eight percent of plays contained a prologue, epilogue, or both (xxvii).

7. For more about Oldfield's epilogue, see Solomon, 158–69 and n. 22.

8. After her death, Jane Cibber was then overshadowed by Theophilus's notorious relations with his second wife, Susannah, whom he sold to another man. For more on Jane Cibber, see Koon, 109–33.

9. Cibber performed the epilogue on 20 August 1731 and 17 May 1732; Miss Brett performed it on 23 May, 17 June, and 22 August 1734 and 11 July 1735. See Van Lennep, et al., Part 3.

10. Thirty-one editions is a conservative count; the 1754 version looks like an impression of the 1751, so although it is unlikely that the publisher, Lintot, left the type standing for three years, the 1754 version cannot be confirmed as an edition.

Works Cited

Auslander, Philip. "Comedy About the Failure of Comedy: Stand-up Comedy and Postmodernism." *Critical Theory and Performance*. Ed. Janelle G. Reinelt and Joseph R. Roach. Ann Arbor: University of Michigan Press, 1992. 196–207. Print.

Bennett, Susan. *Theatre Audiences: A Theory of Production and Reception*. 2nd ed. London: Routledge, 2001. Print.

Canfield, J. Douglas and Maja-Lisa von Sneidern, eds. *The Broadview Anthology of Restoration and Eighteenth-Century Drama, Concise Edition*. Peterborough: Broadview, 2001. Reprint, 2004. Print.

Chico, Tita. "The Dressing Room Unlock'd: Eroticism, Performance, and Privacy from Pepys to the *Spectator*." *Monstrous Dreams of Reason: Body, Self, and Other in the Enlightenment*. Lewisburg: Bucknell University, 2002. 45–65. Print.

Cibber, Colley. *The Prologue and Epilogue of George Barnwell, the London Merchant: To be spoke this Night in the Play-House*. Dublin, 1731. Print.

Danchin, Pierre. *The Prologues and Epilogues of the Eighteenth Century*. 8 vols. Nancy: Presses Universitaires de Nancy, 1990. Print.

---. *The Prologues and Epilogues of the Restoration 1660–1700*. Nancy: Presses Universitaires de Nancy, 1981–88. Print.

DeRitter, Jones. "A Cult of Dependence: The Social Context of *The London Merchant*." *Comparative Drama* 21.4 (1987–8): 374–86. Print.

Dryden, John. *Tyrannick Love*. 1st ed. London: H. Herringman, 1670. Print.

Faller, Lincoln B. *The Popularity of Addison's Cato and Lillo's the London Merchant, 1700–1776*. Garland Publications in American and English Literature. New York: Garland, 1988. Print.

Fisher, Judith W. "Audience Participation in the Eighteenth-Century London Theatre." *Audience Participation: Essays on Inclusion in Performance*. Ed. Susan Kattwinkel. Westport, CT: Praeger, 2003. 55–69. Print.

Freeman, Lisa A. "Tragic Flaws: Genre and Ideology in Lillo's *London Merchant*." *South Atlantic Quarterly* 98.3 (1999): 539–61. Print.

Hall, Edward. *The Hidden Dimension*. New York: Doubleday, 1966. Print.

Havens, Raymond D. "The Sentimentalism of *The London Merchant*." *ELH* 12.3 (1945): 183–7. Print.

Hudson, William Henry. *A Quiet Corner in a Library*. Freeport, NY: Books for Libraries Press, 1968. Print.

Johnson, Samuel. *Prologue and Epilogue Spoken at the Opening of the Theatre in Drury-Lane 1747*. London: Webb, 1747. Print.

Koon, Helene. *Colley Cibber: A Biography*. Kentucky: University of Kentucky Press, 1986. Print.

Lillo, George. *The London Merchant*. Regents Restoration Drama Series. Ed. William H. McBurney. Lincoln: University of Nebraska Press, 1965. Print.

Mazella, David. "'Justly to Fall Unpitied and Abhorr'd': Sensibility, Punishment, and Morality in Lillo's *The London Merchant*." *ELH* 68.4 (2001): 795–830. Print.

Milhous, Judith and Robert D. Hume. "Death in Elizabeth Barry's Dressing Room." *Yale University Library Gazette* 79 (2005): 149–74. Print.

Parker, Andrew and Eve Kosofsky Sedgwick. *Performativity and Performance*. Essays from the English Institute. New York: Routledge, 1995. Print.

Price, Lawrence Marsden. "George Barnwell Abroad." *Comparative Literature* 2.2 (1950): 126–56. Print.

Rodman, George Bush. "Sentimentalism in Lillo's *The London Merchant*." *ELH* 12.1 (1945): 45–61. Print.

Schechner, Richard. "Performers and Spectators Transported and Transformed." *The Kenyon Review* 3.4 (Fall 1981): 91. Print.

Shakespeare, William. *The Riverside Shakespeare*. Ed. G. Blakemore Evans and J. J. M. Tobin. Boston, MA: Houghton Mifflin, 1997. Print.

Solomon, Diana. "Tragic Play, *Bawdy* Epilogue?" *Prologues, Epilogues, Curtain-Raisers and Afterpieces: The Rest of the Eighteenth-Century London Stage*. Ed. Judith Bailey Slagle and Daniel Ennis. Delaware: Delaware University Press, 2007. 155–178. Print.

Steffensen, James L., ed. *The Dramatic Works of George Lillo*. Oxford: Clarendon, 1993. Print.

"The Theatre, Number CXVI." *Town and Country Magazine*. 12 (May 1780): 227-30. Print.

Van Lennep, William, et. al. *The London Stage, 1660–1800*. 5 vols. Carbondale: Southern Illinois University Press, 1965. Print.

Warton, Joseph. *An Essay on the Writings and Genius of Pope*. 2nd ed. London: R. and J. Dodsley, 1762. Print.

Wiley, Autrey Nell. *Rare Prologues and Epilogues 1642–1700*. London: George Allen and Unwin, 1940. Reprint, Port Washington, NY: Kennikat, 1970. Print.

8 Laughter in the Final Instance: The Cultural Economy of Humor

(Or why women aren't perceived to be as funny as men)

Rebecca Krefting

Rebecca Krefting is a Visiting Assistant Professor at Skidmore College in the Department of American Studies. Her research specializes in humor and laughter; gender and sexuality; race/ethnicity studies of visual and popular culture; identity and difference; feminist and disability theater; and pedagogical studies. She is currently working on a book about the ways women use comedy in the service of social justice. Beck performs stand-up comedy sporadically—for money or a cause or a pint.

> *I have suggested that citizenship is a status whose definitions are always in process. It is continually being produced out of political, rhetorical, and economic struggle over who will count as "the people" and how social membership will be measured and valued.*
>
> —Lauren Berlant

In *Vanity Fair*, Christopher Hitchens published the controversial piece, "Why Women Aren't Funny," giving voice to the largely unspoken but generally shared cultural perception that women are not as funny as men. Humor, on and in his terms is best pursued by men, is understood most clearly by men, and should include only those issues pertaining to men. His insight into the gender divide in humor production is as follows: "Male humor prefers the laugh to be at someone's expense, and understands that life is quite possibly a joke to begin with—and often a joke in extremely poor taste. . . . Whereas women, bless their tender hearts, would prefer that life be fair, and even sweet, rather than the sordid mess it actually is." Perhaps Christopher Hitchens has done us the favor of qualifying the category—its scope, pervasiveness, and thankfully, its limitations—of male sexist humor. This kind of humor assumes all women are sexually available and the objectification of women, and assures listeners that what women have to say is less important or valuable than men's contributions (Mulkay). An auspicious genre, which in the wake of the women's movement should be all but outmoded, is, as Hitchens graciously reminds us, quite present and operational in live comedy performances across the US.

His essay articulates an argument that upon closer inspection quickly unravels, not because he is not correct that women are *perceived* as less funny but because he offers biological and otherwise deterministic arguments to explain this largely cultural and economic phenomenon. In doing so, he reduces audiences' reception of humor to something natural, innate, predetermined, and therefore moot, which for him is ideal because it leaves him and every other swinging dick with the upper hand, the "equipment" necessary to incite laughter and be the arbiter of precisely what should elicit laughter.

Hitchens's article sparked a series of public discussion—circulating online and in print—introducing arguments spanning from physiological to sociological to psychological explanations for public estimations of women's *perceived* inadequacy in the realm of humor production. Overlooked in the current public/print investigation of mixed audiences' favoring male humor over female humor, however, is a cultural analysis examining the economy of humor or the way humor is shaped by economic forces, the material incentives shaping popular cultural forms in the US. Related, notions of citizenship, particularly those circulating and enacted socially rather than legally, shape identity and its material accessories, e.g., shoes, musicians, jewelry, cars, and yes, even comics. Citizenship is not simply a legal construct but a social one that necessarily includes acknowledgement, something grudgingly given, if at all, to subordinated populations. Who is acknowledged and accepted and who is not is itself a legend of that nation—its assumptions, attitudes, beliefs, and structures of power. I argue that audiences will affirm the perspectives and identify with (read: invest in and support, laugh or otherwise respond favorably) comics whose categories of identity correspond to ideal citizens, i.e., white, male, heterosexual, able-bodied.[1]

This connection of nation and economy to audience preferences for male comics is conspicuously absent from public and academic discourses on the matter. Contemporary humor scholarship in the humanities addressing gender differences largely focuses on performatic differences between male and female comic performers, such as content and stylistic differences, which still does nothing to address the fundamental question of why—specifically—female content and styles, along with women comics performing in gender neutral ways, fail to meet with success equal to their male counterparts. What are the rewards—material, social or otherwise—for audience engagement with or identification with comics? How do cultural notions of and attitudes about citizenship inform humor production and shape preferences for the consumption of humor? Drawing from my own experiences as a humor scholar and comic performer, along with feminist theories and studies in performance, culture, and humor, this text uses critical discourse analyses to examine live audiences' lack of enthusiasm for women comic performers as symptomatic of power differentials evinced in the cultural economy and a direct product of modern articulations of national belonging.

THE QUESTION . . .

Emily Wilson, journalist and freelance writer for the liberal online news source *AlterNet,* published the piece "Are Men Threatened by Funny Women?" on September 4, 2007, roughly nine months after Hitchens's initial *Vanity Fair* piece. I was interviewed for this article, along with notable Jewish comic Judy Gold, *Bitch* co-founder and editor Andi Zeisler, and well known women's humor scholar Regina Barreca, all of whom affirmed that women struggle to achieve similar popularity and success performing comedy in the US. There are many reasons contributing to this, but Andi Zeisler provided what I believe to be the primary reason for this disparity: "we need to look at *who* is defining what is funny" (emphasis added, qtd. in Wilson). This means we need to pay attention to the prognostications of folks like Christopher Hitchens or other widely read writers defining what is funny and moreover, the *ideal* candidates for humor production (hint: for him that would be men).

Nearly a year later, I received a lengthy email from a cordial engineer living in Maryland who read the *AlterNet* article, located me through the university, and emailed me with questions about why women are not as funny as men. In his email, Ken Winiecki shared that he finds women comics to be irritating, or at least more so than most male comics, and was earnestly "trying to figure out why [he] find[s] a significantly higher proportion of female than male comedians unfunny." The tone was apologetic but firm: many women comics are annoying and he thought my research would lend some insight to the matter. From the *AlterNet* article he became acquainted with one of the leading arguments for why women are more likely to be perceived as not funny, namely that women who are funny are seen as potentially threatening. He found the argument to be less than thorough in addressing his antipathy toward women comics and countered the hypothesis, saying: "Usually when I am threatened I think I feel fear and/or defensiveness, but my negative responses to comedians usually seem to include boredom and/or irritation, which don't seem to me much like a threat response." I considered his queries seriously and placed them in the context of my own work, which, among other objectives, seeks to look beyond the very useful but too oft employed discussion of women's comedy as resistant.[2] It *is* resistant and we can gain much from these thorough and insightful analyses of what women are resisting, the tenor and quality of that resistance, and how visibility of these resistant practices can lead to social change. However, simply elaborating this argument would never address the real question that was publicly framed by Christopher Hitchens, echoed in Ken Winiecki's email, and now the subject of this investigation: Why are men (perceived to be) more funny than women?

THE ANSWER...

To address this query that resounds in various ways in public and personal discourses, I defer first to Andi Ziesler and her question of who is defining what is funny, and second to the cultural economy of humor, which shows us there is simply no reward for engaging with or learning to identify with women whose power is already determined as secondary to men in this society. The willful adoption of views, opinions, and behaviors in contradiction to mainstream ideologies requires incentive, a payoff of sorts. French sociologist Pierre Bourdieu recognized that material gains and advantages are not easily calculable or reflected in one's bank statement. He dissected the many forms capital takes, generating the terms "cultural capital" and "social capital," as forms of capital gain that yield benefits (e.g., prestige, networks, education, opportunities, experiences, proximity to power, etc.) not quantifiable in dollars or relative currency (66). This thinking positions this discussion right where it should be—in the shifting realm of culture as it plays out in the economy, rather than Hitchens's biologically deterministic explanations.

We cannot deny the overwhelming power of our economy—a hyper-capitalist republic—to dictate popular culture forms including who and what we enjoy (read: consume). Shane Phelan, in *Sexual Strangers: Gays, Lesbians, and Dilemmas of Citizenship*, argues that

> [s]truggles for inclusion are shaped not only by the needs of the excluded and the fears or needs of the excluders, not only by whether demands can be framed within the rhetoric of the polity, but by whether state actors have an incentive to include the excluded. The incentives of those actors will not only affect whether a group is included, but will importantly shape the terms under which inclusion will occur. (149)

Based on women's proximity to power, in other words their tacit social standing as inferior to and subordinated by men, there is simply no economic incentive for anyone, men and women alike, to learn to identify and "buy in" to women's point of view. Understanding male perspectives and experiences—which are more recognizable as the standard or norm by which we measure all other experiences—whether or not you are yourself male, bears the promise of incentive, or Bourdieu's social and cultural capital. Women's experiences and identities as marketable commodities will fail every time when placed alongside their male counterparts, whose lives and identities bear far greater promise for cultural and economic viability.

Gender determines incentive because each audience member has to work to identify with and hence share in the humor and laughter. If there is no payoff, no capital gains—culturally or otherwise—to be had, audiences will opt out or experience distanciating or negative emotions much like those described by Ken Winiecki, such as apathy, boredom, annoyance, and/or disapproval. Cultural attitudes affect economic choices and buying tickets to see comics or in other words, purchasing the opportunity to identify in humorous terms with individuals, is no exception.

Successful comedy relies heavily on affirmation of and identification with the comic. A comic leads her audience "in a celebration of a community of shared culture" (Mintz 89), what I am calling a shared national imaginary, similar to Benedict Anderson's definition of nation, which is "an imagined political community," making it an ideal popular cultural form to gauge social constructions of citizenship that include extralegal concepts of inclusion such as social acknowledgement (6). Phelan avers the importance of considering citizenship as central to one's identity and a social and legal construct routinely excluding gays and lesbians. Therefore, the relationship they have with constructions of national identity is one of "sexual strangers," and Phelan emphasizes the imperative of analysis and activism that incorporates sexual strangers into the fold without rendering their differences moot. Central to her argument is the notion that "[c]itizenship is more than theory and constitution, however. The acknowledgement that is its sine qua non requires that one be recognized as being 'like' existing members in some ways" (87). Accordingly, citizenship is more than just a legal construct or a set of rights conferred to an individual, and not all persons believe and feel that, despite status as US citizens, they are treated and given rights corresponding to full citizenship. The appeal of comic performances based on whether audiences identify with the performer reveals not just Phelan's "sexual strangers" but gender strangers and racial/ethnic strangers as well.

The success of live comic entertainment functions as litmus test or cultural index for national belonging. Success stands in for belonging, which is largely predicated on Phelan's idea of positive acknowledgement. Comics must establish some or many points of identification with their audience in order to be successful; laughter signals belonging or affirms that one "gets" where you are coming from.[3] We laugh because we simultaneously appreciate the lawlessness of comedy *and* because we get it, and through our getting it, we also belong. Humor issuing from the mouths of women and members of minority communities that falls flat with audience members can reflect a culture's lack of desire to acknowledge the experiences of the "other," signaling their tacit exclusion from the national imaginary. Group laughter in response to a joke affirms one's position in the national imaginary by signaling group belonging and agreement; this is Mintz's "community of shared culture." The experience of being part of a live audience offers audience members a more participatory and authentic community of shared culture than televised performances, which undergo serious editing to add laugh tracks and remove any unfavorable or lackluster responses from the audience, leaving only a stream of cackling patrons not necessarily laughing at the joke just performed.[4] Thus, the responses of audiences during live shows are the most useful indices of gauging the success of the jokes and the extent to which audience members identify with the comic performer. In sum, audience identification illumines cultural/social outsiders and determines who "sells" and who does not.

The preeminence of cultural discourses and narratives of national belonging emerging out of patriarchy producing white male norms are taken to be the natural order of things. This always already ensures that masculinity, whiteness, and heterosexuality prevail as superior and desirable and determines who belongs and who does not. Loosely translated, this means when it comes to comic performance, socially constructed notions of national belonging or cultural citizenship dictates success with the live audience. Comics occupying privileged social locations in the national imaginary, i.e., white, heterosexual, male, advance a position and bear identity markers audiences recognize as dominant in the shared national imaginary and thus bear the promise of incentive, e.g., if I can understand dominant modes of being I will increase my chances of gaining access to the power and prestige of the dominant class or ideal citizens. Heterosexist, sexist, racist, classist, and ableist ideas of nationhood work to create a cultural economy that supports these beliefs. It comes as no surprise then, that most comics touring the national circuit are heterosexual men.[5] The DC Improv in Washington D.C., where I lived for six years, booked five female comics (Sheryl Underwood, Erin Jackson, Sommore, Aisha Tyler, and Loni Love) in the last three years (August 2008–August 2011) constituting approximately five percent of their bookings (several women returned each year). With some exceptions, I attribute this to the overwhelming majority of folks identifying with a heterosexual male standard because affirming this identity bears the greatest incentive and cultural cache in society.

In *Vince Vaughn's Wild West Comedy Show*, Vince Vaughn hits the road for thirty days of consecutive live shows with four up and coming comics—Sebastian Maniscalco, Bret Ernst, Ahmed Ahmed, and

John Caparulo—most of who have achieved feature status in comedy clubs nationwide. In one city, Sebastian Maniscalco mocks men who wear flip-flops and who order feminine drinks, as characterized by fruit juices and garnishes. The crowd boos him following the flip-flop joke and he commences to cut that particular segment short so as not to lose the audience entirely. Here he is reinforcing what he sees as gender appropriate foot apparel, an opinion not shared by the majority of those in the audience. Maniscalco employs the strategy of using humor to reference concepts of staid masculinity and to ridicule questionable behaviors that undermine "real" men as macho, caring little for their outward appearance and participating only in consumptive practices acceptable for men (i.e., electronics, cars, tools, etc.). In an interview following that show, he shares that he routinely performs this joke because it has proven successful in the past and with audiences in other cities on the same tour. This joke typically meets with success because it draws from stereotypical notions of masculinity circulating in contemporary culture: "[a]nd when a joke bases itself upon a distortion—a 'stereotype' perhaps—and gives the lie to the truth so as to win a laugh and stay in favor, we've moved away from a comic art and into the world of 'entertainment' and 'success'" (Griffiths 22).

Jokes emerging from and capitalizing on gender stereotypes and differences are used frequently and continue to be successful, particularly if they make women the butt of the joke (Crawford). In my own experience performing stand-up comedy there are two surefire ways to get a laugh: use obscenities and make fun of women. Despite drawing from a wellspring of easily identifiable gender conventions, this audience did not identify with Maniscalco's parameters of masculinity as set forth in his jokes because it made questionable the masculinity of a number of those in attendance (most likely those men, Maniscalco's gender truants, wearing flip-flops at the time). In this way, there is a palpable exchange between audience and performer where laughter signals affirmation and negative responses such as booing, hissing, or shaking one's head signals disagreement, disapproval, or lack of identification with the fundamental premise of the humorous material. Both the blessing and the curse of live comedy is that not all audiences will respond similarly and the comic must be prepared for this.

Put simply, live audiences populating the comedy clubs across the nation will identify with and affirm the perspectives of the comics whose beliefs and lifestyles reflect mainstream, socially acceptable norms—values shared, condoned and exhibited by many.

Since these dominant ideas and values arise from a mainly white patriarchal epicenter of power (and based on the hiring trends in comedy clubs across the US), we can conclude that the humor emitting from the mouths of men has been and will continue to be highly sought, an economically viable investment, and a safe bet for mixed race and gender audiences who are well trained in what *should* make them laugh. Andy Medhurst, a humor scholar in the UK, writes in *A National Joke: Popular Comedy and English Cultural Identities*, "nation construction is also involved in the business of identifying internal others, who are seen by those subscribing to an imagination of national community wedded to closed, fixed and impermeable versions of belonging, as threatening groups that are *on* the inside but must on no account become *of* the inside" (28–29). Critical here is the understanding that comic performers situated as outsiders on the inside are going to struggle to establish mutual points of identification with their audiences and in the process be perceived as less competent or funny.

To be clear, I am not arguing that all male comics will be successful and all female comics will be unsuccessful; in fact, there is evidence contrary to this. Many US female comic performers such Wanda Sykes, Kathy Griffin, Margaret Cho, Chelsea Handler, Sarah Silverman, Tina Fey, Ellen Degeneres, Amy Poehler, and Molly Shannon have found national recognition and acclaim. (Though, when placed in their respective performance venues, i.e., national comedy circuits, talk shows, sitcoms, and variety shows, they are the gender minority.) I *am*, however, suggesting success is largely predicated on audiences' ability to identify with the jester in question, and there is a greater likelihood of this when the subjects and topics broached are gender neutral or fulfill existing stereotypes about women, e.g., women are high maintenance, nagging, passive, sweet, bitchy, etc. The women humorists garnering a following have done so by either appealing to broadly dispersed niche audiences comprised of like-community members (e.g., Kathy Griffin enjoys a fan base of primarily LGBT persons, women, and popular culture enthusiasts, of which she belongs to the latter two, and while she is not herself a lesbian, she is very supportive of the LGBT community) or because their comedy is non-threatening and while offering a female perspective, seldom focuses on specifically female issues or overtly challenges patriarchy or the status quo (e.g.,

Sarah Silverman endorses a brand of shock comedy that targets everyone with equal vehemence so as to render any real satire or critique moot).[6] The promise of comedy is that these challenges can be made in subtle fashions; therefore, it is important to note that many of these women certainly strive to incorporate critiques of patriarchy, gender norms and stereotypes, capitalism, racism, and heterosexism into their comic performances, albeit in ways that do not risk alienating audiences.[7]

For many of us not belonging to the mainstream, humor functions as a way to create community and culture among the marginalized. For instance, feminist humor and lesbian humor "affirms the values, beliefs and politics of the in-group and forms part of a shared stock of stories and myths that help form, disseminate, and preserve an imagined community" (Bing and Heller 158). Kate Clinton, a Caucasian lesbian comic whose biting political humor has made her a favorite among liberal and lesbian audiences in alternative performance venues, repeatedly stated at a live performance at Ellington's in Austin, Texas: "You create the world; you invite the people in" (qtd. in Pershing 222). In her case, that world is one comprised of her experiences as female, as a lesbian, as an American, and as an intellectual. The problem she and other subordinated comics face is that mainstream audiences, when confronted with the comedy of the marginalized (by virtue of race, sexuality, gender, ability, class, and age), tend to struggle to find common referents, experiences, and ideologies compatible with their own. If the world created is one based on marginalized subjectivities and experience, you can invite people in, but it does not mean they will understand or value (literally, in economic terms) that world. Audiences tend to enjoy themselves more when they can identify with the comic. Unfortunately, when identification is primed as white, heterosexual, and male oriented, women must struggle all the more to be heard and to legitimate their experiences, let alone have them qualify as being humorous.

One of my favorite bits I perform addresses the lack of synonyms or slang words circulating for discharge, or women's vaginal fluids. This is in direct contrast with the plethora of synonyms in play for a man's seminal fluids, i.e., jizz, spooge, Petey's protein, spunk, etc. I consider this disparity in my stand-up and the way the term itself (associated with the firing of weapons and being released from the hospital) alienates women from their bodies. To improve the situation, I offer the audience my own alternative term for discharge and invite them to use the term as a substitute in the future:

> Instead of using the term discharge, I would like to suggest the term "panty soda." Say it with me now: PANTY SODA! It's fun, it's fizzy, it's *you*. I can't create this kind of change on my own people. I need your help telling others about panty soda. So, tell your family, neighbors, and friends at Bible Study and together we will spread panty soda all over the nation.

Reactions to this joke vary based on my audience. Performing in 2004—for Ladyfest Ohio, a feminist arts festival—for an audience comprised mainly of feminists (male and female alike), this joke brought down the house eliciting cheers, clapping, hooting, and roaring laughter. Performing at the Columbus Funny Bone in Columbus, Ohio the joke elicited nervous titters from a smattering of women and some applause from a group of women (without any men) seated at a table in the back of the club. Like Maniscalco's failed flip-flop joke, I sensed I was losing the audience with this joke and adjusted my set to jokes less particular to the female condition. This joke, by virtue of its subject matter, has nothing to do with men and unless male audience members are willing to imagine otherwise, namely what it might be like to be a woman, to occupy a body pathologized and considered substandard by Western patriarchal medical theories and practices, there is little pleasurable yield from this joke other than the humorous term itself: panty soda. When there is no point of reference listeners can detach, which often leads to negative judgment and alienation, a phenomenon I believe is more likely to occur during the performance of a female comic. Women and men are conditioned to perceive male experience as the norm or template genera, and thus when women take the stage and implicitly request or require your attention and/or identification with female experiences, many find themselves experiencing a kind of distanciation, confusion, or simply an ambivalence toward this performance of "otherness" or what Joanne R. Gilbert calls a "performance of marginality" (xviii). This might explain why Christopher Hitchens struggles with such a myopic and sexist view of what constitutes the humorous.

Conclusion

In April 2008, Christopher Hitchens's invectives against lady humorists were countered in the essay "Who Says Women Aren't Funny?" by Alessandra Stanley, paired with a *Vanity Fair* cover of female comedy greats including Sarah Silverman, Tina Fey, and Amy Poehler. The magazine cover invites you to consider this article in contrast to/with Hitchens's essay published a year earlier. Not to be outdone and certainly unable to allow Stanley the final word on the matter, Hitchens responded to Stanley in a follow-up essay, "Why Women Still Don't Get It," posted exclusively to *Vanity Fair*'s website. The second essay advances a tired reiteration of the first, equally rife with contradictions and misogynistic language that either turns women (including his colleague Alessandra Stanley) into vampish sex kittens or castrating bitches. He reduces Stanley's essay to a flirtatious overture, writing: "Oh Alessandra, oh angel, if you wanted a giggle or even a cackle, you only had to call me." And in the tradition of great bombasts, he gloats that Stanley's essay coupled with a layout of sexy, funny ladies is precisely what he intended: "Did I never tell you this was my Plan A, and was my deepest-laid scheme all along? I forgive you for being so slow to see my little joke because—ah well, just because."

The last line casting Stanley as simple-minded or naive is not meant just for her. Every woman becomes the butt of this joke, though we may not even know it, though we may be complicit and laugh along with it. If there truly existed substantial evidence and objective data (whatever that is) indicating that women are biologically and genetically inferior in the realm of humor production, I would not waste my time concerning myself with these matters. But I am loathe to allow anyone to invoke biological determinism for what is and always has been culturally determined. The premise of Hitchens's diatribe is hardly original; he follows in the footsteps of other notables using science and genetics to support their racist, sexist, classist, ableist, and heterosexist agendas. Fortunately, women have the advantage in this day and age to be in a position to combat these kinds of views and it is imperative to do so. For this, we should applaud Stanley and the other pundits, scholars, and comic performers who argue, demonstrate, and perform otherwise.

As I argue throughout, audiences will identify with performers representative of the most ideal or desirable citizens, i.e., those comfortably situated within the dominant culture and bearing the privileges of not only legal but social inclusion, namely white, male, heterosexual, able bodies. While stand-up comedy may appear an innocuous form of entertainment, successful performers often reflect the status quo. Our beliefs about ideal members of the polity influence whom we support with our time, energy, and money. It is most advantageous to understand and identify with those with the most access to privilege and power. This phenomenon of the cultural economy, at least for the time being, ensures that white, male, heterosexual comics will elicit the laughter necessary for continued advancement in the business of humor production.

There have been many outstanding male comics who are gay, disabled, and/or people of color, e.g., Josh Blue, Richard Pryor, Bill Cosby, Eddie Murphy, Dick Gregory, Eddie Izzard, etc. The history of stand-up comedy is full of exceptions and it is simply inaccurate to say that only white dudes can get a break and achieve success. However, any analysis of the schedules for headliners in the mainstream comedy club circuits reveals white men far outnumber their black, Latino, and Asian male counterparts, and heterosexual male comics are more prevalent than their gay male counterparts. In main, though, what is most important to recognize is that despite occupying a marginalized subject position like being a differently-abled male, a Black male, etc., being male trumps the subordinated subject position, still making them more ideal candidates for identification and yielding greater social/cultural capital than women. *Being white, able-bodied, and/or straight is less predictive of success than is being male.*

Women, try as they might, will continue to flounder when placed next to their male counterparts, as will queer comics alongside heterosexual comics, disabled comics alongside able-bodied comics, and comics of color alongside Caucasian comics. There will be exceptions to this rule, but for the most part those exceptions will be marginalized comics who opt not to discuss or bring their marginality to the forefront—such as Ellen Degeneres, who has gained national adoration for her quirky, girl-next-door brand of comedy. These exceptions will be the fodder for the naysayers (like Hitchens) as they argue either that anyone can succeed in stand-up if they work hard enough or that unequal success between men and women is merely a product of genetic encoding or biology. Both arguments are problematic, the former invoking the myth of meritocracy and placing the blame on the individual for lack of success and the latter making moot any possibility for equity among male and female comic performers. Both are equally strategic and safe arguments to make because neither holds the people or the audiences responsible for their lack of desire or willingness to identify with and collude with women's comic perspectives, which in turn dictates their success in the business of stand-up performance.

In sum, Christopher Hitchens presents an argument for which there is no debate, at least on his terms. In the face of such myopia, Alessandra Stanley can do little other than point to the history of women's disenfranchisement from the industry of humor production and pay homage to the small but growing army of women jokesters active in the world of comedy today. Replacing biological determinisms, which have the unfortunate history of reflecting whichever cultural attitudes are in mode, with cultural determinisms places this debate back into the actual realm responsible for women's *perceived* ineptitude in comic performance compared to men. It also opens the door for change, the possibility that the cultural economy will shift over time, making women's ideas and perspectives profitable investments for audiences, and in turn profitable investments for booking agents and comedy club owners. While I cannot say that it pleases me, I can say with a certain amount of confidence that the extent to which capital—material, social, and cultural—dictates success and opportunity, and the way it determines laughter in the final instance, explains the question of why men are (perceived to be) funnier than women.

Notes

1. My argument will attend more exclusively to parsing out the theory and evidence supporting public preferences for male comics over female comics; however, I include these other categories of difference like heterosexual, able-bodied, and white to reference and recognize the multiple dimensions of power and privilege operating in society and to paint a complete portrait of other privileged categories of identity in the US.

2. Scholars have published extensively on the subject of women's resistance vis-à-vis humor. Some of those I find most useful to understanding the functions and goals of women's comic performance are: Nancy A. Walker, *A Very Serious Thing: Women's Humor and American Culture* (Minneapolis: University of Minnesota Press, 1988); Susan Horowitz, *Queens of Comedy: Lucille Ball, Phyllis Diller, Carol Burnett, Joan Rivers, and the New Generation of Funny Women* (Amsterdam: Gordon & Breach Publishers, 1997); DoVeanna S. Fulton, "Comic Views and Metaphysical Dilemmas: Shattering Cultural Images through Self-Definition and Representation by Black Comediennes,"

Journal of American Folklore 117.463: 81–96; Allison Fraiberg, "Between the Laughter: Bridging Feminist Studies through Women's Stand-Up Comedy," *Studies in Humor and Gender*, Vol. 1, Ed. Gail Finney (New York: Gordon & Breach Science Publishers, 1994), 315–334; Fraiberg "Beyond Indiscretion: Agency, Comedy, and Contemporary American Women's Writing and Performance," unpublished dissertation, University of Washington, 1993; Suzanne Lavin, *Women and Comedy in Solo Performance*, Ed. Jerome Nadelhaft (New York and London: Routledge, 2004); Philip Auslander, "'Brought to you by Fem-Rage:' Stand-up Comedy and the Politics of Gender," *From Acting to Performance: Essays in Modernism on Postmodernism* (London and New York: Routledge, 1997), 108–126; Kathleen Rowe, *The Unruly Woman: Gender and the Genres of Laughter* (Austin: University of Texas Press, 1995).

3. For further explication of laughter signaling belonging and affirmation see Mintz; Allison Fraiberg "Between the Laughter: Bridging Feminist Studies through Women's Stand-Up Comedy," *Studies in Humor and Gender*, Vol. 1, Ed. Gail Finney (New York: Gordon & Breach Science Publishers, 1994), 315–334.

4. For further discussion about the editing of televised comedy to create a simulated comedic effect not necessarily indicative of the experience of the live audience, see Philip Auslander, "Comedy About the Failure of Comedy: Stand-up Comedy and Postmodernism," *Critical Theory and Performance*, Ed. Janelle G. Reinelt and Joseph R. Roach (Ann Arbor: University of Michigan Press: 1992), 196–207 and Richard Butsch, *The Making of American Audiences: From Stage to Television 1750–1990* (Cambridge: Cambridge University Press, 2000).

5. I intentionally do not include White as part of the standard, not because Black men do not experience racism and hence occupy marginalized social strata, but because Black men in particular have achieved an inordinate amount of success in stand-up comedy compared with their female and queer counterparts.

6. Russell Peterson, in *Strange Bedfellows: How Late-Night Comedy Turns Democracy into a Joke*, discusses shock comedy in the chapter, "For Whom the Bell Dings," and makes this argument about Sarah Silverman and the creators of *South Park*, Trey Parker and Matt Stone: "Yet most of the 'edgy' comedy sold and celebrated as such is as nihilistically 'neutral' in its way as the equal-opportunity offender political comedy of the late-night mainstream." Russell Peterson, *Strange Bedfellows: How Late-Night Comedy Turns Democracy into a Joke* (New Brunswick and London: Rutgers University Press, 2008), 149.

7. Margaret Cho, like Kathy Griffin, has achieved and maintained a certain status as female comic icon because she appeals to specific niche audiences like LGBT persons, feminists, liberals/leftists, and intellectuals. She pushes the envelope in ways most televised female comics listed above do not

and cannot, simply because her career unfolds onstage and not in front of the camera (unless taping a live show for a new video). In fact, she overtly fights gender stereotypes and has used her comedy to expose Hollywood's preoccupation with beauty standards and white norms. She can do so because of her position *beyond* the nightclub circuit; however, the material that made her famous and got her to this point in her career was not her more controversial humor, employed now with more gusto and frequency, but the ethnic humor she employed as a Korean-American young woman impersonating her first-generation Korean immigrant mother.

WORKS CITED

Anderson, Benedict. *Imagined Communities: Reflections on the Origin and Spread of Nationalism.* London: Verso, 1983. Print.

Berlant, Lauren. *The Queen of America Goes to Washington City: Essays on Sex and Citizenship.* Durham, NC & London: Duke University Press, 1997. Print.

Bing, Janet and Dana Heller. "How Many Lesbians Does it Take to Screw in a Light Bulb?" *Humor* 16.2 (2003): 157–182. Print.

Bourdieu, Pierre. *Distinction: A Social Critique of the Judgment of Taste.* Trans. Richard Nice. London: Routledge & Kegan Paul, 1984. Print.

Crawford, Mary. "Just Kidding: Gender and Conversational Humor." *Perspectives on Women and Comedy.* Series in Studies in Gender and Culture, Vol. 5. Ed. Regina Barreca. Philadelphia: Gordon and Breach, 1992. 24. Print.

Gilbert, Joanne R. *Performing Marginality: Humor, Gender, and Cultural Critique.* Detroit, MI: Wayne State University Press, 2004. Print.

Griffiths, Trevor. *Comedians.* New York: Grove Press, 1976. Print.

Hitchens, Christopher. "Why Women Aren't Funny." *Vanity Fair* January 2007. Web. 6 June 2011.

---. "Why Women Still Don't Get It." *Vanity Fair* 3 March 2008. Web. 6 June 2011.

Krefting, Rebecca. "Discharge." Presented at the Columbus Funny Bone, Columbus Ohio, 2003. Original material written and first performed spring 2002.

Medhurst, Andy. *A National Joke: Popular Comedy and English Cultural Identities.* New York and London: Routledge, 2007. Print.

Mintz, Lawrence E. "Standup Comedy as Social and Cultural Mediation." *American Humor.* Ed. A. P. Dudden. New York: Oxford University Press, 1987. 85–96. Print.

Mulkay, Michael. *On Humour: Its Nature and Its Place in Modern Society.* New York: Polity Press in association with Basil Blackwell Inc., 1988. Print.

Pershing, Linda. "There's a Joker in the Menstrual Hut: A Performance Analysis of Comedian Kate Clinton." *Women's Comic Visions*. Ed. June Sochen. Detroit, MI: Wayne State University Press, 1991. 193–236. Print.

Peterson, Russell. *Strange Bedfellows: How Late-Night Comedy Turns Democracy into a Joke*. New Brunswick and London: Rutgers University Press, 2008. Print.

Phelan, Shane. *Sexual Strangers: Gays, Lesbians and Dilemmas of Citizenship*. Philadelphia, PA: Temple University Press, 2001. Print.

Stanley, Alessandra. "Who Says Women Aren't Funny?" *Vanity Fair* 572 (April 2008): 182–191. Print.

Vince Vaughn's Wild West Comedy Show: 30 Days & 30 Nights – Hollywood to the Heartland. Dir. Ari Sandel. Perf. Vince Vaughn, Sebastian Maniscalco, Ahmed Ahmed, John Caparulo, and Bret Ernst. MMVII New Line Cinema Picturehouse, 2006. Documentary.

Wilson, Emily. "Are Men Threatened by Funny Women?" AlterNet. 4 September 2007. Web. 6 June 2011.

Winiecki, Ken Jr. "Interested in your thesis." E-mail to the author. 9 May 2008.

9 Rhyme or Reason: Trying to Draw Some Conclusions about Comedy Audiences

Sable & Batalion

Sable & Batalion is the writing/performing/filmmaking duo of Jerome Sable and Eli Batalion. Friends since they were children, Sable & Batalion have been a creative collaboration for eighteen years. The duo is known for their award-winning work in musical film, theater and hip-hop-based comedy, including their critically acclaimed fringe hit retelling of the Biblical story of Job through hip-hop: *JOB: The Hip-Hop Musical*. Originally from Montreal, they have performed in over twenty cities worldwide, including at the New York Musical Theatre Festival, the Montreal Just For Laughs Comedy Festival, and the Edinburgh International Fringe Festival. Among his many accomplishments, Eli is also Judy's brother.

If there's one thing that's for sure about performing live comedy, it's that nothing is for sure. It's not a science by any means, and just when you think you might have cracked the code—just when you think you have a foolproof way to have 'em rollin' in the aisle—something happens that sends you crawling back to square one, depressed and confused as to why no one laughed at your "gold material."

And yet, after years of performing live comedy in dozens of cities around the world, we feel there are some trends that are worth noting. We thought a neat way to approach this would be to describe our best and worst live comedy shows *ever*, and, with some 20/20 hindsight, articulate the factors we think contributed to each getting its ranking.

Our Act

First, a quick description of our act: dressed in full costume, we were a two-man hip-hop duo explaining *Hip-Hop 4 Dummeez* with a PowerPoint presentation and live musical demonstrations. Eli (the guy on the right, pronounced "elly") played the straight man professor, clicking through slides and speaking in overly analytic terms about gangsta concepts, while Jerome (left) played the sidekick clown, bursting on cue into quick comedic snippets of high-energy rapping that purportedly demonstrated the concepts Eli was expounding.

Figure 9.1 Jerome Sable and Eli Batalion, *Hip-Hop 4 Dummeez*. Photograph by Jocelyn Michel.

We performed this show in various comedy clubs and venues around Canada and the US—once in a theater, but almost always in a comedy context; that is to say, the comedy industry. Usually a host would introduce us as our characters, and we'd hop up onstage with our big screen and give our pseudo-lecture to a laughing audience. Some jokes would hit harder than others, of course, but generally it was a success and that's why we kept doing it. But then . . .

Worst Show Ever

Our worst comedy show ever was our New York showcase for the HBO Comedy Arts Festival. It stank. Really. It was terrible. Picture this: it's the middle of the afternoon and we're in a small fifty-seat theater in the middle of Manhattan. The seats are filled with executives from Comedy Central, NBC and HBO, and a handful of our friends. There we are, onstage, doing the act that's worked for us so many times before . . . and *no one is laughing*. Not a soul. We stand there, running through our rehearsed routine, and it's complete silence. Not even one tiny squeak of a pity laugh. Ouch.

How could this happen? Well, looking back on it, there were a variety of factors that might have caused this. First of all, there were three acts on that fateful afternoon. The showcase was one hour long and it was supposed to be comprised of three twenty-minute acts. Of course, judiciously in line with Murphy's Law, things wouldn't go according to schedule, and we were scheduled last.

They say comedy is all about timing, but they're not just referring to split-second delivery—it's about when you approach the audience, how they're feeling at that point, and how you're feeling at that point. That one of us was already close to asleep by the time it was our cue to get onstage, that the audience had already seen around an hour-and-a-half of comedy up until that point, and that no one in the room was anywhere near tipsy (nor would they be, on a Sunday afternoon in a small improv theater in Manhattan) would not help deliver us from that soul-sucker of an experience.

Funnily enough, we'd done really well at a popular comedy club with the same act a week before (and comedy clubs were typically not our forte, with our tech-heavy little act). Could we blame this all on our PowerPoint clicker, which screwed up on us halfway through the show and started displaying all the upcoming slides at high speeds, giving everything away? (The kind of glitch that might give Bill Gates panic attacks, even in his retirement.) Was it the venue space, with its deep and narrow stage forcing us far back from an audience that was just made comedic-love to by a more intimate act? Or did we have to accept the fact we were just plain unfunny?

Hard to tell. The law of averages certainly helps prop up our fragile little egos, but so does the idea that funniness has a lot to do with the ability to know thine audience and work with them. One fatal flaw in our show was that, at least at that time, it wasn't built to fly on improv, a technique which has helped save tanking gigs, probably as far back as uninspired Ancient Greek theater. Maybe improv could have helped us, but our ability to improvise *in character* wasn't developed at that time. So, since we couldn't try to laugh about how bad our show was sucking, we had to drop deeper and deeper into the abyss of awkward. *Awkward*.

Another element that hurt us: critical mass, or the lack of it. Critical mass as a term here should not be used lightly—it often refers to a large lady with an inability to hold back raucous laughter, a.k.a. the cackler. Often it's this woman, or some small audience pocket, that gets some laughter or applause going and influences the crowd as a whole to react. This creates a beautiful illusion of widespread audience response (which may or may not be the case—we as performers are fine to be deluded otherwise). Unfortunately, this woman, whom the comedian longs for so deeply (if only she knew . . .), was either not in the audience that fateful afternoon, or was, but with a wired jaw. Or was dead. Or we weren't funny. Were we?

Best Show Ever

Ok, let's stop brooding. Perhaps we're painting too sad, too harsh a picture of comedy; comedy *can* work, and often, and well, and leaves you feeling great, like you just showered after undergoing the entire Middle Ages in the same sackcloth. One of our best comedy experiences was playing an "underdoggy" position, doing our act at the Montreal Just For Laughs Comedy Festival. We were actually part of the Best of the Uptown Comics series, which is a showcase for many of America's up-and-coming black comics. And of course, then there was us—two short white Jewish guys. But what was great about this show as opposed to the disaster mentioned above was that we were vouched for. Yes, having a festival put its resources behind us and show us love, and being part of the promotion pumping up the show, and having the MC pump us up (i.e., hype us to the audience, not hydraulically inflate us) meant everything to our show. At the very least, it would provide at least a few more minutes of sympathy before being written off, which is the point of no return all comedians fear. And often, it can take a few minutes of greasing up for audiences to understand what the hell's going on, especially for an unconventional act like our own. As it happens, though, this was not even needed—it felt like people were eating out of our hands (which, trust us, is a strange feeling to have in your hands).

[Little sidebar here about the point of no return and the difference between comedy and theater audiences: We estimate that in a comedy situation—e.g., a comedy club with a slew of stand-up acts—the audience is subconsciously giving each new performer a thirty-second window at the beginning of their act. By the end of this thirty seconds an average audience member will have *made a decision* (yay or nay) as to whether the act is funny. From that point on, if the audience member has decided you're *not funny*, reversing this decision is an uphill battle. This goes to a comedy audience member's voting power as a laughing or non-laughing individual in the crowd. In theater, by contrast, no matter how bad you are, and statistically, you probably *really are*, there isn't quite the same decision process for an individual audience member. This is both because s/he has much less voting power (to simplify, it only comes in the level of applause at the very end of the show) and because there is a sort of expectation in theater to respect one's craft no matter what. Put another way, there is always the expectation of sitting there *anyway*, at least until the first intermission. There is no real voting power because even if you're dozing off, the audience response registers virtually the same.]

And let's also not forget the positive role of the ferment, shall we? Many comedy clubs have tried to perfect the alcohol ratio, trying to get the right combination between high drink sales and getting just the right blood alcohol level to have you feel free enough to laugh more than you might otherwise, but not drunk enough to heckle to taboo proportions. When you're dealing with a larger venue like the one in question, which usually has rock acts, the ability to control this balance is even more difficult (then again, the ability to successfully hit someone onstage with a shoe is reduced). Luckily, our timing was such that we arrived onstage at the ideal blood alcohol content, which worked in our favor. This of course was the sheer work of lady luck herself, since often you can't control the alcohol content of your audience (unless, of course, you do shows in your basement, which technically is not legal).

On top of all this, we have reason to believe we benefited from the ultimate synergy effect—the influential large lady with the great cackle. . . . who'd been drinking. Not that we encourage such ladies to do this often—it is the very fact that they do it in moderation that provides the explosive results we, as people of comedy, need to inspire us through the bad shows. Archived footage of the show seems to suggest we were aided by strategically-placed laugh-drinkers, causing ultimate laughter ripples. We are not sure who placed them and how, though we continue to offer our appreciation and a thousand dollar reward to this day.

THE COMEDY OF COLLABORATION

Of course, in speaking about what works and doesn't work in comedy, we should address the fact that our experiences are somewhat unique since we perform as a duo (a white, short, Jewish, and rapping one at that). This has been at odds with a popular modern notion of live comedy stand-up—a non-musical solo performance piece—which is effectively the norm today. As a result, non-stand-up acts have been a bit harder to grasp at different comedy venues around the world, leading to both opportunities and holdups for us. Being unique often has attractive appeal, especially when you stand out from the gaggle of stand-ups out there (there's just too many of them—you'd think the humiliation of playing for three unimpressed people at a time would dissuade some of them over time, but nooooo . . .). On the other hand, the audience needs to know how to receive you, and for many people, at many festivals or in many armchairs the world over, the two-man thing is a difficult sell. If anything, it usually has to be done as a two-man musical comedy duo (i.e., a musical revue of parodies and original joke songs), of which our act shared some basic elements.

The actual comedic execution as two people can also have its advantages and disadvantages. For instance, the cliché of synergy can actually mean something when you're talking about two performers. Audiences internally respect the chemistry between two performers, and secretly love it if the performers are enjoying themselves onstage (though of course, not at the expense of the audience, as many performing groups are apt to do when they get pissed off, and are usually justified in that). A genuine laugh that can come out of one performer (or better yet, is noticeably held back by one of the performers) is one of the most audience-disarming things that can happen in a show, leading to a whole lotta unconscious smiling. Then there's the situation of the off-night—inevitably, sometimes performers don't feel like doing comedy, or maybe do feel like doing it but are too distracted, tired, or intoxicated to pull it off. This is where the buddy system really helps, because inevitably at some point fifty percent of the performers will be carrying more than fifty percent of the show. Sometimes, both performers bring one hundred percent to the table, but the audience just likes the way one guy looks, or sounds (or, doesn't like the one way one guy looks, or sounds, especially if the guy is actually an armadillo).

The main disadvantages of the multi-performers come from the inevitable not-being-on-the-same-pageness, which is bound to happen over time. Usually, this is most detectable in improv settings where there is literally no script page to refer to, but can also be clear in scripted environments as well, where the improv element is more about how to play a scene for *that* particular audience. To get people on the same page takes a lot of experience together (which also means a lot of failures together), some degree of prior mutual understanding, and at the end of the day, just having similar artistic tastes. Of course, sometimes two or more performers don't jive for a whole show or for a single joke because of simple factors like being unable to hear each other, see each other, or speak the same language, the latter reason being why improv is not yet an Olympic sport.

MCs—Masters of Comedy Science?

Ok, we don't really know comedy. Maybe no one does. But we have our little theories here and there. Comedians throughout time have been trying to get at their own audience formula, and judging by the success of some comics—particularly the ones people don't really find that funny and yet manage to get laughs—there's evidence of some good scientific research and experimentation going on out there in the field. Of course, with all due respect to the editor (it's okay, it's Eli's sister), there will never be a textbook for this sort of thing, only years of on-the-job experience. In an industry that often relies on how funny people are within five to seven minutes, overnight success seems very likely. Actually, it's very rare: it takes years to get that perfect five to seven minutes, let alone the hit cable special or derivative blockbuster movie. Like most fields, success is often ten percent inspiration and ninety percent perspiration. In other words, if you breathe one of every ten seconds, then sweat the remaining nine, you may be onto something.

Think of the above ramblings and musings as the thoughts that congealed *for us* over the years, which might very well be highly specific to our act, our way of interacting with audiences, or perhaps can be relevant for other acts as well. We do feel that analyzing these concepts and discussing them between the two of us, to a certain extent, helped improve our act over time. It may have even helped us in writing this piece—or did we lose you in the first thirty seconds . . . Damn! Well, we gotta run—someone's on the other line, rambling about some thousand-dollar reward.

10 Choosing Comedy

Julia Chamberlain
(in correspondence with Judy Batalion)

Julia Chamberlain is a UK-based comedy producer and booker who works for major British venues including the country-wide Highlight comedy chain. On behalf of the Gilded Balloon, Edinburgh, Julia also produces the highly regarded *So You Think You're Funny?* (*SYTYF*) new act competition, which has been responsible for selecting new talent in the UK, Ireland, and Australia.

Judy: Let's start by situating your practice. I know you book acts for Highlight comedy, and are the master judge of the *SYTYF* competition, but let us know if you book for other clubs, venues, or festivals. Please lay out and describe the kinds of audiences you work with.

Julia: I've done various clubs—I used to book for the Red Rose in Finsbury Park, a wonderful longstanding club with a tradition of intelligent, left-wing audiences, a middle-class island in an ocean of horrible estates. My experience was that they were terribly conservative and politically correct and would respond to trigger words without actually listening to the joke, so any routine with a sexual content told by a man and involving a woman would be branded sexist, even when the butt of the joke was the man and the point wasn't sexual but more emotional or social. This material wasn't gross-out, anatomical, or pumping away images—it had context and intelligence. But, no, they'd react first and think later. Except they didn't think . . . This audience enjoyed gay men—Alan Carr before he was huge, and Topping & Butch absolutely stormed the place without the advantage of being a familiar TV face. Other clubs in South London I've been involved in have been less judgmental, but no more rewarding—they were so laid back and quiet it's very disconcerting for the performer just to have people smiling contemplatively.

I also book for an English-speaking club in Munich, mainly for expats. English, Irish, Canadian, American, and a few Germans. They love intelligent, mainly clean comedy and don't like audience interaction at all. It's a Monday night, so people aren't rat-arsed, and they're not spoiled for choice for live comedy, nor are they inundated with it on TV. They have a regular return audience, and they're very discerning and proper connoisseurs! I sometimes look at their online comments and they really are on the money—if someone was a bit too casual in their approach (between ourselves, drunk), it doesn't go unnoticed. They are so appreciative of the good acts.

Planning the *SYTYF* heats in Edinburgh, when I will have seen all the acts at least once and there will be judges selecting someone to go to the final, is quite a job. The judges are all industry-related—reviewers, TV producers, and comics. I have to plan a show where to my mind there's an obvious winner and a couple at least who'll give them a run for their money. I try not to bunch up lots of Irish, women, music, or double acts. There needs to be a spread of ethnicity and styles for the night. I've found that the professional audience always enjoy music acts but rarely give them top place. I guess it's because musical comedy still falls into the "spesh act" category and by definition it's hard to have a whole evening or program of spesh acts unless you're jumping into the burlesque/cabaret arena. However, for the first round at the London showcases, I don't know what I'm getting, so apart from putting musical or double acts to close the first half or the end, it's pretty much a surprise to me how things turn out.

Judy: Along these lines—and I'm jumping right into it here—how do the different audiences you work with respond differently to comedians? Do audiences vary depending on context/place/club/time? Do you book particular comics for particular audiences?

Julia: The main difference working with a big company like Highlight, you see at Christmas; that's when the audience is made up of big parties, and a proportion of them may not have been to comedy before and have little interest in it—they're there for the party. I'm astounded how ill-mannered audiences can be—people who wouldn't dream of talking through a play or a concert will happily conduct a conversation through an act. So you need someone loud, confident, and who won't get too rattled by an audience with a short attention span. It's here musical acts can come into their own, but you still only want one on the bill. They are by definition louder; everyone responds to a tune or a song and the laughs are easily cued for people not used to listening!

You may be asked to book for a family audience, or a business audience where content has to be clean and swearing is out. That's a challenge for bookers and many comedians—even when material is clean, sometimes the rhythm of a routine requires some swearing as an intensifier. There are remarkably few comics who can perform a twenty- to thirty-minute set without sexual references or crude language. There's a gap in the market!

Judy: Following from that, can you characterize different types of audiences? Are some sophisticated? Are some rowdy? Can you know in advance what kind of audience you might have on a given night? What factors are important in determining the *type* of audience, if such a thing exists?

Julia: Unfortunately, you rarely get a sophisticated audience. Maybe that's not such a bad thing, as sophisticated doesn't sound like an audience that will let itself go, too cool to laugh is more like it. A nodding, jazz audience: grim to perform to. What you want is an intelligent bunch who want to come and haven't been coerced into being there, relaxed, not too drunk. Rowdy occurs when you've got a lot of single sex parties, typically hens and stags, but not necessarily; they can also be post-rugby, or post-football. You do try not to sit single sex parties alongside each other to prevent them talking to each other and either copping off or picking a fight. You're aiming for the focus to be on the stage, not on the girl in the micro mini clutching a cocktail.

I know many comics who dread performing to an all student night. The audience is probably so young they don't have the same terms of reference, common experiences, or anything much beyond school. They're often ridiculously PC, but will go mad for anyone who looks like a pop star or they have seen on telly. This is also where some of the clever-clog comics who are vastly impressed by their own learning go down well, superciliousness being a bit of a student trait. Conversely, said comics wouldn't cut it in a more wide ranging room.

Judy: Can you tell us a bit about the specifics of production, or the curation of a comedy show? For instance, how do the ordering and lineup affect the show? How important are they vis-à-vis audience reception?

Julia: It varies—with a compere and three acts, you might have the third person do a longer set at the end. They should be someone very experienced, maybe a bit larger than life, and definitely a strong headliner. The openers can be more verbal—someone funny, a bit gentle—followed by someone more risqué or musical or high energy. With a compere and four acts, you'd split the show into two halves with everyone doing an equal length set. The extra person straight after the interval is in "the sweet spot." It's nicely protected, the audience is warmed up thoroughly and they'd get to run slightly shorter than everyone else. It's good for people making the transition into full sets, or for open spots doing ten minutes. The audience gets an extra act and there's still a strong headliner to wind up the night. The comp-and-four nights are long and audience concentration may begin to wane—drink takes its toll, but so does anxiety about getting last trains, babysitters, etc. So you have to have a rock solid closing act. That's not the place to experiment. Comparably in the opening section, you're wanting the evening to build, so the first half needs to end on a high so the audience is still excited about coming back after the interval and has a lot to talk about.

Judy: Do audiences respond differently to male and female comedians? To comedians of different nationalities?

Julia: Yes, they do. I hate to say it, but sometimes there's a palpable sense of disappointment when a female comic appears onstage. Women do have to work harder and be better than the men just to maintain ground. The preconceptions that an audience has about women are staggering—they think it's going to be all tampons and "aren't men shit?" and it never is. Most of the period jokes you ever hear onstage come from the men, but nobody ever remarks on that. I think men would rather look at a woman onstage, and find it slightly intimidating when she's clearly highly articulate and opinionated and not passive. It's a bit of a shock to the system for them when the woman answers back if they interject with something dumb and irrelevant.

As to responding to different nationalities, I guess it depends where the club is. In the northwest of England, they seem to have a genuine dislike of either posh southern or London-sounding comics. Even some of the northern hosts aren't particularly supportive. Irish comics are welcome everywhere, as are Aussies, Canadians, and Americans—but they have to deliver the goods. You can't cruise it on a cute accent alone. Scottish audiences will judge you by your material alone, wherever you're from. They like a good story, well told. London clubs will take all comers. There is a smattering of European comics appearing now, Dutch, Swedish, German, and you can just see how the audience will have to really concentrate on the accent. We're so used to TV's American and Australian English that it's second nature, but a European inflection is still challenging, even when there's no real difficulty in understanding. The audience treats these comics like a special child—they should trust themselves more to understand.

Judy: What sorts of comics make good comperes?

Julia: Friendly, quick thinking people with natural authority who don't get rattled. I prefer ones who know their job is to host the party and make the stage a great place for the rest of the acts. It is not their solo show interrupted by colleagues.

Judy: I wonder if you could say something about your role as an arbiter of comedy taste for the masses—you book comics for major clubs and also run new act competitions that are trend-spotting events. Do you feel responsible to comics? To your audiences? Or do you consider only your own instinct and taste? When you select acts, especially new acts, what guides your choices? Do you consider what your audiences want and aim to please them, and if so, who are these audiences? Or do you aim to make new audiences?

Julia: That's a massive question! But here goes. With big club booking I am not my own woman. I sometimes book acts I personally wouldn't be that bothered about seeing, but I know they are successful in the club and audiences respond well to them. It's not my position to stop booking someone because I don't happen to like their style, and simultaneously make a huge dent in their income.

With new act comps I can indulge personal taste a lot more, but I do try to get out of my comfort zone and choose people that aren't necessarily just economical gag writers with a bit of dash—I'll embrace the surrealists as well, as long as I think they really have a commitment to what they're doing and aren't just writing waffly stuff because they can't do the "proper" material. I detest people who get up and think they can just riff off the audience by doing surveys or insulting someone in the front row, or by using anecdotes that may be true, but that aren't necessarily funny. If I'm judging a final, I'll be very definite about my preference and dismiss the ones that don't do it for me; but if I'm actually looking to populate a whole semifinal, I'll grant a bit of leeway and sometimes take notice if the audience went nuts for someone who left me cold, as long as I'm sure it wasn't their clique. On the whole, the audience doesn't influence much, but usually we're not in conflict so there's not a lot of influencing needed.

Anyone who knows me knows I'll go out of my way to encourage people I really think have a germ of something special that a gazillion more gigs will help to bring out, or just knowing somebody has a bit of faith in them will boost their confidence. And I've never told anyone to stop doing comedy, no matter how much I think they shouldn't. My personal preference is for a well-written gag, no blathering, preferably clean—although I love a bit of filth if there's something fresh to say about an old subject. A well-turned phrase or an original and unexpected image is what excites me. Tight writing, crisp delivery, and personalized style. I'm sick of the sub Eddie Izzard imitations and all the American imitators, the acquired persona. Thank god you can't smoke onstage anymore, that get rids of some very affected posturing.

Judy: Please add any other general reflections you might have, from your unique perspective, on the performer-audience relationship. What works, what doesn't, and how do comics and audiences interact? How do comedians assess, respond to, control, love and hate their audiences? How do they deal with hecklers, with audiences in different contexts and countries?

Julia: When things are going well the audience seems to forget they are being told fictions—they believe the person onstage is the same bloke who is sitting having a beer at the back. If someone does "single" material, it's assumed they are, and same goes for "married." Nobody makes up stuff about having children, so that's where the two worlds do meet successfully. Conversely, if it's not going well, the audience would barely trust the act to tell them the time and there's a genuine hostility— "Why would I believe that?" So suspension of disbelief ties in with actually liking the stage persona. If the audience buys into the persona, they're prepared to laugh at the bits between the jokes, the silences, the minute expressions, the nonverbal communication. It's absolutely magical when that happens, for the performer and the crowd. Everyone glows as a result. That's really being in the moment for all concerned.

Comics always notice the one person near the front who isn't laughing and are drawn to them like a moth to flame, with miserable results for all. Three hundred people can be roaring and guffawing, but the one who is smiling on the inside is somehow spotlit. They're humiliated by the attention, and the comic looks like a bully at worst, or a cheap point scorer at best.

Heckling. Audiences don't really understand this particular art. Heckling is not intended to step on the punch line of someone's material. It is a witty interjection that invites a wittier response. As the putdown says, "The point of heckling is for you to make me look like a c**t . . ." However, the mindless abuse and catcalls people now call heckling is like listening to a radio go out of tune. It spoils the joke, the flow, and the atmosphere. It's nearly always unclear and distracting, but the tone is unmistakable. And of course there is the irritating "drive-by" heckle, where something is yelled, but not repeated when requested, for being too dumb to be worth the effort. I think hecklers should be hooked up to the national grid. They add nothing. Comedians will field these badly bowled balls with speed and grace, but they shouldn't have to. In Australia, they just heap fairly graphic abuse on the offender and leave them buried under piles of unsavory implications about their intelligence, their parents, their sexuality, and their ability in bed. I'm not qualified to say how heckling outside of the UK and Oz is dealt with.

Judy: Finally, how do you feel about audiences? How often do you love them? Hate them? Agree with them? Do they baffle you? Are they smart?

Julia: I wish audiences were all like me! That sounds unfeasibly arrogant, but I go to comedy wanting and expecting to laugh, prepared to listen, bringing some intelligence to the event, and not wanting to talk over the performance. Even after decades of going to live comedy, I still get an absolute thrill from watching it work well and can get helpless with laughter. It's wonderful to look at an audience who are all having a good time, leaning forward, facing forward, eyes gleaming, drinks on the table, hands free and ready to clap. Sometimes they do baffle me when there's a wonderful act doing really funny, clever material and they're just glassy-eyed and unreceptive. It makes me depressed that you can see they react just to noise—sometimes somebody is about as funny as bone cancer, but they're loud, they're emphatic, and they throw themselves about the stage and it makes people react. I suppose people giggle as a nervous reaction to a loud noise sometimes, but it doesn't make for a bonding experience among the audience or between audience and performer. These sorts of acts think they are killing night after night, but it's just people responding to the big retarded kid onstage, worrying that unless you humor him he'll not go away and harass someone else.

That being said, I feel hugely protective toward performers. It's like walking the plank above a load of crocodiles every night, putting elements of your personality on the line. Of course nobody makes them do it, but it takes years to conquer the nerves and go and risk reputation and confidence with a bunch of people who have nothing invested in you. If the audience is not willing to meet them halfway, it's heartbreaking.

Conversely when a performer is just being vulgar, aggressive, and crude but likes to think of themselves as edgy and transgressive, you really want to knock them down a peg or two. Comedy is about entertaining people, not a manifesto. Good luck to the blokes who think they can get mileage out of rape or pedophilia or the current UK trend for racism—the French, Muslims, and Jews all seem to be considered fair game on a regular basis, negative stereotyping still prevails.

Audiences: sometimes the majority are smart, and that's great. But could you take a cross section of three hundred people in a Tube carriage and ask if they're smart? Sometimes they will be, sometimes they won't. Depends if you're on the Northern Line at Elephant and Castle or Hampstead, to really polarize it. Context is all.

11 Seven Steps to the Stage: The Audience as Co-creator of the Stand-up Comedy Night

Kevin McCarron

Kevin McCarron has been a stand-up comic for over ten years, and an academic for over twenty. As a comic, he has performed at clubs across the UK, has written and performed in five one-man shows at the Edinburgh Fringe Festival, works as a resident MC, and is co-promoter of Laughing Horse Comedy, the largest chain of grass roots comedy clubs in Great Britain. He was also the first stand-up comedian to perform in Monaco, where he out-sold Chris De Burgh (Chris sold forty-one tickets; Kevin sold forty-six). He is currently Reader in American Literature at Roehampton University.

> *Comedy, more than any other art form, is a communal experience. Laughter unites an audience, transforming an untidy hotch-potch of strangers into a single entity.*
>
> —William Cook

When I first began writing and performing as a stand-up comedian, I came across this observation by the American novelist Kurt Vonnegut: "every successful creative person creates with an audience of one in mind. That's the secret of artistic unity" (111). At this early stage of my stand-up career, I thought Vonnegut's advice was irrelevant to the way stand-up comedians write. However, not long after I began performing regularly, I changed my mind.

Over the last twelve years I have written five completely different one hour shows for the Edinburgh Festival: *A Joke Too Far* (1999); *Jest Kidding, Folks* (2001); *Jestation: twelve months in the making* (2003);

Jesting Pilot (2005); and *Nuclear War! Followed by the total extinction of every single living organism on the planet* (2007). Three hundred minutes of jokes—that's a lot of material. In addition, hundreds of other jokes I have written, many of them actually quite good, did not make it to Edinburgh, or beyond. Until a few years ago I used to think my own joke writing practice was essentially syntactical and even solipsistic. Like many stand-up comedians I write routines that are extended stories, with, ideally, jokes scattered strategically throughout, but I also write what I think of as *non sequitur* jokes, free standing, one or two liners, disconnected from one another. These are the opening three jokes from my fourth Edinburgh show *Jesting Pilot*: "I'm impressed at the balls of recruitment consultants. They can't even get themselves a decent job;" "I've got two kids—ten and eight. Yeah, odd names, but we know who they are;" and "On the train coming here this evening, an official announcement informed us that there would be a delay because of a 'passenger under a train at Piccadilly Circus.' I couldn't help thinking, if you're under the train, then technically, you've ceased to be a 'passenger.'" Like the cultural theorist John Limon, I, too, am "impressed by the beautiful, abstract geometry of stand-up ... the appeal of comedy for me is akin to the appeal of math, except that the formal abstraction of a gag retains as its subject matter the pollution of the liminal ... " (6). My own *non sequitur* jokes have, for me, a similar mathematical quality, like the balancing of an equation.

Once, I thought such jokes were unaware of an audience; they were just "right," satisfying themselves sometimes more than they actually satisfied me. However, years of performing stand-up comedy and writing jokes and routines have shown me that I was wrong; I had failed to recognize the contribution of the audience not only to a comedian's set but also to the individual jokes and routines of which that set is comprised. Limon too, while sharing my pleasure in the "abstract geometry" of stand-up, is fully alert to the crucial importance of the audience to the comedian:

> It is simple to intuit in this ideal structure (the audience cannot err, it cannot feign, it cannot be misled) why comedians might, above all other artists and entertainers, hate their audiences; but the most comprehensive way to put the matter is that they hate their audiences because they are not, as performers, entirely distinct from them. Audiences turn their jokes into jokes, as if the comedian had not quite thought

or expressed a joke until the audience thinks or expresses it. Stand-up is all supplement. (13)

With experience, I realized Vonnegut's assertion about the importance of writing for an audience might be equally applicable to a stand-up comedian; I came to learn that the relationship that exists between stand-up comedians and their audiences is so intense, so unique, that audiences actually shape the content and direction of individual comedian's sets, and thereby actually co-create the entire stand-up show.

I have found there are seven stages during which audiences are co-creators of stand-up comedy: conception, contemporary construction, cumulative construction, anticipation, perception, auditing, and performing. Five of these responses to an audience occur before the stand-up comedian even walks out onstage. Indeed, there are no stages at all in the construction of a stand-up comedian's routine, or even during the composition of an individual joke within the routine, when an audience is *not* contributing.

CONCEPTION

I could not *conceive* of writing a joke that began, say, "These three niggers stroll into a bar." Why? Only a tautology can answer: "It's not just that I, personally, don't use this kind of language, it's also because I know the audiences I am comfortable with wouldn't find anything that followed such an opening in any way amusing." An audience is present when I embrace or reject even the outline of a joke; the very *possibility* of a joke is subject to the scrutiny of this invisible audience.

CONTEMPORARY CONSTRUCTION

Although many stand-up comedians may not care to admit it, even when comics, in ostensible isolation, write immediately satisfying (to them) jokes, this invisible audience has also constantly been present during what is, actually, the "performance" of the joke and not the writing of it. As they are writing the joke, comedians *see themselves performing it*, and they envisage the audience's response. When I write a joke that is immediately "good to go," as comedians say, I acknowledge that not only does it satisfy itself, in the sense that it is balanced mathematically, like an equation, I also know the reason it is "right" is because, like a properly balanced equation, it cannot be challenged by an audience. It's right! However, now I also know this assurance itself originates in the joke's "awareness" that precisely because it is mathematical, it will not be delivered to an innumerate audience. In this case, indeed, in every case, a particular, invisible audience has contributed to the joke from its inception to its punch line. I now think Vonnegut is right, with this caveat: I may not write "for an audience of one," but I do write for "one audience" —often I write jokes for an "Ideal" audience, a Platonic Ideal of an audience, and every now and then I'll get the opportunity to tell some of these jokes. As an example, the following is one of my own favorite jokes; I am very proud of it, and yet I can tell it very rarely, perhaps one in thirty gigs—usually when I have been booked to perform after an academic conference to a particularly well educated audience: "I've noticed those who can spell insouciant—aren't!" Or this one: "I wrote a great joke about Marcel Proust, but I've forgotten it." Another favorite of mine can be used much more frequently, but hardly always: "Any Jane Austen fans in? I love that line in *Pride and Prejudice* where Austen writes, 'Good morning Miss Bennet, ejaculated the vicar.' Obviously vicars didn't get out much in those days."

CUMULATIVE CONSTRUCTION

I begin what I usually envisage as a longer routine, however, by understanding that the material is only the inchoate, written expression of an idea destined to be spoken, not to stay written. I see the shift from the written to the spoken as one that is, in this specific context, incontestably evolutionary, and one that lies at the heart of stand-up comedy. Ultimately it is the various audiences who co-create the finished (if it ever is) routine for me. It is only by performing the routine to, say, a dozen different audiences, in at least as many different stand-up comedy clubs, and carefully evaluating the responses to each variation that I realize what particular combination of vocabulary, rhythm, inflection, emphasis, and elision (to note only the most obvious) is required to achieve the maximum comic effect for this particular routine. Comedy club audiences effectively co-create a stand-up comedian's material from the first time the comedian road tests the material. They continue to do so throughout the routine's evolution—it evolves because an audience, several audiences, signals their approbation or their displeasure by laughing, or by not laughing.

If, and it is a very big if, apprentice stand-up comedians eventually become good stand-up comedians it is not because they have become better *writers*. All appearances to the contrary, it is because they have become better *listeners*, and they have been listening, most intently, not to their friends or their relations, not to other stand-up comedians, and, emphatically, not to critics; they have been listening to their audiences. The American writer Betsy Borns notes:

> Comics tag the ability to distinguish between what works and what doesn't as "laugh ears" . . . Listening is, for the comic, one half of creation; the other half is writing. The two are not mutually exclusive; to listen without writing is to be an audience, to write without listening is to be a bore, neither of which make one a comedian. Laugh ears are grown, not inherited. (247)

A comedy club audience unarguably contributes to shaping a stand-up comedian's routines, but a particular audience may also determine in what order the routines or jokes will be performed, and indeed *what* routines a comic decides to use on a given night.

ANTICIPATION

Equally, of course, this means a particular audience may dictate what material an act will *not* use. Steven Jacobi writes, "Satisfying a comedy audience's expectations—it does, after all, expect to laugh—is one of life's more daunting tasks" (21). This is undoubtedly true, but comedians, too, have expectations. If I was booked, for example, to do a full spot (twenty minutes) at any one of several central London comedy clubs on a Friday night, I would be aware, like every professional stand-up comedian in the UK, that there will be large numbers of people in the audience who will have little experience of "alternative comedy," little idea of its conventions and etiquette, and who will have been drinking sedulously since five p.m. My expectant preliminary knowledge of this audience's attitude and manner actually shapes my set even as I travel on the London underground toward the gig. Long before I get there, this anticipated audience has ensured that I drop my Bush/Blair/Gulf War/Al Gore/Global Warming material; the audience has also determined that because my Proust routine is unlikely to take the roof off, it, along with a number of similar routines, has to go. My stuff on ecstasy, night busses, tattooing, and Australian tourists, however, is in—this now forms the backbone of the set I loosely anticipate delivering.

Perception

Once I'm actually at the venue I will look the audience over, and my perception of them, visually, will also influence what material I might use, or drop. I will be thinking, perhaps, they look rough, there's a lot of drinking going on, there are very few women, most of them look no older than eighteen, and so forth. The next stage, auditing, or editing my material *in situ*, will take shape depending on whether I am doing a set or compering the entire show.

Auditing

As a compere . . .

The compere's job is to begin, and end, the stand-up comedy show. Mark Lamarr says, "I feel the audience are part of the show, and I think that comes from compering" (qtd. in Cook 21). The compere will usually open by what, in the UK, is called bantering: talking to the audience. Opinions are, and always have been, divided on this thorny issue of audience interaction. Jack Dee is vehement in his opposition:

> I never go into my audience, unless someone takes a swipe at me first . . . because I hate nothing more than audience participation. It's a betrayal of trust—it's a breach of contract. I've paid to come and see someone else being funny—I haven't paid for them to attack me . . . If I'm sitting in the audience and some comic says "And you, sir! Where are you from?" I have to leave. I cannot take it. I absolutely loathe anything of that nature. That will ruin the night for me. (qtd. in Cook 197)

Jack Dee is a very gifted stand-up comedian, but speaking as somebody who has compered several nights a week for a decade, I am mystified both by his objections to audience interaction and by his curious logic. I cannot see a connection between asking a member of the audience where they are from, and being "attacked." However, in America, too, Dee's view finds considerable support. Borns writes, for example:

> Budd Friedman says that, with the exception of one or two comics who do it well, talking to the audience is the "height of amateurism . . . and is used as a crutch by all the rest, including myself [in addition to owning the Improv, he is also the emcee] and a good comic doesn't have to do that." Whether or not one agrees with this opinion, comic/audience interaction has managed to become a fixture in the clubs, despite its continuing absence from television. (193)

I would argue, though, that comic/audience interaction has not "managed" to become a fixture in the clubs—it is the lifeblood of stand-up comedy clubs, and the primary reason for their continuing existence. It is also the reason that both in Great Britain and in America, stand-up comedy rarely works on television for more than a few minutes. When I am compering, and I ask members of the audience exactly the type of questions to which Dee so violently objects—"Where are you from?" or "Are you two married?" or "Has anybody got any children?"—I am performing three tasks simultaneously. Firstly, I'm demonstrating my improvisational skills to the other acts and to the audience. I may well be, after all, the resident compere, perhaps there onstage every week in a comedy club popular enough to attract regulars—I cannot use pre-scripted material all the time. I must often improvise! Secondly, when I ask such questions, the answers from the audience provide the other comedians with information on the audience demographic. Like me, the other acts have seen the audience and their perceptions of the crowd will have affected the set they plan on using. Now, while they are listening to me bantering with the audience, the other comedians are further reevaluating the set they had expected, loosely, to perform. They are now restructuring, deleting, editing, perhaps even spontaneously writing new material, so that when they go onstage themselves, their material will be perceived by the audience as having emerged organically from the unique and peculiar circumstances of the night. Finally, perhaps most importantly, my questions assume a proleptic role—they dramatize for the audience that stand-up comedy is, above all else, interactive; the audience is an integral part of the performance. This relationship is precisely where the magic of live stand-up comedy resides. If I was doing a routine and I noticed, for example, a woman prodding her partner at something I had said, I would drop my material and ask what the prod was for. I would have every confidence I could get a laugh from this situation and come back to my routine. Stand-up comedians are not actors—our job is to react, to interact, *now*, with whatever is happening in front of us; in other words, with the audience.

When performing a set . . .

If I am *not* compering I will be listening to the compere talking to the audience, and the audience's responses will further impact on my processes of selection, structure, and exclusion. If the audience is responsive to the compere's banter, I will be encouraged to banter myself. If they are resistant, I will expect to just do my set. If I see that it is a predominantly young audience, I will drop my material on having children, say, and use my routines on "pulling" in nightclubs, smoking weed, and horrible flatmates. Equally, if the audience is older I will use my giving-up clubs and drugs to look after babies material. If the audience laughs at any of the compere's topical material I will be encouraged to use some of my own. If they don't laugh, I will still quickly need to gauge the strength of his material against my own, then make a decision.

Performing

When I am onstage myself, the audience's reactions to my opening jokes will almost certainly determine the entire trajectory of my set. If they don't laugh, for example, at two jokes about the American election, I drop the other two on the same theme and move other material up. These are not the responses of a hack, but those of a seasoned, professional stand-up comedian aware he is just one act in an entire night of stand-up comedy. Lenny Bruce was, deservedly, renowned for his courage and determination as a stand-up comedian, but he was also always alert to his audiences. Albert Goldman writes of one of Bruce's performances at the Gate of Horn night-club in Chicago: "He did some of his punchy new bits, but seeing lots of people walking out of the club, he switched in the middle of the show to sure-fire material . . ." (398). Goldman is always aware of the crucial contribution the audience makes to a stand-up comedy performance: "Incredible, isn't it, how the audience shapes the performer!" (397). Indeed, he is so aware that although his comment is framed as an interrogative, it concludes not with a question mark, but with an exclamation mark.

THE DEAD CAT EXAMPLE

I offer here an account of these seven stages and the importance of the audience throughout them with reference to one of my own most often requested routines: "Dead Cat."

Conception

I first saw "Dead Cat" as, essentially, a comic true story, an *objet trouvé*. I never thought of it as a story about marriage, or the differences between men and women. It was the audience's responses to early versions of the routine that made me realize what my story was really about. In its early versions the story was simply this (and true): my wife found a cat outside our house that had been run over by a van and she nursed it back to health—naturally, it became her favorite. A year later she had some exams to pass so she could progress in her job as an HR consultant, and while she sat a series of very demanding exams over the course of the week I looked after both our children and all six of her cats. Unfortunately, the very first day she was away at her exams I went outside and found this favorite cat lying dead in the back garden. So I buried it, not wanting to upset her with all her exams still to do—but, obviously, meaning to tell her when the exams were over.

That first night she came home depressed, believing she had not done well, and wanted to know where her favorite cat was. I professed ignorance. My wife gave me the cat's biscuits and I called out for her, all the while standing no more than a foot away from where I had buried her. On the final night, when I was at last able to break the grim news, my wife came home with a box of new cat biscuits. As I shook the box up and down, I saw written on the side of the box, GIVES NEW LIFE TO YOUR CAT. The routine, initially, ended with me thinking, "Well, here's a real test." However, the version I do now is at least four times the length—virtually all of it co-constructed with the audience.

Anticipation

Having written up the routine, and memorized it, I went onstage anticipating a small laugh here, a larger one there, and so forth. The *actual* response of the first few audiences I performed the routine in front of, however, were instrumental in shaping my subsequent performances of it. I initially anticipated, for example, that my hyperbolic physical mimicry of digging the cat's grave would get a big laugh. It didn't! Not in four separate performances. I then saw that it was too graphic, almost brutal. This act of mimicry has long gone. Now I bury the cat without any accompanying physical gestures at all. Equally, in the routine's early days I threw in a fairly unambitious joke about sex and my wife's lack of interest in it, and got an absolutely huge laugh. It has stayed!

Contemporary Construction

This issue, too, is linked to its predecessors. After a few performances of this routine I lost my anticipation of when I thought the audience should laugh, and started becoming aware of when they actually *did* laugh, and also, just as importantly, when they did *not* laugh. At its most basic level, this is how a comedian's material is altered by an audience. One night, a woman in the audience told me her cat had to have its leg amputated. I realized so could my wife's unfortunate cat. This would require a vet, so I developed the routine. I had my wife coming home late, cuddling the wounded cat, suggesting we take it to the vet, but I did not want to be charged a huge fee and offered to hit the cat over the head with a shovel. This meanness on my part expanded, and became a microcosm of the somewhat adversarial relationships often experienced between men and women: particularly over money and priorities.

One night at a club in Camden there was an Australian vet in the audience and I saw I could make the vet himself an amusing character. I could also make him team up with my wife against me. When I hear the vet will charge one thousand pounds to save the cat, I ask how much to have it painlessly put down: "They both turned to glare at me, as if I was a mix between Osama bin Laden and Adolph Hitler. And my wife's eyes carried a further message: 'If you don't go along with me on this there's no sex for a year and a half.' And, ladies and gentlemen, the thought of that extra six months just did my head in!" This was also the right time, I realized to crank the routine into fantasy: "I'm going to have to take off that back leg, umm, stick a new spine on it, and um yes, bolt on a new head." I also always get a big laugh when I eventually describe finding the dead cat, "her three legs pointing up at the sky."

Cumulative Construction

One night when I was compering at a university in London, I realized, after chatting with students onstage, instead of my wife being in HR (about which I had nothing comical to say anyway) I could make her a student. This would enable me to further extend the routine by offering a comic critique of modular degrees, and especially of the subjects I decided she should study: psychology and counseling. On a night with a lot of students in, I often extend this particular aspect of the routine, giving her friends who study sports sciences, for example, or aromatherapy. Even when there are no students in, though, my wife now is always a student.

Auditing and Perception

At the Laughing Horse in Kingston I realized the subject of cats is strongly gendered. When I spoke of my wife's love of cats, numerous men in the audience nudged their partners, or pointed to them, or even shouted out, "Boo!" Not long after, one night in Soho I realized an unusually large percentage of the audience was male. While I was chatting to them, I became convinced most of these men preferred dogs to cats. I was right. Since then I have bantered with the audience using dog/cat, male/female at the beginning of the routine. It always gets good laughs.

Performing

Performing a routine in front of an audience is the only way to learn how the material works. Although I was getting big laughs from "GIVES NEW LIFE TO YOUR CAT," I knew deep down that the audience expected, well, a bit more—actually, a punch line. I also knew it was a reasonable expectation. One night in Richmond, a woman shouted out over the laughter at the end of the routine: "Was she [my wife] happy? [when I told her about burying the cat]." It had not previously occurred to me the routine could go beyond me reading the words on the cat food box. Now, though, a number of possibilities opened up.

It was while deciding my wife would be *unhappy* at what I had done that I saw a possible punch line to the routine. I also realized more audience interaction was possible here. Since then I have always asked audiences to vote on a scale of one to ten whether my wife was happy or unhappy when I told her the truth. I play married against single, male against female, and, right up to the punch line, I look like a well-meaning chump. I end now, though, by saying: "Actually, I got *minus* ten for doing it. My wife was so cross that she's busted my balls about it for nearly ten years. I swear to you there have been a lot of times during those ten years when I wish I hadn't poisoned that fucking cat!" If I were a joke writer instead of a stand-up comedian, I would have lost the enormous input offered by my numerous audiences into that routine.

Phil Jupitus, stand-up comedian and television and radio broadcaster, talks of the ideal energy exchange between audience and performer in a comedy club:

> You're just like a lightning rod for the feeling in the room, really as a stand-up . . . And it's two way. Cos you need them as much as they need you. There is *nothing* like a good stand-up comedy gig, for that kind of unique, *what-the-hell-just-happened there?* kind of night, you know. It's like alchemy. (qtd. in Double 213)

Indeed, the experience Jupitus refers to here *is* like alchemy: at its heart lies transformation, irrationality, and even magic—none of it possible without the stand-up comedian's awareness of and continual interaction with the audience.

Works Cited

Borns, Betsy. *Comic Lives: Inside the World of American Stand-Up Comedy.* New York: Simon & Schuster, 1987. Print.
Cook, William. *Ha Bloody Ha: Comedians Talking.* London: Fourth Estate, 1994. Print.
Double, Oliver. *Getting the Joke.* London: Methuen, 2005. Print.
Goldman, Albert. *Ladies and Gentlemen—Lenny Bruce.* London: W. H. Allen, 1975. Print.
Jacobi, Steven. *Laughing Matters.* London: Century, 2005. Print.
Limon, John. *Stand-Up Comedy in Theory, Or, Abjection in America.* Durham, NC: Duke University Press, 2000. Print.
Vonnegut, Kurt. *Palm Sunday.* London: Granada, 1982. Print.

12 Hecklers: A Taxonomy

Nile Seguin

Nile Seguin is a Canadian comedian based in Toronto. He has written for the CBC television series *This Hour Has Twenty-Two Minutes* and *The Hour*. He has performed at the *Boston Comedy Festival* and the *Just For Laughs Festival* and writes, produces and co-hosts the popular podcast *Total Request Comedy*.

People are usually impressed when you tell them you do stand-up comedy. There are a lot of cool things about being a comic: keeping your own hours, living by your wits . . . er . . . I'm sure there's a lot of other cool stuff I'm forgetting right now. Anyhoo, there are however some really uncool things about being a stand-up and one of them is having to deal with hecklers. For some reason, people assume heckling can actually help a show since it gives something for the comic to play off of, but that is just the weirdest rationale I've ever heard. Nowhere else would we assume this. I can't punch a cop in the face and say: "Hey, you can't arrest me! I was making sure your reflexes and combat skills were sharp. If it wasn't for me you wouldn't have known your taser needed new batteries! For god's sake, stop hitting my face."

Hecklers are bad enough as it is, but they get even more annoying when you realize they aren't even that original. There are maybe three species of hecklers in the world. They haven't been catalogued or studied extensively so I could be wrong, but here is the classification I have developed so far.

The heckler most people believe is the most common of species is, of course, the Loudmouthed Yellowbellied Douchebag. He's the guy who yells, "You suck!" at the top of his lungs when you're in the middle of your set. This species is kind of like the Christian right in that they aren't as common as you're led to think, they just seem that way because they're loud, judgmental, and usually wrong. This is the guy—

and it's usually a guy, but I like to think as our society progresses, "Douchebag" will become a gender-neutral slur . . . You can do it, ladies! Look at Ann Coulter—who feels the cover he paid means he can do whatever he wants to whoever's onstage. For the record, that's not how comedy clubs work, that's how strip clubs in Russia work (which incidentally, is probably where this guy was conceived). The Douchebag is usually found in the mid to back section of the audience, as the darkness makes him braver (and probably better looking). He is usually at the show merely as a warm up to his going-out-clubbing where he can attempt to attract a mate using his incredibly powerful pheromone, or Rohipnol, as it's called in the pharmaceutical industry. If he isn't too drunk, the Douchebag can usually be easily put in his place with a few stinging jabs. He'll generally shut up, since, much like his dating life, he was only looking for someone who would put up with his bullshit and not fight back.

If he is too drunk, it means he's evolved into the next species: the Doubly Hammered Chatterer. This is the person who is clearly just so polluted out of their mind that their blood alcohol level would look like the score of a double overtime basketball game. Within seconds of starting the show every comic on the bill can tell that the Chatterer has been drinking since seven . . . the age not the hour. The Chatterer is especially annoying because they choose to do this at a stand-up comedy show rather than any other performance. If they'd done this at a music concert they'd not only not be a problem but would also probably come away with an unwanted bass player baby. But they come to the only show that could be stopped by one loud-mouthed drunken asshole. No, not the MTV Europe awards featuring Kanye West, but a stand-up comedy gig.

The Chatterer is an especially dangerous species of heckler since, although they are very vulnerable to mockery, they are too hammered to know when they've been beaten. So a lot of times they'll just keep chattering away, trying to burn you while everyone sits awkwardly until security comes and takes them out by force. It's just like Christmas at my place—only in my case, replace the Chatterer with my mother, who's trying to burn me with a hot poker and not her wit. Also, there's more booze at Christmas.

The next of the species of hecklers is most commonly known as Bob From Accounting. Bob is the office joker who is convinced he could have been and still could be a stand-up comic if it wasn't for all that silly "having to be funny" and "not being afraid to go onstage" bullshit. Bob has been looking forward to this office outing for weeks and thinks this is his time to shine. He hopes if he can cross swords with the comic, he'll be able to impress Judy the copy girl and maybe they can eventually go home to his parents' place and dry hump on his *Star Wars* sheets while his parents watch television downstairs. Of course, you usually end up making him look stupid, Judy leaves with Jennifer from Sales, and Bob ends up at home angrily masturbating to a Miley Cyrus poster he found on the subway. Bob From Accounting is the saddest of the heckler species because he's a victim of his own fear. He doesn't want to be an asshole, he just really wants to be a comic but his inability to do it properly means he merely does this half-assed and messy version of the real thing. In that way he's like former President Bush only not as funny.

So there are your three species of hecklers. Even as I describe them, however, I realize there is a bit of a contradiction in what I'm writing. I have to admit there are times when I don't mind heckles or hecklers. When I first started performing, hecklers made me very nervous and I felt the need to prove to them and everyone there that I was indeed the funniest person in the room. But now, if I'm in the middle of a run of shows and am feeling bored, a moderately interesting heckle might bring a little excitement to the job. And sometimes—very rarely, but sometimes—someone will say something very funny and when that happens, I call them as they are and say something clever like: "Okay, that was pretty funny." There have even been times when someone will come up with a clever tag for one of my jokes, at which point I will say: "That was very funny, consider that stolen," and move on with the show. And yeah, I can see how you might think it's okay to heckle if that comic has been asking the audience questions the whole show, but know this: most of the time when you heckle you're basically giving the comic the same feeling you have when your boss walks up to you ten minutes before the end of the day and adds twenty minutes of work to your pile.

Back to our accounting, and the three species of heckler: I know, it's disappointing since you probably wanted there to be more or maybe you think there are. If so, feel free to yell them at me while I'm onstage the next time I'm performing. That way I'll be able to add the next species: The Irony Free Jackass.

13 The Comedy Clubbers: Photographs

Sarah Boyes

Sarah Boyes is a Brighton-based artist who uses photography as a medium with which to explore how the act of viewing forms part of human relationships. For this project, she organized a lunchtime comedy event at Joogleberry's in Brighton and captured her impressions of the audience. These photographs, along with the rest of the series, have been exhibited in the UK.

The Comedy Clubbers 191

The Comedy Clubbers 193

14 Audience

Michael Frayn

Michael Frayn is an English playwright and novelist, best known for his plays *Noises Off, Copenhagen* and *Democracy*. His works have appeared in London's West End and on Broadway, winning Tony and Laurence Olivier Awards. His book *Spies* won the Whitbread Novel Award and the Commonwealth Writers Prize, and his novel *Headlong* was shortlisted for the Booker Prize. Frayn's work often blends questions of philosophy with humor and farce. He has also written nonfiction, memoir, screenplays, and has translated works from Russian. *Audience* (1991) is a one-act play.[1]

Characters

Joan (F 13)
Helena (F 14)
Quentin (G 12)
Lee (G 13)
Wendy (G 14, later G 15)
Charles (G 15, later F 15)
Reginald (G 15, later G 14)
Amanda (G 16, later F 16)
Eileen (G 16)
Keith (H 18)
Bobbie (I 16)
Merrill (I 17)
Usherette

A proscenium arch, seen from behind. In the last few minutes before the start of the play, the lights gradually come up to reveal, rather dimly, a kind of mirror image of the auditorium, with members of an audience being shown to their seats by an usherette, buying programmes, taking off their coats, and chatting.

All that can be seen of this second auditorium, in fact, is a section of the stalls with one of the aisles and the entrance doors at the back. Twelve seats are defined in various parts of the central block: four side by side in the row nearest the front (Row F); five side by side in the row behind (Row G); one, way off to the side in the row behind that (Row H); and two side by side in the backmost row (Row I). [See Figure 14.1, Plan 1.]

By the time the play starts, nine members of the audience have taken their places in these thirteen seats.

In I 16 and I 17 at the back—an American couple: **Bobbie**, *in her fifties and in command, and* **Merrill**, *in his seventies and no longer in command of anything much, not even his faculties.*

*In H 18—***Keith**, *in his forties and wearing seedily casual clothes.*

*In G 12—***Quentin**, *who is in his fifties and knows everything about the theatre. Beside him, in G 13—***Lee**, *who is in his late teens and knows nothing about anything.*

*In G 15—***Charles**, *a middle-aged man being remarkably attentive to his companion,* **Amanda**, *in G 16, who looks as if she is being hunted by the police.*

*In F 13—***Joan**, *in her sixties and, beside her in F 14—her daughter* **Helena**, *a distracted woman in her forties.*

G 14, and F 15, and F 16 remain unoccupied.

The **Usherette** *has taken her place by the double doors at the back. [See Figure 14.1, Plan 2.]*

Music. The **Usherette** *closes the doors. The house lights begin to go down. So do the house lights onstage. A moment's darkness, then the audience is illuminated again by the spill of light from the stage they are facing, which is where we are sitting.*

Joan (*sotto voce to* **Helena**) . . . So I told her. "Forty pounds," I said . . .
Helena Shh. (*She indicates that the curtain has gone up.*)
Joan (*faces front*) Oh, yes.
Pause.
Joan (*whispers to* **Helena**) "And that included delivery and fitting" . . .
She reluctantly abandons the conversation. Everyone stares at us in silence for some moments.
Amanda (*to herself, puzzled and irritated, in normal conversational tones and at normal conversational level*) Where's this supposed to be?
Joan (*to herself, likewise*) What's all this?

Quentin (*likewise*) What in heaven's name . . . ?
Bobbie (*likewise, delighted*) It looks just so real!
Charles (*likewise*) We *are* in the right theatre?
They try to read their programmes.
Helena (*reads*) "Act One . . ."
Amanda (*reads*) "An auditorium . . ."
Charles (*reads*) "Evening."
Amanda Oh no.
Helena Oh dear.
Quentin God help us.
Charles I thought it was a musical.
Bobbie I can't believe we're here! Our honeymoon, day two!
Merrill (*aloud, sotto voce, to* **Bobbie**) Where's the popcorn, baby girl?
Bobbie (*aloud, sotto voce, to* **Merrill**) You just hush now, baby boy.
Quentin (*to himself, gloomily*) These are supposed to be *ordinary people*, are they?
They all continue in the same manner—each person speaking to him or herself in normal conversational tones, and each inaudible to all the others.
Lee (*suspiciously*) These people—they're supposed to be all like, symbolic or something, are they?
Amanda (*darkly*) This is supposed to be us, is it?
Bobbie They're so lifelike!
Charles (*gloomily*) They look as if they've just walked in off the street.
Helena It all looks a bit *modern* to me.
Quentin They did this in that play, what was it called, in the thirties.
Charles I think this is going to be rather a yomp. Better break out the rations.
He offers **Amanda** *a box of chocolates.*
Joan Well, I suppose it's the kind of thing *she* likes.
Charles Seems to hold some morbid fascination for *her*, anyway.
Amanda (*brushes the chocolates away*) I read something about this somewhere. It's supposed to be all about—I don't know, something—what was it . . . ?
Charles And we might just manage twenty minutes in the car on the way back.
Amanda (*to herself*) I wish they'd stop staring! I hate plays where they peer out at you. Why don't they just look at each other? We're supposed to feel got at, are we?
Helena It was Jane who recommended it. Of course it was Jane who

recommended that one where they all took their clothes off.
Joan (*thoughtfully*) Chap there loosening his tie already.
Amanda They can't actually see us, can they?
Merrill (*sotto voce, to* **Bobbie**) What are they saying?
Bobbie (*sotto voce, to* **Merrill**) Shh!
Merrill What?
Bobbie They're not.
Merrill Not what?
Bobbie Not saying.
Merrill Not saying what?
Bobbie Not saying anything! They're thinking.
Merrill Thinking?
Bobbie Shh!
Merrill Thinking what?
Bobbie You have to work it out.
Merrill What?
Bobbie I'll tell you afterwards! Shh!
Merrill (*to himself*) Thinking? We're supposed to sit here thinking, "What are they thinking?" I know what they're thinking. They're thinking, "What the hell are *these* people thinking?"
Keith Funny, isn't it? You do your best to make a play relevant to the lives of the audience. You try to write about people they can identify with. What happens? Do they identify? Do they make the connection?
Amanda But why do they all look so actorish?
Keith I think they're just trying to recognise the actors.
Quentin I don't recognise any of them.
Lee They're all famous, are they? We're supposed to recognise them, are we?
Quentin Oh, not *her*! She was in that thing at the whatsit.
Lee Oh, yeah, he was in that commercial with that bloke who's in that other thing.
Keith Why do I have to sit here and subject myself to this humiliation? (*He sees the empty seat in Row G.*) Oh, and an empty seat. Only been running four months, and already there's an empty seat in Row G ... My God, there's two more in Row F ...
Quentin I'm just waiting for poor Roddy to come on.
Keith I'm only here because poor Roddy's off.
Quentin That's the only reason I've come—to see Roddy.

Keith That's the only reason I've come—to see the understudy.
Quentin Four months of this thing—it's a wonder he's not back in the clinic already.
Keith Laugh coming up here, by the way . . . *Should* be a laugh here . . .
Merrill Shut my eyes for a bit. That'll wake me up.
Keith No? Well there was a laugh there. You take your eyes off a show for two minutes, and the next thing you know the theatre's half empty and all the laughs have gone.
Quentin Oh, and there's dear old what's-her-name. But what *is* the poor poppet wearing?
Bobbie I just love the dresses they wear.
Helena Ridiculous, wearing a dress like that at her age.
Amanda (*shaken*) I've got a dress like that.
Joan I might try that pattern in the downstairs loo.
Bobbie Everything taken care of. That's what I love. All the people so beautifully arranged. It's all going some place. Someone's got it all figured out.
Merrill's *head jerks forward. He opens his eyes.*
Merrill Nowhere to put your head. That's what I hate.
Keith I think they're beginning to settle down. Perhaps we'll get the next laugh.
Merrill (*eyes closing again*) One of these nights it's gonna roll right off.
People begin to stir in their seats again.
Keith No? What's worrying them now?
Helena I suppose there's going to be language. It's that sort of play . . . I mean, I don't mind. I'm just worried about Mother. I know what *she* must be thinking.
Joan I wonder how often they have to clean that upholstery . . .
Quentin Anyway, it's a treat for him.
Lee I mean, like, what's going on? Am I supposed to be *enjoying* this, or what?
Quentin I know how much it means to these boys to get their first taste of live theatre.
Lee Like, why just me? I'm not the only one doing a Drama A level . . .
Quentin So valuable for them to be taken off on their own once in a while.
Lee Soon as it's over he's going to be on about, what did I think? What did I feel?
Quentin Given a chance to say what they really think and feel.

Lee I mean, how do *I* know? We haven't done this one, have we?
Silence.
Keith All right?
Helena (*suddenly*) What *I* resent is that there they are, all having a wonderful time swearing and taking their clothes off and sitting around as if they owned the place—and they get a great kick out of it because here we are watching them. Yet here we sit, with our clothes on and our mouths shut, and not so much as a thank you—no one taking the slightest bit of notice!
Keith Good. Yes. Fair point. We'll talk about it afterwards. Now . . .
Pause.
Merrill (*opening his eyes*) Great stuff. When's it over?
Charles They ought to put the finishing time in the programme.
Everyone shifts around again.
Keith Come on! Don't start thinking about supper.
Quentin I've booked a table at that little place across the road.
Charles Or if we left at the interval . . .
Helena Could leave at the interval . . .
Joan Go at the interval . . .
Helena Only she won't, of course.
Joan Only she paid for the tickets.
Helena She insisted on sitting there to the bitter end even in the one where they all took their clothes off.
Joan Taken his jacket off now.
Charles Say eighty minutes in the car, eighty-five minutes . . .
Keith If you're not careful there won't *be* an interval. You want an interval? You want to go home tonight? All right, then, you buckle down to it and start thinking about the next laugh. Silence. Concentrate.
Merrill *opens his eyes and coughs.* **Keith** *turns round and gives him a look.*
Keith Right. Thanks. Hold it. Stop there.
No one notices **Keith**. *He faces the front—and immediately* **Merrill** *coughs again.*
Keith Oh, no!
Keith *jumps to his feet and stares at* **Merrill** *until he stops. But by this time* **Charles** *has started coughing as well.* **Keith** *comes leaping over the backs of the seats to hover behind* **Charles**, *unseen by anyone, as if about to murder him.*
Keith You'll start them all off!
Charles *stops.*

Keith Right. That's it. No one else.

But now **Lee** *has started.* **Keith** *goes leaping back to threaten him in his turn. But* **Lee** *is already acutely aware of causing a disturbance. He stuffs a handkerchief into his mouth and shakes silently, letting no breath escape.* **Keith** *watches over him vengefully.*

Keith That's right. Just suffocate in silence.

Gradually everyone becomes aware of **Lee**'s *sufferings, and makes great efforts not to turn around and look.* **Keith** *watches, agonised.*

Joan Is someone having a fit?

Keith No one's having a fit.

Helena Is someone going to be sick?

Keith No, no, no! Just keep your mind on the play.

Amanda Someone ought to do something.

Charles It's probably just one of the actors. It's that sort of play.

Seating plans for *Audience*

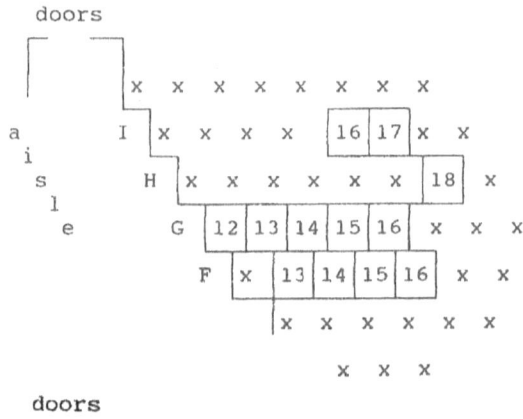

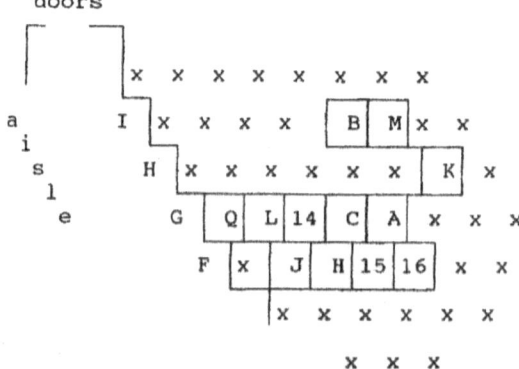

Figure 14.1 Plan 1 and Plan 2 for Michael Frayn, *Audience*.

Note

1. © Michael Frayn, *Audience* and Methuen Drama, an imprint of Bloomsbury Publishing Plc. Extract from *Audience* by Michael Frayn published by Methuen Drama © Michael Frayn 2007 and 1991 is printed by permission of United Agents LTD (www.unitedagents.co.uk) on behalf of Michael Frayn.

15 *Ugly Betty* and the (Live) Comedy Audience

Elizabeth Klaver

Elizabeth Klaver is Professor of English at Southern Illinois University, Carbondale. She has published widely in drama, television, and cultural studies, including two books, *Sites of Autopsy in Contemporary Culture* (SUNY Press, 2005), and *Performing Television: Contemporary Drama and the Media Culture* (University of Wisconsin, Popular Press, 2000). She has also edited the books *The Body in Medical Culture* (SUNY Press, 2009), and *Images of the Corpse from the Renaissance to Cyberspace* (University of Wisconsin Press, 2004).[1]

Perhaps the reader is wondering what the television show *Ugly Betty* (2006–2010, currently in syndication) has to do with a book on live comedy audiences. After all, *Ugly Betty* is a filmic television show; it does not use a live studio audience or even a laugh track. While it is true I am embarking on somewhat different terrain than the other essayists represented here, I want to take this opportunity to consider how *Ugly Betty* might enable a discussion of the comedy audience of various media, specifically the question of live versus unlive. In what ways does television comedy offer a similar vehicle for joke telling as, say, live venues like stand-up comedy and theater? And does the television audience respond to jokes in any way similar to the audience of live performance?

Though virtually any comedic television show could anchor my discussion, I'm choosing *Ugly Betty* simply because it was such a remarkable phenomenon, especially in its first year.[2] Clearly, the show built a large comedy audience over the course of the 2006–2007 network season. According to the Nielsen ratings, *Grey's Anatomy* and *Ugly Betty* catapulted ABC into the number one network spot for

Thursdays, and all of its original episodes won in the category women aged eighteen to thirty-four (ABC Media Net). Nevertheless, while the Nielsen data is useful, it is also quite limited, for many more sectors of audience are needed than women aged eighteen to thirty-four to account for so large a television viewership. Moreover, one cannot draw many conclusions about an audience of several million based on a house of three or four viewers. This situation is quite different from live venues where the house may hold several hundred; here, one can assume if everyone is laughing, something must be funny to everyone. Knowing the empirical information about the audience of *Ugly Betty* is so limited, I want to take a cultural studies approach rather than a sociological one, attempting to see its audience through the lens of *Ugly Betty* itself by utilizing theories of humor and spectatorship. This analysis will, in turn, found a comparison of how humor works across various live and unlive media.

SITES OF ANXIETY

Ugly Betty, as we know it, was drawn from the highly popular Colombian telenovela, *Yo Soy Betty La Fea*, which began running in 1999 (Booth) and is similar to the film, *The Devil Wears Prada*, though without the Faustian legwork. As in the American version, *Betty La Fea* places its titular "ugly" heroine in the glamorous world of a fashion design company. Such an awkward situation would certainly prove to play well in the American television market, for it appropriates the fish-out-of-water genre developed so adroitly, however differently, in such situation comedies as the CBS shows, *The Beverly Hillbillies* (1962–71) and *Newhart* (1982–90). Dubbed a dramedy, along with *Boston Legal* (2004–2008), *Ugly Betty* combines the hour-long, serious drama format with extensive comedic undercurrents minus laugh track.

The dramedy is part of the format shifting television comedy has continually undergone since its inception in the 1950s. Television comedy has always tinkered with different genres of skit comedy and their concomitant audiences. Right from the beginning, sitcoms were basically structured in either a play format with studio audience as in *The Honeymooners* (1955–56), or a filmic style with laugh track like the one-season *The Hank McCune Show* (1950). The two types continue to the present day in *Two and a Half Men* (2003) with studio audience, and *Everybody Loves Raymond* (1996–2005) with laugh track. Interestingly, a third type has started to emerge as the sitcom without a laugh track or studio audience, perhaps the best example being the highly acclaimed Canadian *Corner Gas* (2004). The "no laugh" sitcom may, in fact, be an outgrowth of the dramedy, which first appeared in 1985 with *Moonlighting*.

In part because each episode is longer than a sitcom, dramedies may be better suited for the sort of comedy that constructs "sites of anxiety." According to comedy theorists, certain forms of humor are dominated by sensations of "existential absurdity and human suffering" (Pye 60, 55). In other words, comic forms do not necessarily work simply because they are funny, but also because they negotiate the types of serious philosophical, social, and/or political issues the audience may be finding stressful. It is clear live performance has a history of constructing this sort of space; consider, for instance, the droll absurdity of Samuel Beckett's post-war wasteland in *Waiting for Godot* or the political satire of Lenny Bruce. To what extent does television offer similar sites of anxiety? Certainly, *Ugly Betty* is exemplary of the sort of television show that does cover many of the anxieties found in contemporary US (and other western countries) culture: anxieties associated with being gay at work, being gay and young in the family unit, even being straight (male or female) in a predominantly gay community; anxieties associated with single motherhood, especially the raising of a gay boy; anxieties associated with feminism and postfeminism, diversity, and interracial sex and romance; and perhaps the most daring of all, certainly one of the hot topics of American politics today, anxieties associated with immigration policy, represented by the "scary" Mexican undocumented worker, who is rendered (to my mind) as the most adorable of all the characters, Betty's father Ignacio Suarez.

One major anxiety forms the premise of the show, as in *Betty La Fea*: the ugly in a world of beauty. The pilot establishes this situation when Betty is hired by CEO Bradford Meade at *Mode Magazine* to be his son's assistant, not because she is competent (she is), but because her homely appearance will not tempt Daniel's libido (it doesn't). To its credit, the show does not saddle Betty with the sort of self-deprecating humor classically associated with the underdog, especially when the underdog is a woman. As Frances Gray points out in *Women and Laughter*, funny women, particularly stand-up comediennes, often rely on the art of self-deprecation (137). To the contrary, Betty's character displays a high degree of self-confidence. Even so, the world is still beautiful, and Betty is still ugly. After the pilot, the show's title sequence takes over to remind the audience at the onset of each episode of this premise, as well as to "suture" the audience not only to Betty as the main character but to her as the right character. The notion of suturing in visual media comes from film theory developed by theorists such as Christian Metz, Laura Mulvey, and Kaja Silverman some years ago, but nevertheless still provides a useful explanation of how a film signals to the audience who is to be the main character or subject and aligns the audience's perspective with him or her. In the classic scenario, the audience is shown a series of shots that stem, quite obviously, from someone's point of view. Once the audience understands they have been gazing through someone's eyes, the camera turns around to show the audience who has been doing the looking. This process sutures the audience to the subject's point of view and establishes the subject as the protagonist. Alfred Hitchcock used this method to a high degree of effect.

A form of suturing can also be recognized in live venues such as theater and stand-up comedy. In these situations, suturing functions through some technical effect such as lighting or even voice. Though in the live venue the audience's gaze is free to wander wherever it will, usually the gaze will adhere to whatever is given the focus. It is important in a play then, to light the main characters early or to give them the first lines. Of course, in stand-up comedy, the comic is always encircled in a spotlight and miked. With this combination of light and voice, the audience's gaze is as good as riveted. The title sequence of *Ugly Betty* goes for the same riveting effect, but in a somewhat different manner of suturing, perhaps better to suit televisual discourse, which is generally much more fragmented and repetitive than either film or theater. After all, the filmic or play narrative is developed once in a single sitting, whereas the narrative of a television series is developed week after week over a long, even very long, period of time. Each episode of *Ugly Betty* begins with opening credits scenes that review the previous week, launch the situation for this week, and figure Betty prominently. These scenes are designed to catch the eye of the viewer by focusing it on an eye-catching character (in braces, glasses, clashing fabrics), a technique that substitutes for the point-of-view shots of classic film.

The opening credits then cut to the title sequence, a series of images in the guise of a puzzle reminiscent of the children's game in which a series of incongruent parts must be sorted to produce the correct picture. Here is a *face* looking directly into the face of the viewer, but it is compiled as a series of rapidly moving, incongruently juxtaposed, and mismatched facial parts.

Not these eyes.

Not this nose.

Not this mouth.

Early on in the sequence, the face resolves briefly to that of a photographed model that provides the world of beauty image for the show, but nevertheless is instantly discarded as somehow wrong, for the puzzle starts back up. Just before the final image, the capitalized words "UGLY BETTY" slide into the eye and nose slots. When the face finally resolves correctly, it is of course Betty's, plain and real. The final shot, then, provides viewers with the last step in the suturing process, equivalent in film to turning the camera around to show us, under the banner of the title, who is doing the looking, align our perspective to her point of view, and establish her as the subject.

At the end of the title sequence, we know it is Betty looking directly at us, as we are looking at her, in an exchange of gazes that constructs an extremely powerful form of identification. The sort of direct looking used here would rarely be seen in the filmic suturing process unless for metadramatic purposes, for it breaks verisimilitude, and indeed, it only reappears in the actual running of *Ugly Betty* episodes when the scene is rendering an internal television news or news entertainment show. In fact, such direct looking is most often utilized in theater, in the asides of Shakespearean and Renaissance comedy and in some postmodern plays such as *Wit* by Margaret Edson, which, oddly enough given its subject matter of ovarian cancer, has a number of funny moments. However, because the title sequence of *Ugly Betty* is outside the frame of the program, the directness of its final image can be used to address viewers personally. It's as if Betty is saying, "I may be the main character, but you and I have a special affinity."

Discourse Competence

The special affinity created here between subject and viewer in *Ugly Betty* has to do with the construction of "discourse competence," a useful concept in humor theory that allows us to see, in both live and unlive venues, how subject and viewer together gain power (see Pye 57–59). Discourse competence in humor situations follows from the play of incongruity at the level of the signifier. According to Susan Purdie, when several "definitionally different" signifiers are launched in a single semantic space, a clashing of information is produced. Further, in order for both participants to get the joke, the incongruent signifiers must be understood by the subject and recipient as "aberrant usage." The subject and recipient thus demonstrate their command over the semantic space and emerge as "master of discourse" (qtd. in Pye 56).

One can see incongruity underlying the humor of many forms of comedy in a variety of media. In *Waiting for Godot*, incongruent signifiers befall Didi and Gogo every time they say, "Let's go," and then do not move. The signifiers of the statement clash with the signifiers of their bodies. As the play proceeds, this vignette gets funnier each time it occurs because the audience not only understands just how aberrant the usage is but also begins to anticipate it. A similar strategy was at work in David Letterman's running joke on *Late Night* during the George W. Bush presidency, "Great Moments in Presidential Speeches." The first several examples truly are great speeches from such presidential heavyweights as Franklin D. Roosevelt, John F. Kennedy, and Ronald Reagan. The last one, however, is always delivered by a bumbling, incoherent George W. Bush. His language not only clashes with the inspiring words of the previous speakers but also contradicts the very title of the joke. Interestingly, without the foregoing speeches, which set up the play of incongruity (the juxtaposition of proper with aberrant usage), Mr. Bush's lines would be rather more embarrassing than humorous.

In both of these examples, incongruity among the signifiers sets the stage for the construction of shared discourse competence between the teller of the joke and the recipient, between playwright or comedian and the audience. Most audience members will "get" the aberrant usage and recognize it as humorous (though *Godot* certainly has a history of audience irritability), developing a rapport with the joke teller that enables them to attain parity of power over the discourse. And the more often the joke is played out, say week after week on *Late Night*, the more discourse competence the audience gains. If we consider again the title sequence of *Ugly Betty*, we can see this show offers the same vehicle for telling the joke, and we can surmise the television audience would be responding similarly.

In this case, the puzzle forms the semantic space in which the series of incongruous signifiers—facial parts—are being rapidly juxtaposed. Since it is clear the signifiers are not harmonizing—the eyes of the model don't go with a mouthful of braces—a clashing of information occurs. When the signifiers eventually harmonize to produce the right face, subject and recipient can share a wide smile in knowing just how aberrant the usage of the previous signifiers truly was. Betty and the viewers "get" the irony of the joke, thus emerging together as discursively powerful. This power over discourse is perhaps key to understanding how the show builds relation with its audience. No matter how many times Amanda and Marc remark cruelly on Betty's appearance, the audience not only remains positioned as recipient of the joke but grows in its identification with Betty. (As an effect, Amanda and Marc are positioned as "discursively incompetent.") Like Betty, we've all been out-of-place at some time, so placing the subject in such a discomforting venue should resonate with a considerable number of people, certainly enough to form a large television audience.

In fact, there are at least two instances in the *Ugly Betty* first season that reinforce subject/recipient discourse competence on this joke of being out-of-place. The first instance occurs in the pilot, when Betty tries to enter the *Mode Magazine* conference room and smashes face first into a glass wall. The question posed here is pretty clear: will Betty be able to break through the invisible barriers erected around the world of beauty? And if she can, won't she be terribly out-of-place? By the end of the pilot, both questions have been answered, more or less. The second instance is more complex and dangerous because it flirts with viewer competence over the televisual discourse itself. This scene occurs early in Episode 18, "Don't Ask Don't Tell," and consists of one of the internal television vignettes that are inserted occasionally into some episodes. Here, a news reporter is speaking directly to the audience about the arrest of Mrs. Meade for the murder of Fey Sommers. He tries to ask Betty a few questions just as she is hurrying into the Meade building and, reminiscent of the pilot, she ends up slamming into the glass doors. What is so strange, though, about the scene is that Betty's slamming into the glass doors is immediately repeated, in its exact form, four times. Before the viewer has time to say "videotape," Betty's nephew, Justin, is shown watching the scene on television, replaying it over and over with the remote. Meanwhile, he is laughing: "it just gets funnier every time."

Actually, the scene is rather more astonishing than funny until viewers are let in on the joke, and we would be unlikely to find it funny without the addition of Justin's laughter. In humor research circles, laughter is understood to be one of the most important features in joking that makes a joke work, whether the venue has a live audience or not. If the teller of a joke laughs heartily at the punch line, she is more likely to have the recipient follow in kind. Even more effective is chuckling throughout the telling, a strategy often used by Jay Leno and Bill Maher in their stand-up routines, and the basic idea behind the laugh track. Of course, there are many deadpan comedians like Sarah Silverman who rely instead on the absurdity of the persona to provide the humorous context. Nevertheless, even in these cases the live audience is laughing, which helps make the joke funny. Such laughter is termed "keying," for it quite literally alerts the audience to the context as humorous (Kotthoff 274).

Keying falls under the rubric of "meta-message," for it stands outside the frame of the joke proper but is part of the context that announces, "this is play" (Kotthoff 288). Clearly, then, the video replaying in Episode 18 of *Ugly Betty* is utilizing keying, a method of joke telling most often associated with live performance. As a form of meta-message, the video replaying also announces, "this is play." Indeed, the meta-message as the replaying is actually part of the joke itself. Together with Justin's laughter, it opens a set of citations that would be unavailable if the scene were played "straight," as it is in the pilot when Betty crashes into the conference room wall. Besides reminding the audience of our position of being out-of-place, literally unable to get into the Meade building, the meta-message cites forms of physical humor such as slapstick and the pratfall developed in vaudeville and farce, and even shows in the television encyclopedia like *America's Funniest Home Videos*, also on ABC, which are based on real situations made funny as physical comedy.

Indeed, without the television citations and the audience's ability to grasp them, this joke would be in real danger of falling flat even to the point of offending the viewer, for it could easily render the recipient as a fool or dupe and undercut his or her discourse competence. Contrary to the similar joke in the pilot, which may indeed have set viewers up for this one, the joke here is based on the notion of "pulling the rug out from under" the recipient, for our belief in the initial verisimilitude of the scene is brutally exposed as unsophisticated. In order to work, somehow the joke must right the world and reposition the viewer as discursively competent, and it does so by showing the very apparatus of the meta-message, the replaying of the video. Thus, rather than ending with an audience of disgruntled butts, the joke manages to correct our position by aligning us with the subject's side, suturing us to Justin's point-of-view, allowing us to identify with the puppeteer and share in his discourse competence. (Interestingly, the scene utilizes the classic filmic form of suturing.) We end up positioned as competent with respect to the televisual discourse because we recognize our own television viewing habits. We (should) leave the scene in a state of identifying with our own viewership.

Indeed, such a complex process taps into the sort of visual sophistication developed in the postmodern era, though certainly audience self-consciousness has been played upon at least since Shakespeare and the many metadramatic moments in his comedies. Nevertheless, from novels such as Thomas Pynchon's *The Crying of Lot 49* to the language poets to *Chicago*, the notion of making readers or audiences aware of their subject position is a hallmark of contemporary literature, elite and popular. Michael Frayn's play, *Noises Off*, comes to mind when thinking about visual self-reflection and the live comedy audience, in this case a theater audience. *Noises Off* is about a theater group producing a play entitled "Nothing On." As the first act opens, the audience is led to believe it is watching the performance of a play, no metadramatic tricks involved. Out of the blue, the scene is interrupted by the director, who walks down the house toward the stage and begins to criticize the action. His sudden appearance operates on the audience in a manner that recalls Justin's role in Episode 18 of *Ugly Betty*. Having had their discourse competence abruptly yanked, the audience must quickly yield the original point of view to the director. Now realizing they have been watching something "staged," the audience is obliged to suture to the "stager." (As with Justin in Episode 18, the director is the one who turns out to have been doing the looking all along.) The first act must now be recognized as a rehearsal for the play, "Nothing On." Act Two proceeds to show "Nothing On" in a performance, except the set has been turned around, making the audience privy to the hilarious infighting going on behind the scenes, of course in dead silence for there is a fictive audience on the other side of the "house."

In Act Three, the set is returned to its original position, enabling the audience to witness what has happened to the production of "Nothing On" after months of disruption by the cast.

Having seen the play twice, I can verify just how funny it is in performance. Clearly over-the-top in exploiting the jokes and pratfalls of the English farce, the play is nothing less than a farce about the conventions of farce. The audience laughs not only at the hilarious spills and double entendres of the players but is, furthermore, asked to grasp the meta-message, "this is play," to recognize the play's citation of the farce. Going even further, though, the play draws on the discourse competence of the audience to identify the conventions of theater production, certainly those involving rehearsal, backstage, and performance. And finally, the play puts the audience in the subject position of recognizing not only its own sense of viewership but three specific types of viewership: directing in the first act, behind-the scenes in the second, and (fictive) general audience in the third. It takes a high degree of theater sophistication on the part of the audience for this play to work and a high degree of confidence in the audience's discourse competence to believe it will work. The video scene in Episode 18 of *Ugly Betty* relies on the same tactics as such a live performance. Its success also depends on the audience's ability to recognize and embrace their own discourse competence and to enjoy visual self-reflection.

In a sense, though, the scene in Episode 18 also corrects a situation that had developed earlier in the season, through Episodes 6–12, in a plotline I call "the Daniel/Sofia affair." Played by Salma Hayek, who is also the protagonist of the internal telenovela and one of the executive producers of *Ugly Betty*, Sofia arrives at Meade Enterprises to launch a woman's magazine. Beautiful and sexy, she immediately attracts Daniel's attention, but due to his history as a womanizer, she refuses to fall for him. After a turbulent courtship, she eventually agrees to marry Daniel. In the last episode of this plotline, Betty discovers the ugly truth behind Sofia's intentions, but not soon enough to prevent Sofia from announcing on a morning news show that she has manipulated Daniel into a marriage proposal for the sole purpose of writing a "how-to get-a-man" article for her new magazine. As in the video scene with Justin described above, viewers have had the rug pulled out from under them. There was little reason to suspect the verisimilitude of the Daniel/Sofia affair, and certainly no reason to believe the demise of the affair, if that were to happen, would be so humiliating. And not just humiliating to Daniel, but humiliating to the audience as well, for our discourse competence is considerably called into question.

In fact, to turn the knife just a little harder, viewers are treated to a set of flashbacks whose reading changes drastically with the addition of this new information: for instance, we are shown again the scene of the coffee mishap in the elevator, but rather than the innocent encounter it initially appeared to be, it is now revealed to have been a cunning scheme on Sofia's part for whetting Daniel's sexual appetite by giving him a peek at her breasts. What makes these flashbacks different, though, from the video scene with Justin described above, is that the flashbacks are not in the form of meta-message. Though outside the actual frame of the joke, a meta-message must occur during the telling and key the recipient to a humorous context. Here, the flashbacks occur after the punch line. And rather than keying a funny situation, they expose just how gullible the recipients have been. Moreover, there is no laughter to help the audience through this situation and no way to align with the joke teller's point of view. In fact, viewers are aligned with the butts of the joke—Daniel and Betty—and like them, rendered discursively incompetent. It is Sofia—bad girlfriend—who has emerged with discourse competence.

Perhaps what saved the denouement of the Daniel/Sofia affair from completely alienating the audience at the time it was aired was its contextualization as another instance of the show's unpredictability. *Ugly Betty* has so many plot twists that unpredictability could be considered one of its keys. Could viewers regain their discourse competence simply by recognizing and enjoying the surprise? We'll never know, for the network then did something only television has the capacity to do: it reran the episodes of the Daniel/Sofia affair during the early spring. Armed with the new information about Sofia's real intentions, the audience was given the opportunity to reread and reinterpret the relevant episodes.

And, of course, the episodes of the Daniel/Sofia affair look completely different in rerun. Viewers can't help but see the episodes in a new light, which deploys a competence over the discourse they did not have previously. By broadcasting the reruns, the network gave viewers, perhaps unintentionally, the opportunity to rebuild discourse competence. Rather than romantic, the Daniel/Sofia affair now seems utterly sordid, with Sofia emerging as cruel and opportunistic. Oddly enough, though, the reruns also enabled viewers to complicate Sofia as one of the most interesting and socially pertinent characters on the show, for she concentrates our attention on a site of anxiety the other women characters have only been able to circle: post-feminism.

SITES OF ANXIETY REDUX

Exactly how women are supposed to behave, supposed to desire, supposed to advance in career and romance in the early twenty-first century is a topic of real concern, perhaps most especially to that group, women aged eighteen to thirty-four, who are dedicated to watching *Ugly Betty*. This is the sort of serious social issue media venues are taking up across the board, certainly seen in theater—*Vagina Monologues* comes to mind—as well in the feminist and post-feminist routines of comediennes like Janeane Garofalo, Sandra Bernhard, and Sarah Silverman. As a professor, I often run into these issues among women students on campus. For instance, one topic under discussion is whether it's okay for women to take strip-cardio classes where they learn to pole dance under the guise of aerobic exercise. One side argues that strip-cardio is not only good exercise but empowers women to feel good about their sexuality; the other side argues that it simply reinforces women's internal sexism to see themselves as sex objects. On a more general level, the discussion revolves around the status of feminism today. Is the type of feminism initiated in the mid-twentieth century, what is called second-wave, still pertinent? Or has second-wave feminism evolved to a third-wave? Or should we consider ourselves in a state of post-feminism?[3] Before returning to Sofia and *Ugly Betty*, I want to digress briefly in order to outline the contours of the current "woman question," certainly a site of anxiety television, like live comedy, regularly examines.

Contemporary theorists seem to agree second-wave feminism has given way to something new, though whether it should be considered third-wave or post-feminism is open to debate. According to Janelle Reinelt, second-wave feminism is most often criticized today for having been too narrow and extremist and, I would add, for putting the blame too often in the male corner. Indeed, one of the major complaints is that second-wave feminism was responsible for fostering the ideology of women as hapless victims (Reinelt). As criticism of second-wave feminism was building in the 1990s, Susan Faludi published the book *Backlash: The Undeclared War Against Women*, which countered the rising notion that women had attained civic and economic equality, contrary to statistical evidence, thus rendering feminism obsolete. As Reinelt documents, Faludi at this time solidified the term "post-feminism" to describe this position. However, "post-feminism" is an umbrella term for a range of positions. In popular culture, as Sarah Gamble writes, post-feminism has been associated with women who have "claim[ed] male privileges and attitudes," represented by "the Spice Girls, Madonna and the Girlie Show" (43). Post-feminism, here, finds it perfectly acceptable for women to use their sexuality and feminine wiles, if that's what it takes, to succeed. Indeed, those who hold this position view themselves as liberated from the bluenoses of second-wave feminism who condemned sexual and feminine opportunism. The persona presented by Sarah Silverman, for instance, might be considered post-feminist. This persona is not a second-wave prude when it comes to talking about sex, and certainly, while one can say her remarks about sex come from a specifically woman's point of view, it would be difficult to argue they are strictly feminist. In fact, as Gamble notes, post-feminists in this vein tolerate pornography, and I might add strip-cardio, for the most part because they reject the feminist ideology of victimization (44). (In *Jesus is Magic*, the Silverman persona makes a call for more Jewish strippers.) Moreover, having developed in the heterosexual community, post-feminism does not target men as solely accountable for what happens to women.

To their credit, post-feminists recognize women do have agency and responsibility. The sense of women's agency and responsibility is also shared by those in the camp of third-wave feminism, which is offering an alternative politics to post-feminism. Though sharing some of the same positions as post-feminism, third-wave feminists see themselves as being derived from, and less opposed to, second-wave feminism. Recognizing social and economic equality is still unrealized, third-wave feminists nevertheless have a more global vista than second-wave feminists. They understand most women in the world have not achieved even the modest advances made by white women in the industrialized west. Third-wave feminists recognize the factor of race, as well as class, has an enormous impact on women's lives. As a result, they tend to be highly pluralistic in their outlook and constitute a remarkably diverse women's movement (Gamble 52–53). Again, with her racial slurs the persona utilized by Silverman would go against this grain.

To return to *Ugly Betty*, it is the character Sofia who offers the most complex treatment of these sorts of feminist questions. In the first running of the episodes of the Daniel/Sofia affair, the audience sees Sofia as smart and competent, gorgeous and cosmopolitan. Born into a poor family in Mexico, starting out as a maid, and achieving the position of editor-in-chief of an American women's magazine, she embodies the "rags to riches" narrative always popular with American audiences. Not only is she representative of a meritocracy in which women's competence is valued, she wants to aid other women, especially Betty, whom she recognizes as particularly talented. In terms of the men in her life, she clearly has the upper hand, riposting cleverly with Daniel and portraying herself as someone who knows quality lies in the person rather than in the image. In fact, Sofia is very close to achieving super-woman status, the final goal in her quest, by adding a husband and children to her already fulfilling life.

All of these characteristics would be thrilling to contemporary women, whether post-feminist or third-wave, certainly in the first running of the episodes. Sofia gives all of us hope that women, even one woman, can achieve the second-wave goal of social and economic equality. She is certainly more than the female equivalent of Daniel, equal to him intellectually, socially, and vocationally, but superior to him morally. To third-wave feminists, she demonstrates the diversity of today's women's movement. Not only are women of color fully involved in third-wave feminism, they can also make, and represent, the huge strides desired by all women. In this initial interpretation of the episodes, perhaps the most important trait of Sofia to third-wave and latter-day second-wave feminists is her sense of solidarity with other women. Unlike Amanda, who wants Betty's job, or even Wilhelmina, who wants to run the magazine, Sofia does not feel competitive with other women. And let's not forget she does all this without giving up her femininity or her sexuality.

Of course, this interpretative edifice comes crashing down with the revelations of Episode 12. True, Sofia is still beautiful, sexy, Mexican, accomplished, and cosmopolitan. But her moral code proves to be worse than Daniel's, for at least Daniel, no matter how shallow, is honest. And her feminist solidarity is thoroughly compromised. If befriending Betty was one way to get to Daniel, then Sofia's solidarity with Betty means that solidarity is just another means to an end. Here's the recipe: use every means available, including the traditional craft of sexuality, duplicity, and betrayal. In post-feminist terms, this is the route to claiming male privilege. Nevertheless, it is perhaps a bit unfair to post-feminists to call Sofia a post-feminist. Once the reruns of Episodes 6–12 commence and we read her narrative as one grubby scheme after another, it becomes hard to imagine anyone, even the most opportunistic career-climber, willing to condone her actions. I would rather claim Sofia's demise more likely falls into the arena of a critique of post-feminism in much the same way Silverman holds up her persona for the audience to critique. From this angle, Sofia can be seen as a caricature, an extreme version of the type that has been constructed to focus the audience's attention. She's too "bad" to be true, just as she was too good to be true as a third-wave feminist. Sofia's life on the show, then, ends up representing the range of discussion on feminism today, the politics of third-wave feminism in the first running of the episodes and, in the reruns, the extreme edge of post-feminism. Moreover, presenting the discussion in such a concentrated fashion enables the organizing of the more ambiguous women characters into a sort of graduated spectrum of feminist politics by inclining characters like Amanda and Wilhelmina toward the post-feminist camp and our titular heroine striving to ride the third wave.

Nevertheless, the high degree of scrutiny of contemporary feminist politics enabled by the reruns may have been the unintended effect of a much more dangerous game the show was playing with the viewer's competence, particularly over the televisual discourse. As in the Frayn play, *Ugly Betty* suddenly unraveled the viewer's trust at the end of Daniel/Sofia affair. But whereas the play gamed the audience for no more than five minutes, the television show presented the misleading narrative for numerous weeks, which is a much more serious subversion of the viewers' discourse competence. In part, this difference between *Ugly Betty* and *Noises Off* results simply from the medium in question. While a play lasts one evening, a television series goes on for seven or eight months, which allows a luxury of time not available to live performance for all sorts of twists and turns in the narrative to be developed. The downside to this sort of joke, though, is the difficulty in reestablishing the audience's trust after such a lengthy and profound deception.

It may be that showing the reruns in the spring turned out to be a strategy (unconscious or not) for rebuilding discourse competence over the Daniel/Sofia affair by authorizing a way for viewers to remove their misplaced alliance from Sofia, the teller of the joke, in order to gain power over the joke. While revisiting the narrative through rerun is distinct to the televisual medium, it may follow from the same desire in audience members to attend a live performance more than once. Comedy goers often return to a comedian's show, wanting to hear again the same jokes, perhaps as a way of experiencing a sort of live rerun. The loss of the surprise factor would be compensated by a gain in authority and discourse competence, and may be one of the reasons I went to *Noises Off* a second time. If this interpretation holds water, then the joke in Episode 18 of Justin replaying the video of Betty slamming into the glass doors is meant to reinforce the rehabilitating work of the reruns of the Daniel/Sofia affair. And in both instances, it is the television apparatus itself—the media-specific ability to replay and rerun episodes—that makes, or repudiates, the joke. Most importantly, the viewer's mastery over the televisual discourse is not only reestablished but actually celebrated.

Conclusion

Most television shows work hard to hide the wizard behind the curtain of illusion, ignoring in any metadramatic way an audience is watching. To the contrary, *Ugly Betty* showcases the televisual discourse, not only recognizing its competent audience but also making this recognition part of its showmanship, sometimes taking perilous risks with the audience, sometimes simply being playful. Since it takes two to make a joke, this sensitivity to the audience implies the existence of recipients who must also be willing to play with the televisual discourse. A fundamental trait of the audience, then, would be media sophistication, for in a very real sense *Ugly Betty* is about viewership.

One of the major ways *Ugly Betty* foregrounds viewership is through its use of replays and reruns, a technical capacity that clearly makes television different from any other medium. Yet being about viewership is also a subject *Ugly Betty* shares with plays like *Noises Off* and other live venues. In this case, the medium is less important than the fact that the performing arts have an audience and therefore apply similar methods for engaging that audience. Particularly with respect to comedy, theories of humor suggest telling a joke, whether to a million recipients, a few hundred, or several, requires the same tactic of constructing, and even subverting, discourse competence. By analyzing the way discourse competence is produced in a recipient, one can draw some conclusions about the response of an audience. And in the case of *Ugly Betty*, the Nielsen ratings confirmed for four years the show worked for millions of viewers.

The Nielsen ratings also indicated *Ugly Betty* was particularly strong in the category of young women. This was undoubtedly because the show navigated some of the sites of anxiety experienced by such members of the audience, young women who are concerned with how they fit into the culture of the early twenty-first century. Nevertheless, *Ugly Betty* also manifested a number of anxieties that have to do with being out-of-place. Certainly, one can see an audience that materialized out of viewers who have experienced anxieties, ranging from immigration policy to diversity, at one time or another. A comedy audience of this sort, even though televisual, shares much in common with audiences who attend live comedy performance such as plays and stand-up. Such viewers are eager to seek out venues, live or not, that provide a stage for critical social and political issues.

Notes

1. I would like to thank Judy Batalion and the editorial staff for their helpful comments on this essay.

2. The television writers' strike in the second season made judging the show's success more difficult than in the first season.

3. Feminists have recently begun to discuss the possibility of a fourth wave of feminism, engendered by the misogynist treatment of Hillary Clinton during her 2008 run for the Democratic Party presidential nomination.

Works Cited

ABC Media Net. Web. June 11 2007.
Booth, William. "Building 'Betty.'" *Washington Post* 22 October 2006. Web. 11 June 2007.
Frayn, Michael. *Noises Off.* New York: Samuel French, 1985. Print.
Gamble, Sarah. "Postfeminism." *The Routledge Critical Dictionary of Feminism and Postfeminism*. New York: Routledge, 2000. 43–54. Print.
Gray, Frances. *Women and Laughter*. Charlottesville: University Press of Virginia, 1994. Print.
Kotthoff, Helga. "Pragmatics of Performance and the Analysis of Conversational Humor." *Humor* 19 (2006): 271–304. Print.

Pye, Gillian. "Comedy Theory and the Postmodern." *Humor* 19 (2006): 53–70. Print.
Reinelt, Janelle. "States of Play: Feminism, Gender Studies, and Performance." *S&F Online* 2.1 (2003). Web. 18 May 2007.
Ugly Betty. ABC. WSIL, Carbondale IL. 2006–07. Television.

16 Watching Me, Watching You: Sitcom and Surveillance

Frances Gray

Frances Gray is former Reader in Drama at the University of Sheffield, and has written plays and comedy for the BBC. Her books include *Women and Laughter* (1994) and *Women, Crime and Language* (2003).

This essay is based on a lecture delivered at the Third Summer School in Humour Studies at the University of Bologna, 2007.

"Who are *you?*" said the Caterpillar.

This was not an encouraging opening for a conversation. Alice replied, rather shyly, "I—I hardly know, Sir, just at present—at least I know who I *was* when I got up this morning, but I think I must have been changed several times since then."

Who Are the Audience?

I sit in front of the television and wonder who I am.

On the one hand: I am English. Therefore a major part of my self-definition is tied up with the notion of humor. In more jingoistic times Frank Richards, creator of boys' magazines *Gem* and *Magnet*, saw humor as directly responsible for the British Empire: "[F]oreigners. . . . lack the sense of humor which is the special gift to our chosen nation" (qtd. in Paxman 36). The sense of destiny in the word "chosen" may have vanished, but the English still have a high investment in the belief that there is an English sense of humor; for example, lonely hearts ads continue to prioritize GSOH (Good Sense of Humor) over kindness or passion. Nor have we relinquished an unspoken assumption lurking in Richards's panegyric that humor means power. To define *what is funny* in a culture obsessed with the need for GSOH is to hold sway over the whole process of signification.

On the other hand: I am English. Therefore I am under constant observation, part of an endless live show. More than twenty percent of all the CCTV cameras on the planet are watching me—four million of them, one for every fourteen of the population (*Independent* 12 Jan 2004). Our relationship with them is uneasy, but there is also terror about the point where surveillance stops. Some of the most disturbing images in the media are of murderers and their still living victims— CCTV footage no longer live but frozen at the last visible moment before the unimaginable act. Detecting, not preventing, the cameras provide the media with images of accusation to frighten the innocent as well as the guilty. We do not like the idea of our image becoming the property of someone with the power to frame it in a compromising way, but nor do we want to disappear from the screen into the unimaginable. Small wonder that since the publication of Foucault's *Surveiller et Punir* in 1975 scholarship has been increasingly preoccupied with our ever-increasing visibility and the power with which it invests the state. As Foucault himself pointed out, one form of entertainment that explores our ambivalent reaction to this phenomenon is an English specialty, the detective story, and crime shows currently outnumber comedy shows on English terrestrial TV by almost two to one.

The humorous and the criminal/detective aspects of the English self-image combine in a phenomenon that has burgeoned since the start of the new millennium—Foucault lite. You can observe this in action at the Galleries of Justice in Nottingham, a highly successful museum converted from a former courthouse. As you walk the galleries, bobbies in old-fashioned helmets and Victorian warders leap out to become your guides while staying in character. While there is much to be learned about the history of crime and punishment, the lesson most forcibly pushed home, because the exhibits and the experience both reflect it, is that we inhabit a panopticon, an endlessly observed carceral network. It is necessary to find a way of negotiating our relationship with these people in authoritarian costumes. There are ground rules. The pretend bobby is expected to instruct, even if he treats us (politely) as felons. And it is assumed we will not offer even pretend violence; if we do, we will not be thumped with truncheons but courteously escorted off the premises. The whole contract is highly self-conscious, which always makes the English uncomfortable. The space itself, however, provides a hint how we should behave:

> Travel with us on an atmospheric tour through three centuries of crime and punishment. . . . Witness a real trial in the original Victorian Courtroom and put your friends and family in the dock, before being sentenced, and "sent down" to the original prison cells, laundry, medieval caves and authentic prison exercise yard—with its chilling last views from the gallows!

Stuck in a space between performance and spectacle, we become self-conscious and muck about for the camera, giving our "role-playing tourist" on a live comedy show for the benefit of security staff. It is this newly created space I want to examine in relation to comedy, and, in particular, situation comedy as opposed to and as extending from live performance.

English narrative comedy, like detective fiction, has always depended on the idea of *being found out*. It can be seen at its simplest in English farce, which puts respectable men in compromising cupboards and deprives vicars of their trousers. This is not the same as the comedy that derives its energy from the exposure of hypocrisy; characters rarely have terrible sins to hide—in fact, they are often doing a good deed that circumstances conspire to render suspicious. Although the plot often seems to involve sex (as a possibility rather than a fact), its real root is the English class system. This is not synonymous with economic position but rather it is a complex system that depends on the knowledge of arcane social rules and highly specific languages designed to keep outsiders outside. (My personal favorite is the language of fox hunting in which you can betray your outsider status simply through the definite article—one should always speak of "hounds," never of "*the* hounds.") The arbitrariness makes it a minefield for anyone attempting social mobility or even communication between classes. Things are further complicated by an unspoken rule that familiarity should be effortless: positive effort implies a *desire* to fit rather than the fact of fitting, while failure to conform implies effort is diverted to a priority higher than fitting. Hence there is a constant risk of exposure and embarrassment. It is said that the English welcome death because it means you can never be embarrassed again. And while in the post-Thatcher world there is less risk of being embarrassed because you say "*the* hounds," there are still arcane rules to navigate. English comedy continues to depend on the exposure of the private, imperfect, and desiring face.

EAVESDROPPING AUDIENCE?

Steve Neale and Ben Krutnik have usefully extended Freud's analysis of the relationship between joker, victim, and audience in the smutty joke to embrace sitcom. There is the teller or mediator of the joke: this may be one of the cast, but, in the broader sense, it is the camera that shows us the situation; there is the target, there to be embarrassed; there is the receiver in front of whom he or she is embarrassed—identical, they suggest, to the audience at home who are constructed as eavesdroppers. Initially sitcom was broadcast live, aiming for responses like those of a theatre audience for trouser-dropping English farce—indeed sitcom took over from farce the idea of embarrassment, closely related to class politics. However, this changed as TV developed its distinctive contribution to the genre—a comedy of failure, grounded in an eccentric character with aspirations we know to be hopeless because they are in excess of his talent or maybe just his luck. Actor-comedian Tony Hancock, whose character combined snobbery, belligerence, and vulnerability in equal quantities, was its earliest exponent, and one of his first innovations was to abandon the business of going out live. Recording allowed him to use the camera in a more fluid and hence more naturalistic style. Thus in one sense he was more distant from his audience in that he was not "present" as they laughed at him. However, compensating for this fact with a sophisticated use of cameras to offer intimate close-ups, he was able to render himself arguably *more* present in that he was more available to his audience. The comedy of failure was kept alive and kicking for decades—by the socially aspiring rag and bone man Harold and his down-to-earth dad in *Steptoe and Son* in the 1960s and *Fawlty Towers* in the 1970s, while what was arguably its last hurrah, *One Foot in the Grave*, showed a grumpy pensioner, Victor Meldrew, at odds with the yuppified world of the 1990s.

These sitcoms could never simplistically endorse the codes their eccentric heroes tried in vain to negotiate. Because they went out to a broad class and income spectrum, the interpretative community watching the humiliations of Hancock or Victor Meldrew did not necessarily share the code of the people that crushed them. The intimacy of the new recording techniques and democracy of television meant that at some point in the comedy of eccentricity the audience was given a different position within the "joking relationship." A classic example occurs in *Fawlty Towers*. Hotelier Basil Fawlty is generally the object of the joke as he fawns upon the local bigwigs of Torquay flaunting his scrappy social graces—as in this moment where he fails to master winespeak:

> BASIL: It's always a pleasure to find someone who knows the boudoir of the grape. I'm afraid most of the people we get here don't know a Bordeaux from a claret.
>
> WALT: A Bordeaux *is* a claret.
>
> BASIL: Oh a *Bordeaux* is a claret. But *they* wouldn't know that. You obviously drink a lot. Wine, I mean. Well I don't mean a lot, not too much, the right amount for a connoisseur, I mean, that doesn't mean you're . . . does it, I mean some people put it away by the crate but that's not being a connoisseur, that's just plain sloshed, oh Bordeaux's one of the clarets all right. (Cleese and Booth 130)

However, at the end of his tether as his "gourmet night" is in jeopardy and the car stalls fetching emergency supplies, he addresses it in a different style:

> I'm going to count up to three. One. Two. Three . . . right! That's it! I'm going to give you a piece of my mind. I've never liked you, you son of a bitch, you've never run right, you've had it in for me from the beginning, haven't you? Well you've had this coming to you. I'm going to give you a damn good thrashing. (Cleese and Booth 215)

This time Basil is not observed by Walt the wine-snob or any of his ilk. The camera shares this moment only with us. The effect is not to demean Basil by inviting the shared contempt of Freud's "joking relationship." Because Basil has nothing to lose, because there is no on-screen embarrassment at stake, he can engage in an overflow of completely pointless creativity. He finds a memorable image to encapsulate a kind of frustration many of the audience will have shared, and in turn it is shared with us. This is not achieved by Basil acknowledging our presence but by the intimacy the camera has permitted. It is a marked contrast to the live comedy available in clubs and on television in the 1970s, which opted for a stylized delivery of jokes by comedians sharing little of themselves. Rather, it resembles an "aside" in the theater, the imparting of a confidence—even though it is involuntary. While we stand back from the rage and enjoy the picture framed by the camera, Basil transforms himself from comic object to comic subject for us alone to see. It's a tiny victory.

The sitcom of eccentricity has a frightening subtext: "You'll never get out." The characters, however powerful their energies, are stuck in the mundane—jobs they hate, marriages they loathe—wistfully hovering at the edge of a social class, a romantic relationship, or a cool image they will never quite reach, and are always embarrassed when their efforts fail. But those solitary moments are a guarantee that they won't go under. They are, of course, fictions that have been carefully shaped to foreground the talent of the performer: that *Fawlty Towers* "car-flogging" moment taps into John Cleese's physical agility in controlling extremely long limbs to give the effect of a deranged spider. Because such moments *are* set pieces, the audience doesn't assume they can easily be achieved in real life. But they function as powerful suggestions that, however absurd people can be, they deserve a better world than the class-ridden, bureaucratic, and selfish one they live in.

However, this depends on evading the usual conventions of the three cornered joking relationship and occupying that private space for a moment. Our place in this sitcom world of the last century varied—sometimes we were consciously invited to join the joking relationship with the onscreen receivers, sometimes we pretended we had the privilege of spying into the private space beyond the possibility of embarrassment. But because it was so common a feature of the genre from Tony Hancock onward, it was never difficult to know what response was demanded and it was always clear which space we as audience were expected to inhabit.

Awkward Audience

As the millennium approached, surveillance continued to proliferate and develop technologies that transformed TV documentary. This had once entailed considerable disruption to its subject and the camera continually reminded us that editorial choices had already been made. Live broadcasts were rare and their presentation made clear that they were uniting the country as a live audience—for the Coronation, the Cup Final, the moon landings. However, the newer technology enabled the camera to transmit a stream of apparently unmediated reality. The power of the media to do this became ever clearer as the *Big Brother* series unfolded on Channel 4 from 2000. Here surveillance was ubiquitous and permanent. A group of people were placed in a closed environment where the only place not equipped with hidden cameras was the lavatory and where their activities were broadcast on a twenty-four-hour basis on the internet. To surveillance the program added competition and a cash prize. The contestants were thus in a double bind: they needed to "perform" to attract viewers, but also needed the appearance of spontaneity in order not to seem competitive. They swung between self-conscious comedy, like shoppers mugging for the cameras in a mall, and negotiating relationships in a hothouse of gossip, often resorting to the language of agony aunts to dissect their egos.

But as competitors revealed their pasts, got drunk, and fooled about, the editors responsible for the primetime segment of the show transformed the recorded footage and its relationship to the audience. Rather than the live mistakes of silly but vulnerable people that could be swiftly forgotten, *Big Brother* solidified into sitcom with a narrative line. However, in place of the techniques with which Hancock and the rest gave the illusion of living and vulnerable characters, we now had real vulnerability given the illusion of unreality. The other media joined in to raise the stakes. *The Sun* foregrounded Jade Goody as the comic target of the 2002 series, gleefully relaying her gaffes (such as asking whether Greece had its own moon). While in a sitcom the three cornered joking relationship does not outlast the thirty-minute episode, the mockery of Goody became a sustained process. Much of the embarrassment she might have felt—for instance, being seen naked after a game of strip poker—was deferred; while she might have faced the mockery of her co-competitors at the time, other incidents would always arise to deflect it; but the outside audience, egged on by a *Sun* that still reprinted her gaffes five years later, could continue as long as it chose.[1] A performer like John Cleese could feel only gratification when his character remained "live" to an audience on a ten-year-old video: a real person whose mistakes were endlessly recycled as entertainment could only feel the humiliation again and again as an old clip or quotation was treated as live entertainment all over again.

The power assumed by the *Sun* made it apparent that, as Ben Thompson puts it, "the commodification of the self which reality TV entails is also a comedification" (397). Docusoap, carving out a story about real people from recorded footage while continually providing updates about its characters in order to offer a sense that it was "live," rapidly became the new sitcom. Channel 4 made its role in this process clear with the 2007 docusoap, *Chaos at the Chateau*, about a couple who convert a castle in Slovakia into a luxury hotel. This story was marketed by its website as "*Fawlty Towers* for real," and even its credits mimicked the lettering on Basil Fawlty's hotel. The parallel is evident in the structuring of episodes. When the couple's ignorance of the language led them to buy a whole dead pig instead of a live piglet for a petting zoo, David organized a "Pork Night." While the parallels with Basil Fawlty's "Gourmet Night" were not exact, the episode chose to focus, exactly like *Gourmet Night*, on the couple's relationship with their volatile chef who abandoned them at the crucial moment. The media joined the game, the *Times* invariably referring to the couple by the names of their *Fawlty Towers* counterparts. "The owner of the Slovakian Fawlty Towers is looking forward to the local magnate dining at the chateau in the hope that he will invest in the hotel. Unfortunately, he claimed that it was a thriving business, whereas in fact there is not a guest in sight. Undefeated, Basil and Sybil dress up all the staff to look like guests" (*Times* 3 May 2007).

Arguably, some of the more extravagant episodes involved the cooperation of the couple: it doesn't seem likely, for instance, that Ann would use her own bedroom to accommodate a gay couple without telling David or that he would enter it at the exact moment the men were undressing. But the process leaves the audience uncertain of its role. On the one hand we are encouraged by the credits to construct scenes like these as self-conscious artifacts, Ann and David mugging for the camera—indicating that they have a sense of humor, that they are being English in the face of the embarrassment of surveillance, and that we have permission to laugh. On the other hand the series showed Ann and David at times of genuine unhappiness—for example when their dogs were killed in the course of a row with the neighbors—and created an anxiety about them that had to be allayed with new, live interviews. However, such revelations are at the discretion of the editors. You cannot help wondering whether only an incident as painful as this could have ruptured the *Fawlty Towers* flow. What is conspicuously lacking in the whole thing is a space for private silliness, one that allows targets to claim the right to control the laughter. The talent of performers like Cleese made the creation of such a space for their characters inevitable. On reality TV it is not inevitable, but it is, perhaps, as worth fighting for as the cash prizes.

As an audience we are doubly complicit in the joking relationship; the sitcom narrative painstakingly carved out of the footage makes us identify with the camera as teller of the joke. Instead of a genuinely fictional private space, a fiction is created that in mugging for the camera the subjects are "asking for it" —not just for the period of their visibility on screen, but for as much of their subsequent lives as the media choose to examine, so that they remain a kind of permanent live show. As Foucault warned, visibility is a trap. But falling out of sight of the cameras is also a frightening prospect in a world of surveillance. It makes you nobody. Visibility can all too easily collapse into celebrity as something to be desired. Mugging for the camera may be the only way of coming to terms with the fact that it is equally dangerous inside or outside the trap.

GUILTY AUDIENCE

Docusoap instant sitcom is vastly cheaper than the real thing and it was not difficult in the cash-driven post-millennial media to promote the idea that no fictional comedy could match real life. When sitcom innovation *did* occur, however, it confronted docusoap head-on. The new generation of sitcom writer-performers had grown up in the 1980s, a period when stand-up comedy—or at least in the incarnation known as alternative comedy—was known as the new rock 'n' roll. Whether it was live in a club or on TV—often also live—alternative comedy changed both the matter and manner of performance. While its most obvious impact lay in its challenge to the sexist and racist material of an earlier generation, alternative comedy also had a more confessional, intimate relationship with its audience. Instead of seeking to tell a string of jokes, the new comedians talked about their insecurities, their politics, their struggles as women in the workplace, as gay men in a world of uncomprehending straights, as new men flummoxed by feminism. The tone of voice was relaxed, seeking a laughter of recognition, rather than stylized joke telling. It could slip into the hypernaturalism needed for a narrative comedy that critiqued docusoap not by broad parody but by imitating the behavior of those continually "live" to a TV audience. *The Office*, opening in 2001, was set in a typical trap, a boring workplace, but one that was the setting for a fictional docusoap with a fly-on-the-wall camera. Hence the relationship of the characters to the camera had to be negotiated as part of the plot, making it a participant rather than the teller of the joke. There were deft reminders of the camera's new status, such as the paralyzed terror overtaking a maintenance man suddenly aware of its presence while delivering the toilet rolls. When the camera was involved in a *Big Brother* strategy of following a consistent "plotline" —such as the likeable Tim's shy attempts to romance the receptionist, Dawn, it was shown to fail to take control of the narrative. Tim and Dawn show their feelings largely through subtext: they share a love of practical jokes against the pompous deputy manager, such as setting his stapler in jelly. This enables them to avoid the embarrassment of direct declaration; we are laughing partly at their jokes, but also in support of the way they subvert the camera to gain emotional privacy. Things reach crisis point at the end of the second series when Dawn announces she is leaving. Tim starts speaking to camera, and then walks out of frame; wobbling shots of him walking toward her indicate that the camera is following. He pulls Dawn into another room and closes the door. He unhooks his microphone and the sound vanishes. All that can be seen is shadows on a Venetian blind. The two emerge, blank faced. Tim clips on his mike and tells us, "She said no" (Gervais and Merchant *Series 2* 249). Tim's shyness is not the target: rather, we are encouraged to mock the way the camera puts the possibility of private play at risk.

However, the most sustained relationship with the camera in *The Office* is that of David Brent. While Brent may not have been the first sitcom hero in a show grounded on the idea of reality TV, he was the first to have a complex relationship with his own comedification. Brent is throughout eaten up by the desire for visibility—although he would probably define it as "celebrity;" his strategy for gaining it is "humor." In the post-Thatcher world of "classless" office politics, humor offers a means of upward mobility. To define it means power. For Brent, to be live to a reality TV camera does not mean surveillance but celebrity status. Consequently Brent never enters the space of private play; not only are his jokes aimed at a visible audience in the office, they are consciously aimed at *us*. But we are not the vapid live audience he imagines we are. We never laugh. Brent flaunts his GSOH by trying to put some new employees at ease with a carefully rehearsed racist joke, only to have the punch line deflated by the entry of sophisticated black Oliver, wearily remarking, "It's not the black man's cock one again, is it?" (Gervais and Merchant *Series 1* 36). Rebuked by his boss, Brent can't really grasp that he has offended, but tries to make it up to Oliver by announcing how much he admires Sidney Poitier.

The joking relationship is radically reconfigured. Oliver is not the target, nor are fellow employees passive receivers of the joke they visibly reject. And like them, we are embarrassed by it. However, we are not laughing at the exposure of a racist—if we believed Brent had genuinely hostile feelings toward black people the situation would not be comic. What is exposed here is Brent's lust for power, and it is comic because not only does he fail to understand his own motives but he also has virtually no concept of exposure in a life lived entirely in pursuit of visibility. His awareness of humor as a discourse of power is not matched by an understanding of its complex codes, as hard to navigate in a world sensitized to racial and gender politics as any of the arcane language of the class system. For Brent humor remains a monolithic construct whereby a joke is funny just because it is labeled "joke" —hence he cannot control his discourse. He has no idea that he has transformed himself into a target as absurd as Basil Fawlty at his most snobbish.

However, our relationship to him is not quite the same as our relationship to Basil Fawlty because we are made aware of a different boundary to laughter and embarrassment, one Brent never sees. Among the new staff is a young woman in a wheelchair; Brent, in charge of fire drill, starts to haul her down the emergency stairs, gets tired, and abandons her on the stairs. The camera pulls away as if *it* is embarrassed. It allows us to share a kind of moral perspective. It is as if the camera itself realizes its very existence is the problem. At the end of the second series this took on a moral dimension new to situation comedy. Brent, who has persistently tried to undermine the authority of his bosses with humor at the expense of doing any work, is made redundant. He receives this news on Red Nose Day, dressed in an ostrich outfit. Briefly, the camera reveals his utter panic and terror. We are aware for perhaps the first time that he might be a decent private individual, but cannot detach himself from his own comedification. In short, the trap wins. However, it is Brent's choice to mug for the camera rather than looking for a private space of play; this isn't the camera's fault, and it sometimes seems to struggle with the fact that it has been positioned to entrap him. Through those moments when it turns away, it reminds us that we are *always* free to do so, that even if we do not have a choice about the surveillance around us, we have a choice about our relationship to the camera. And we also have a choice about the way we construct ourselves as an interpretative community.

Private Audience

If the camera could sometimes take an admonitory role in *The Office*, *Peep Show*, which made its debut in 2003, gave it a more radical function still. Effectively it dislodges the teller of the joke from the relationship by shooting every exchange from the point of view of the person addressed. Cameras are placed on the head of the actor out of shot, so we see exactly what they see. The two protagonists, whose point of view we most often share, are twentysomething flatmates bound by the remains of an uneasy relationship that began at university and which has become a trap: Mark, the pathologically uptight loan manager and Jeremy the utterly selfish and childlike wannabe musician. Our intimacy with their point of view is enhanced by allowing us to eavesdrop on their thoughts. This takes the intimacy of alternative stand-up to a new level: although our relationship with them might lack the immediacy of live performance, it brings us closer to the characters in that their thoughts—like everybody's—are unspeakable.

Their immaturity makes for a comedy of embarrassment and the plots tap into a number of situations almost clichéd in their potential for exposure—nakedness, sexual betrayal, and drunken pranks. The pair has no more chance than a vicar in a 1920s farce of not *being found out*. When Mark scores a rare success with a woman by playing one of Jez's terrible records to make her laugh, Jez inevitably walks in; later, Mark lifts his bedcover to find the word JUDAS spelt out in sausages. But the personalized cameras virtually remove the teller from the presentation of these moments—we see both incidents from the point of view of the victim and the perpetrator separately; it is impossible to identify with one rather than the other, so guilt and laughter are as inextricable for us as for them. Sometimes the camera seems willful in its refusal of the obvious joke, as in the episode where Mark and Jez go skinny-dipping. Inevitably, it is Mark who finds it difficult to strip down, although he has set his heart on showing the fanciable

Sophie how liberated he can be, and he hovers on the diving board in his underpants as the others call to him from the lake. But when he is finally naked, we see the action from his perspective: a pair of pants around trembling ankles, followed by a lurch into dark water. At no point do we see him framed as the target (and given how funny the English seem to find bare bums, this sacrifice of an obvious laugh is remarkably radical). Similarly we miss a potentially climactic comic moment when Mark and Sophie are locked together prior to a charity bungee jump and the scene cuts to black. We only learn Mark has chickened out when we see his arm holding an envelope of money they have collected by pretending he *did* jump.

This sacrifice of the narratively obvious not only gives us the sense we are part of a process of surveillance akin to watching *Big Brother* live, it forces us to interrogate the nature of our relationship to the surveyed. Confined strictly to a single perspective, we are confident conventional modesty will be preserved: this means we can observe the most private moments without a sense of voyeurism in the *literal* sense. Whether we feel like another kind of voyeur—as a shot of an accurately directed stream accompanies Jez's reflection that now that he's been deserted by his girlfriend, he can pee with the seat down ("your reign of terror is over, Big Suze")—is a decision we have to make on our own. It is no coincidence, though, that these two emotional incompetents in a surveillance culture are themselves obsessed with spying. Mark watches Sophie on the workplace CCTV and even hacks into her email to see what she thinks of him; caught, he protests that they can't throw their relationship away "just because I spy on you." But because Mark and Jez are never framed as targets by the cameras, and because we are empowered to eavesdrop inside their heads, we cannot adopt the traditional comedy audience stance of superiority about their lack of self-awareness. If their moral standards can be lax (invited to sleep with Sophie's mother, Jez thinks of his absent girlfriend and reflects "It's a moral dilemma, only not really, because she won't find out"), the embarrassment and self-loathing we overhear in their heads give them a kind of perverse heroism. When Mark ceases to fancy Sophie almost as soon as he has won her, she discovers the engagement ring he has been hiding and accepts his non-proposal of marriage. Yes, he tells the incredulous Jez, he *is* going to marry her "because of embarrassment," reflecting hopefully to himself, "this me-not-loving-her business will sort of put me in a position of power in our marriage. Yes. I win."

The dimension of fantasy in the heads of Mark and Jez mean the space of private play is reclaimed. However, it's a rather darker place than comedy is used to because the playfulness need never penetrate the outside world to the point of being voiced aloud. Jez worries about his girlfriend Nancy getting off with Glyn and hopes the van will crash: "If she got disfigured, she'd be more likely to stick to me." It is also a space of fuzzy thoughts that open up fields of comic possibility. Mark has occasional lustful thoughts about his male boss, Johnson, and wonders whether this means he's "repressed even to myself." Johnson's taste runs to other men's girlfriends, but his most sexually charged speech is reserved for management technique—he offers Mark the chance to be "Camilla to my Charles." "Johnson's Queen!" trills Mark in his head. While another series might hammer this home with a plot or two, this is funny because it remains another unfulfilled aspect of the unadventurous Mark. Diffuse, inarticulate, and even violent as these images are, they are also creative. The eccentrics of older sitcom were embarrassed in front of us, but they also found a place outside embarrassment to play. The newer ones preempt the camera as joke teller and invite us right into their heads where the embarrassment is actually experienced. Under perpetual scrutiny ourselves and encouraged by the media to laugh at others mugging for the camera, we can't help feeling a profound relief at this. It's not just the holiday from logic or rules postulated by Freud as the source of comic relief. In a country that has no privacy laws and continually informs us that the live show in which we endlessly and involuntarily take part is good for us, the knowledge that there are no cameras inside the head, alongside the permission to climb, just for the moment, into another head, fuzzy and anarchic and fraught with embarrassment though it might be in there, is a tiny victory.

Notes

1. I have not dealt with the disgrace of Jade Goody after a racist comment during a reality show was followed by her very public struggle with terminal cancer. To incorporate this into the text would not do justice to her complex relationship with the media, but I feel the basic point still stands.

Works Cited

Chaos at the Chateau. UK Channel 4. Dir. Simon Greenwood. 2007. Television.

Cleese, John, and Connie Booth. *Fawlty Towers*. London: Contact, 1977. Print.

Frith, Maxine. "This Britain: How the Average Briton is Caught on Camera 300 Times a Day." *The Independent*, 12 January 2004. Print.

Gervais, Ricky and Stephen Merchant. *The Office: The Scripts: Series 2*. London: BBC Publications, 2003. Print.

—. *The Office: The Scripts: Series 1*. London: BBC Publications: 2002. Print.

Neal, Steve and Ben Krutnik. *Popular Film and Television Comedy*. London: Routledge, 1990. Print.

Paxman, Jeremy. *The English*. London: Penguin, 1999. Print.

Peep Show. Series 1-3 (Episodes 1, 4, 19, 24). UK Channel 4. Writ. Jesse Armstrong and Sam Bain. Dir. Jeremy Wooding. 2009. DVD.

Thompson, Ben. *Sunshine on Putty: the Golden Age of British Comedy*. London: Fourth Estate, 2004. Print.

17 Obscene or Absent: Literary versus Comedy Audiences

AL Kennedy

> AL Kennedy is a multi-award-winning Scottish writer of novels, short stories, and nonfiction, whose credits include the prestigious Costa Book Award. In 2006, she decided to take to the stage as a stand-up comic, and has since then performed one-woman shows at the Edinburgh Festival each year.

I was four or five. I was visiting the Ideal Home Exhibition—the one in Dundee. I can no longer recall how appalling the entire exhibition must have been. The Ideal Home is Not In Dundee. I know my parents were very excited. This was in 1969 or 1970, so fondue and brown settees were exciting, as was *orange*. All I remember is the man who was selling prawn crackers.

He was probably more of a student than a man. He had a stall, he had a deep fat fryer, and he had patter, which he ran through while he transformed something that looked and probably tasted like poker chips into something that looked and probably tasted like those peanuts of expanded foam they use to pack around delicate items in parcels.

I loved the patter. I listened to it with three, maybe four different audiences. I'd never heard a grown up being professionally funny before. I'd never heard that kind of almost-repetition before, that adjustment to audience, improvisation, before. I watched the last audience drift away. This was Dundee, after all—Dundee doesn't do enthusiastic mobs unless there's a witch to burn. (Our Millenium Fireworks happened without prior notice—people just thought there'd been some kind of colorful accident. There were complaints.) And although they are fond of bad pies, Dundonians have little interest in eating expanded foam. Dundee has high figures for incest and child-murder—we keep our enthusiasms for the home.

Back to the Exhibition, I kept waiting. Faced with a short but determined audience of one, the poor guy had to run through his entire patter again, just for me. Eventually my mother came along and rescued him, buying a bag of greasy expanded foam crackers out of guilt. I couldn't understand why she also wanted me to feel guilty—the man had needed an audience; I'd provided one—I'd been on his side. I had figured out that whatever he was doing wouldn't work without someone else being there.

That was probably my first experience of words being out in the world with people. I already loved them being inside my head, but this was like suddenly discovering your best friend was a secret agent, or had domination over snakes. I was impressed. I was slightly offended that words had some kind of other existence going on without me, but mainly I was impressed.

Obviously, as a writer of literary fiction, I could sum up my audience in one word—absent. But that's rarely actually true and my own relationship with words has never been that fixated on the page. I spent my teenage years watching and dabbling in theater, I went to university and studied theater and drama. I performed other people's work, I recited other people's work. I'm not sure what I was looking for, but I can say I loved being in a specific place at a specific time with others and having something happen that would never happen in quite the same way again. I loved that one human being could alter the shape of another, alter their breathing, make them sweat, produce noises, feel feelings, without ever touching them. I loved that I could sometimes do that to other people. I loved it when people did it to me. (Bear in mind I was discovering sex during the same period and AIDS hysteria was just breaking loose, so the whole performance thing seemed a lot simpler, less dangerous, less clumsy, and easier to walk away from alive than other types of physical interaction. Not that I wasn't trying both and not that they didn't get glued together in a disastrous and maybe permanent way.) I was obsessed with the idea that theater could become an alternative form of government and that communal experience could alter people for the better, not just turn them into a mob. I loved that people could build things out of words and that what they produced would be greater than the sum of those noises, those marks on paper.

But I hated most directors, I was not visually appetizing, I couldn't be bothered with all of those other people who were onstage and who meant that I had to remember their cues, I'd got used to writing and directing and having an amount of control and room for experiment that is unusual in the real world, I didn't like a great many of the words I was being given, I didn't fancy the idea of endless repertory performances of "An Inspector Calls" and "Oh, Vicar, Where's My Trousers," and many actors just gave me a pain.

I'm not sociable. I like communicating, but it wasn't that hard for me to move further into writing and further away from having to interact with people.

So I spent a few years doing awful jobs that involved puppets and double glazing and I wrote at home because that gave me some kind of creative satisfaction and it has a meditative quality, a possibility of taking me out of my head. (At that time I did have other ways of doing that, but they were all variations on a theme of car crash.) One night, I made a decision to write as if I were surrounded by people—I genuinely really did picture them sitting on the ground, as if they were kids and I was telling them a story—and I imagined *telling* the story. I'd worked out that an audience, like being hanged in the morning, concentrates the mind. Long term, sustaining the idea of an audience can be a huge distraction if you're trying to put your energy fully into prose—if I put mental effort into imagining a crowd with any clarity while I'm writing I wouldn't be able to write. That first time was also the last time they were clearly defined, but it did help.

So almost since I began writing professionally I've had the idea of an assembly of listeners vaguely set at the back of my mind. I also have the idea of one individual into whose head I am speaking. I have to assume that this person is interested in the same things as I am, that they're about as bright as I am. I have to make the decision to love them—rather than like them, liking is pointless and uncommitted—so then they get the best I can do. I don't think about markets, or even particularly about my editor, who has been the first person to read my work for around fifteen years. I know he's bright and quite possibly sociopathic, so that helps along the last couple of rewrites, but mainly there's just a sense of someone to whom I owe my best.

This isn't because I am loving or outgoing, it's just practical. And it's not hard to transfer a bit of fellow feeling on to the potential recipient of something that is pleasant to make and a psychic and emotional release.

Of course, an actual audience does turn up fairly soon—particularly if you live in a country where there is still (clichés apart) a strong sense of language as being a musical thing, a thing to be shared. In Scotland it's probably still true that your first reading will be well ahead of your first publication. Readings can help you recognize and develop your "voice," they can help you hear and finish individual pieces, they can build confidence.

The mere thought of the first reading I had in an art centre of any importance sent me right back to write something new so I could face all those people with an adequate effort. I knew the story worked when the audience laughed at the moderately funny bits—humor thresholds for literary fiction are unbelievably low—and when what a comic would call a *call-back* worked and the audience gave a little wriggle and a murmur when they recognized the loop had folded in on itself.

Literary audiences are, of course, not always friendly or helpful or confidence building. They can leave you bleeding internally in a foreign hotel room more effectively than the Mossad.

So let's get to that. When you begin your career you may quite often be slapped on the bill with other, bigger writers and will be thrown on before them when nobody wants to hear from you at all. Literary audiences may simply be determined to be emotionally uncommitted and cold. As you get better known they may decide to be in awe and may refuse to leave awe, no matter what you do. If you get through at all to an audience like this people may actually weep, which just alarms and confuses everyone. It takes at least five years of touring to build an audience that turns up knowing and expecting what it wants and understanding that you're the person to provide it. This seems to be the case in any country, the only variation being the size of the landmass—quicker to get things sorted out in Germany, slower in the US. Clearly, there are parallels with the comedy world. I can now do writing-related comedy gigs at literary festivals where we all seem to want the same thing for an hour or so and we have fun and it feels nice—healthy and free. Plus, I can feel the material has an underlying level of proper meaning.

For literature, audiences in London seem the hardest to reach, the slowest to understand, and the most likely to cry. Audiences in Ullapool, Nairn, and Brighton listen well. Canadian, Australian, New

Zealand, and German audiences are very warm. French audiences are willing to be warm with persuasion. New York can be tricky or ridiculously friendly, ditto Michigan and Portland, Oregon. Santa Fe provides possibly the best crowd in the world for anything. The West Coast around L.A. and San Francisco can be hard—too laid back, somehow, or with a weird taste for grit and being shouted at. I can sometimes feel grubby after having a good night in America because it will just have seemed too easy—as if I've molested a bunch of strangers and they've thanked me. Scottish audiences accept dark material, as do German and Eastern European audiences. Germans will sit for events that last three or four hours in all kinds of conditions—this seems to be true in Eastern Europe, too; once they're out of the house, they're staying and they appreciate any kind of a laugh—they seem to have the happy assumption that horror, death and famine are just around the corner, it's good to stockpile some chuckles. London and US audiences avoid the dark, or want very specific types of mindless nastiness, rather than anything genuinely disturbing.

With comedy, the pattern has repeated wherever I've gone. What I would call "polite" comedy audiences can actually be taken over to quite dark places as long as they only affect me, or we're all doing something political and therefore "worthwhile." Edinburgh audiences are generally very comedy-literate, but Glasgow audiences will often be happy to go further off the rails into Darkland. Both literary and comedy venues get repeat offenders, regulars who turn up and give the place a particular flavor. Big single-interest parties or particularly high levels of devotion can throw an evening off in either case. Some audiences are quite narcissistic—in comedy they'll want banter with you rather than material, in a reading, they'll want less of the reading and more of their questions, which turn out to be mini-theses of interminable length and tediousness. Some audiences want to be taken away from themselves and temporarily saved; I tend to be more in sympathy with them because I'm that kind of audience myself.

The venues for literary events may be conventional theaters, or halls—apparently chosen to lack intimacy—but often they will be entirely unsuitable arenas, such as noisy, still-open bookshops, quiet, still-open libraries, marble hallways, odd corners in community centers and green houses. Sight lines may be dreadful, acoustics may mean that you could reenact the Battle of Vimy Ridge and no one would hear it. If there is any amplification it may simply add to your woes. Speakers will be positioned badly. Sound checks will rarely be done and mikes are often embedded into lecterns, so that readers have to choose between eye contact and audibility. Many venues are phased if the reader wants to stand—they prefer something static, academic, low-energy, and with the author struggling to get any noise at all out of their lungs. (The hearing-impaired and feisty will always sit at the back, as is their right; they wouldn't be able to complain if they were at the front.) It continues to amaze me that people pay money for this kind of thing. Audience members are still often astounded and frankly grateful if they aren't stricken by venue-related pain throughout and don't actually lapse into a tedium-induced coma within minutes of the event beginning.

Literary audiences don't heckle because they don't have to—they know the second half of most events will be given over to a Q&A session that means they can accuse you of saying things you never have, of doing things you've never done, tell you your work is dreadful, tell you *you* are dreadful, complain about remaining unpublished themselves, or simply manifest a variety of unusual mental states. The ground rules for these sessions generally mean the writer isn't allowed to respond in kind. He or she just has to stand there and look polite, if not imbecillic.

Let's be more specific—your average ghastly evening will see you arrive at the venue and find you are under dressed—and sadly you can't slip into that little something you wore when you sat at the captain's table on the way back from Port Said, because that doesn't exist beyond your own limbic area. The host/ess looks at you as if you are going to steal things. There is no green room, there is nothing like a green room. You mingle with the audience while they look at you as if you are going to assault them and then steal things. You are yanked into a standard box of a hall, the echoes of your feet arriving do not fade, even as you leave. There is fizzy water to drink—so you will burp all the way through. Or there is no water at all. The lighting state isn't. Your already disappointed audience troops in while four or perhaps as many as seven people give interminable speeches about each other, about sponsors, perhaps taking a few hours out to summarize your work in the driest of terms, or to mention a local charity that involves dying children and sick dogs. And then you're on. The audience already hate you. No one can hear you, even if you scream. They don't want to hear you. You do want to scream. You proceed to read as much that is obscene and offensive as you can, just for the hell of it. Questions such as, "When did you sell your soul to Satan, you wanton whore?" and "What kind of mental impairment is it that you suffer from?" are asked. You leave as soon as you can, given the bad weather, the poor roads, and the inconsistent public transport. Or you are consigned to the Overlook Hotel and sit up all night feeling sullied and inadequate, while waiting for an axe to come hacking through your door. You will borrow the axe to kill yourself if they're tired after all that hacking.

Much or some of this will be familiar to anyone who's done comedy, or indeed musical touring. And there are many good venues out there and very fine and welcoming festivals and I've had a blast in them and been grateful. In many areas the same rules seem to apply to spoken word, comedy and music. But there are differences.

A literary audience can actually seem quite unsure of its role: Do they adore, do they concentrate very hard, do they have to seem clever? They may not be clear. A comedy audience does at least know it wants to laugh. It may also know very clearly what kind of laughs it would like and who should deliver them. In the world of literature it will be an advantage to be a man, you will have natural authority; women have to be much cleverer and faster and self-deprecating, or dressed to impress/give hand jobs and be self-deprecating. The same rules apply in comedy, except you've never really lived unless you've experienced the waves of instinctive loathing that will greet the simple fact of your existence if you happen to be a woman. One of the loveliest facts about blind prejudice being that it emerges precisely when you do. You know before your tiny hand grips the mike that your arse is out the window and very few options are open to you—beyond having a MASSIVELY AUTHORITATIVE and DOMINATING personality with a bit of mumsyness thrown in. Or you could try SEXY/CUTE AND SEXY. I tend not to be mumsy and my dominating gets scary quite fast—my versions of sexy and cute are absolutely funny but in many of the wrong ways, so I have certainly been left trying to talk to whoever's up for it—wives, girlfriends, men who are desperately ugly, people I've made up in my head. Sometimes a spokesperson will have a pop and if you can batter them back with your own pop everyone accepts you and it's fine. But sometimes there will just be a lot of silence. Huge, youdon'texistandneverhaveanddeservenotevenourhatredbutourinabilitytoseeorhearyou silence.

It's a little like being unexpectedly dumped by 150 boyfriends at once.

At least the prejudice is right out there in comedy and you can tussle with it. In the literary world you should be RP and from somewhere in Surrey. (I'm not.) In Comedyland you should be working class and will have to work much, much harder if you're not. (I'm not. I even sound English, which can be such fun in Scotland.) In the world of literature writers and academics are given a great deal of leeway to create personae that are etiolated, precious, clearly false at some level. In certain circles this kind of construction is regarded as tasteful—the real man or woman shouldn't be shown. In Comedyland there is almost no tolerance of anything that smacks of pretense—if the words and the flesh don't match, audiences get very restless and resentful. "Character comedy" is, of course, a whole other world, but it rarely plays well unless it has the smell of genuine sweat, or pain, or warmth, or humanity about it (if I'm in the audience, anyway). In the literary world you can say the word "cunt" constantly as long as you've written it down first and speak with great and challenging seriousness. In your intervening chats, you can't swear at all. In Comedyland a bright audience won't be delighted by the simple fact that you're swearing, but they will appreciate elegant blasphemy.

A good audience for comedy will appreciate elegant anything—they always seem to show an appetite for expression (and if they can see you bouncing off something and be sure you've made this up only for them they will be even more happy). Even a drunk barn full of stag parties will respond better to something that's rhythmically tight and well phrased. It seems human beings have to be too drunk to walk before they lose their grip of poetry. A literary audience will listen quietly and nicely and be very tolerant of boredom. Plainly, a comedy audience won't—but they can be drawn into listening and will lean in and hold their breaths for a long riff of one kind or another. Audiences will applaud something simply because it runs melodiously and is well-phrased to a conclusion. There is also a brand of heckler that will simply get overexcited by a long run and have to interrupt—usually with something entirely unrelated. It's kind of premature ejaculation. It seems odd that the appreciation of language in a comedy night can seem more intense and tangible than it is in a reading, perhaps because watching comedy can be like watching writing, watching thought, being in someone else's mind, their dream, their skin—maybe it's just nearer than the page as a communal experience. A good reading will tend to set people back into themselves, as if they've had their story and they're off to bed now—it will produce reflection, even if that turns into enthusiasm in the Q&A or the signing afterward, there's a sense that a literary audience is about going in as well as out. With comedy there can be inward moments, but there may not be many, and need not be any.

The comedy interaction can easily feel more honest than the literary one. But, given that I have a long-established audience for readings, people who turn up for a reading with me will have something closer to a slow paced comedy evening and many of the same rules apply: some kind of intro to get everyone comfy, to MC your way in, possibly some chat, a laying of whatever ground rules there might have to be. Obviously, in a reading you're getting an immediate reaction to something that would normally have no tangible feedback. Then again, when you write you're not expecting immediate feedback. Feedback can be useful in rewriting, but it's not essential. Comedy material doesn't necessarily work in any other context; part of the deal would be that it does get an immediate reaction, that it is partly formed by an immediate reaction.

If a reading is to have very serious or dense material then humor will lift it and move it along. Most writers who read well produce some kind of balanced evening, supplying whatever is missing from an evening built around parts of something that's supposed to be a whole. (Poets have an advantage here, given that they're throwing out completed pieces, but they still have to balance up the total and ease things along.) With a comedy audience, similar decisions have to be made: trying to bang in with something strong and quick, settling down, varying pace, getting a rhythm of climaxes, working to a strong finish—whatever. I don't have much of an established audience for comedy, so I go out there being the average hole in the ground that you can tell nothing from and work from there, which gives a certain liberty—if people who like my stuff do turn up that's a plus, but portions of a literary crowd may turn up expecting Steven Fry or Joyce Grenfell and then there will be a falling out—I seem to lack the capacity to go down that road unless it's what I've been booked for. Comedy isn't my career, so I can say I have the freedom to only do the stuff I want in the way I want and wait and see if people like it, but I suspect I would make that decision even if it was my primary way of earning a living. Faking it is uncomfortable and sickening—and ultimately a kind of failure—better to find out who you are and what you want to say and how you say it. Despite having done rambly, funnyish evenings about being a writer, it took me two years to actually feel comfy doing comedy about my writing job. I do love writing and I do believe in it, but it takes a good deal of drafting the material to prevent the event descending into a big wank. Of which there is more than enough in the wonderful world of literature.

It's interesting (only to me) that as a writer you "find your voice" and that as a comic you do precisely the same thing, but literally. There will be a first evening when you really hear who you are—surrounded by folk listening at about ankle level—and it will feel better, and that process continues. I don't think you can hide your mind on the page, or hide your fears. You are physically more exposed as a comic, you have to know what you look like, how you sound, how you move, how you seem and how you are, but it's not an unfamiliar exploration. Just as a written piece lives or dies from the first sentence—do you have authority, are you going somewhere, do you sound as if you have something to say, or some way of saying that matters? —the comic lives or dies between walking on and getting hold of the mike, getting out the first couple of words. You can pull it back, but it's nice to not have to. Both worlds are savage, but they're fascinating to inhabit and once you've lived in them for awhile, you begin to learn where your particular authority lies. Writing to someone, even someone you don't know, is quite intimate, and there are lots of things you have to be careful with because of that intimacy—the equivalent of not shouting. Oddly, although you may have racks of folk in a hall or a club for comedy, it's still an intimate conversation—you can shout, you may well shout, but you're not shouting at them, only past them, at the bad things. You're still intimate, chatting.

Comedy venues, even when they're small and rattly, tend to have some kind of commitment to making a theatrical/performance type event happen. Good clubs understand that an audience that's physically cold will be emotionally cold, that if they're too hot they'll get cranky and apathetic. The ideal temperature seems to be from thirty-two degrees Celsius up to forty. I think good people can raise the temperature while folk are having fun, but if you kick off at forty that could be tricky. Venues and MCs understand that having people sit close together is helpful and that setting the right tone and atmosphere is going to help everyone. Bad MCs in the literary world tend to just be inept and there are very few that will actually "warm up" an audience. Bad MCs in comedy are more usually actively trying to sabotage the people they present. A good comedy venue will have a low ceiling and will feel like a basement even if it's an attic. It will feel like night, even if it's lunchtime. Even if the walls are painted a migraine of colors, everything will blend to black and reddish black. Comedy seems to need the permission of darkness and body heat, and a good many literary events would benefit a little from some of the same treatment. If a literary event maybe gets you ready to go bye bye after your story, the comedy event is more like being in bed—with strangers, or your own head, or both. Comedy venues smell: good venues smell as if something disreputable happens there often.

Comedy audiences touch each other, relax in the dark, shout things they wouldn't under other circumstances, sweat, drink. Literary audiences may get alarmed if things get too biological. Couples in a literary audience are on an early date or have been married for a hundred years. Couples in a comedy audience are trying to hurry into sex, or are still enjoying having sex, and they're preparing for the rest of their night. Audience members at a comedy club who were pleased with what you've done will shake hands with you, touch your forearm, hug you, kiss you. Being made happy is an intimately pleasing thing and a physical thing—it creates a physical reaction. Literary audiences will maybe say they've had a nice time, and very occasionally they will shake hands. This may be why they can react so well to comedy about literature—then they can get their hugs. A comedy audience that dislikes you will reject your physical existence entirely and the feeling will be mutual. A literary audience that hates you will restrain its loathing to a slow chill.

In both comedy and literary performances I've found that a persona develops—the aspects of your character that are useful come to the fore as you fit yourself to your voice and subject matter and the demands of the form. The persona may look exactly like you, it may not be far off, but it will not be you. The press will create an additional version of one or more personae. They will generally seek to intervene in an unhelpful manner. I write using my initials and I have come to be glad of that—the person who isn't exactly me doesn't exactly have my name. Comedy clubs, even when I ask them not, use the AL Kennedy name, although sometimes I'll be introduced as Alison Kennedy, which seems more appropriate. I now tend to be called "Al" in comedy clubs. So now I have three names, which maybe was inevitable. "Alison" does the shopping, AL does the typing, and Al hangs out in sleazy dives with people whose pupils have dilated to the size of blintzes.

As *Al* has to be physically present, that persona has a much higher level of physicality and the vocal delivery has a greater range. And I get my hair cut more often. Plus, I now overdress often with little provocation. Some of the style and energy has transferred over to the readings and, I think, assisted them. I now do more radio and have, for goodness' sake, what we might call a voice coach, for various reasons. (I would recommend any serious writer to look seriously at voice.) I think mostly what matters to the audience is that you engage with them with some kind of honesty, or a very convincing appearance of honesty. Literary audiences like you to be in control; comedy audiences are more interested in loss of control. As an author, you should be wise and in charge of the evening so that no one will die from being overexposed to art. Being drunk and incoherent is not welcomed, although it makes for entertaining stories afterward. Comedy audiences seem fairly happy if the comic is dog eared and dysfunctional—again, if they're too pissed to speak, it gets old pretty quickly. Comedy audiences are also more up for losing their own control—they're partly drinking it away—but they seem pretty willing to talk to strangers, or have their hair cut, or lift middle aged women over their heads. If they trust the comic, they'll basically do anything for them—like the crowd for a comedy Hitler.

Author photographs tend to involve smiling—so the author can undercut their highbrow, serious profession. Comedy photographs tend to be deadpan—so the funnyman/woman can prove they have depth behind it all. I prefer deadpan for both because it's less tiring and my teeth are too big.

It may be that working in both areas allows one to balance the other. I tend to be of the opinion that each can improve the other—each draws off what suits it best at any given time. Physical, contemporary, unhinged, reactive, communal, obscene, bewildered—that might go to comedy. Absent, cerebral, meditative, reflective, solitary—that might go to literary. Or not. Really not. The same areas can be explored in different ways in different forms. I don't think it's a coincidence that my first novel produced under the influence of comedy won a number of major prizes. The interesting thing is that all the elements you might put in a literary gig can be altered and happen in comedy and vice versa. And if I'm having a good day the interaction with an audience can be just as much fun or warm or whatever whether I'm in a club or a reading or on a patch of tarmac outside Faslane Nuclear base. If I think of the things that interest me in comedy and literature the list of qualities is the same—compassion, liberation, intelligence, outrage, humanity, sex, politics, religion, belief, truth. It's all just people speaking to other people.

18 *The Daily Show*'s Studio Audience

Scott Jacobson
(in correspondence with Judy Batalion)

Scott Jacobson is an Emmy-award winning comedy television writer, currently staffed on *Bob's Burgers*. He has written for television shows and specials including *The Academy Awards*, *The Colbert Report*, and *Saturday Night Live*. This interview was conducted while Scott was a writer for *The Daily Show with Jon Stewart*.

Judy: This book is about the live comedy audience, but of course, your main work is for television. At *The Daily Show*, however, you do have a live studio audience as well. I'm curious about the role of this live audience in responding to your written material and influencing TV spectators.

Scott: *The Daily Show*'s studio audience is pretty raucous, and though the show is typically pragmatic and moderate in its politics, there's no denying our fans lean to the left, so one thing we're conscious of when writing is something we call the "clapper." A clapper is a joke that isn't funny but still gets a strong and—some might say—cravenly Pavlovian response.

Say the setup for a joke is a sound bite from former President Bush. For instance, President Bush: Blah blah blah, heh heh heh.

A clapper punch line might go something like, "Really? Well you didn't say 'blah blah blah' when you LED US INTO WAR UNDER FALSE PRETENSES."

Now that's not really a joke, seeing as no wit is involved, no socially conditioned expectations are defied, and no genitalia is gratuitously invoked. But audiences explode at stuff like that, which, if you wrote the joke, makes you feel good for a second, then not-so-good, then frankly cheap.

I saw the made-for-TV movie *Behind The Camera: The Unauthorized Story of Mork and Mindy*. In it, the legendary (?) writing staff of Robin Williams's breakout sitcom discuss comedy writing, mentioning something called a "joke-like substance." It's a bundle of words that bears the markings of a joke but isn't really funny. A placeholder, basically, that passes for a joke but lacks inspiration. I try not to pad out my joke packets with too many of these, but it happens.

Judy: How important is the live response in fueling the energy of the show and in priming the televised audience to laugh? Are there warm-ups for the studio audience before filming? If so, what kind? By whom? At what time of day are shows recorded? And what mood is the studio audience led into? As a writer, are you at all conscious of this?

Scott: We have a warm-up comic. His name is Paul Mecurio, and he's good at what he does. He whips the audience into a frenzy, primarily by insulting individual audience members. (When my mom and dad came to the show, he made some joke about my dad's weight; my dad was mortified, but the crowd loved it.)

Who knows why feeling at risk of being torn to shreds by a stand-up comic in front of 175 people puts an audience in the mood for a TV taping? Maybe it's a good cop/bad cop thing, and Paul's the bad cop. By the time Jon comes out for his audience Q&A, they just want to laugh at anything besides themselves. Even our jokes.

We tape in the early evening, usually around six p.m. By the time the theme music starts up and the show begins, the audience has been waiting for approximately an hour and fifteen minutes. When friends come to the show I feel like I should apologize for that stretch of tedium, but they don't seem to mind. It might be part of the warm-up, actually. For the same reason people are hungry for Jon after a few minutes of our warm-up guy (who, for the record, is very funny and does more than just insult people), they're hungry for entertainment after an hour plus of listless standing and waiting.

I can't say I'm conscious of the audience's mood on a day-to-day basis, because I usually leave work after rehearsal. But on a night when I have stuff on the show, I'll watch at home and when the audience is particularly tepid, I kind of cringe and brace myself for my jokes. A lot of the time they don't go over so well in those situations, and it's disappointing, but not in a way that sticks with me the next day. The thing about working on a show that's on every day is you always have a chance to redeem yourself, so you learn to not take anything too personally.

Judy: What is the audience in your head as you write? I believe you once told me your writing process involves the writers being audience for each other. Can you elaborate?

Scott: The audience is definitely in my head when I write, much more so than when I started at the show. Our viewers are smart, and probably better informed than your average comedy show viewers, but there are still a lot of references that get nixed because they might not be familiar to a broad audience. We also have to remind ourselves frequently that not everything we find funny in our insular comedy writer world translates to outsiders, to use an alienating term.

And yes—we don't exactly sit around a table and perform our jokes, but the writers are a sounding board for each other. More and more we've been writing headlines in pairs, which means both writers have to like a joke or it doesn't go into the script. That working method forces you to think more about what you're writing, and about how things will play in front of an audience.

When you're writing solo you sometimes get self-indulgent. I personally love writing alone for just that reason (more of your own voice comes out, and you feel more attached to your writing), but it might be bad for the show for the same reasons it's good for the individual writer.

Judy: Are you conscious of differences in your American and international television audiences? Same for *The Daily Show* book audience? Does the particular satirical type of humor of *The Daily Show* lend itself to any particular audiences?

Scott: The show is broadcast pretty much worldwide now, but our biggest following by far is still in the US. Makes sense, because we typically deal with American politics. I've always been curious about how much of an international following we have. There's something called *The Daily Show Global Edition*, which broadcasts on CNN International, and from what I can tell is typically watched by Americans staying at exotic, far-flung Holiday Inns.

The book is even more America-centric. It's even called *America: The Book*. It's come out in a few other countries, and even spawned an imitator in Mexico, but I suspect Americans get the most out of it.

Judy: For how long have you worked at *The Daily Show*? I assume, as the show has become hugely popular, its audience has changed. Have its expectations and sense of loyalty altered? Does your writing have to adapt with time to meet the shifting needs/wants/challenges of your audience? Does it get easier? Harder? Please share any insights about the sustained or long-term relationship between comedy writers (who are constantly producing new material) and their audience.

Scott: I've been at the show for nearly five years, and it's changed a lot. We work differently now—there's a lot more collaboration, as I mentioned, which isn't a bad thing. I don't feel like our audience has changed immensely, though. And from their perspective, aside from a few obvious differences (correspondents come and go, as do regular segments), the show probably hasn't changed much.

Judy: Have you written for other live productions? Can you share any insights about the different strategies you might use when writing for live audiences versus television audiences?

Scott: I wrote jokes for the Oscars and a couple other live award show-type things. It was definitely a different experience. The Academy Awards audience, of course, comprises mostly celebrities waiting in terror for their categories to be called. They aren't in a mood to laugh, necessarily, and they're especially not in the mood to laugh at themselves. So: tough crowd. But Jon got them on his side, which was more a testament to his ability as a performer than ours as writers, I think.

It's hard to talk in terms of strategies, since at this point writing is pretty intuitive. If it's a big, heterogeneous audience, you keep your jokes big and broad. If it's *The Daily Show* audience, you have some latitude to try out weirder stuff. As writers, we can't easily gauge the mood of any particular audience since we're not the ones onstage; we have to anticipate. If we thought about it too much, we'd probably be paralyzed by fear of bombing vicariously. But instead we focus on making each other laugh, and hope the things that make us laugh (within reason—there are plenty of inside jokes that simply wouldn't translate) will make the audience laugh, too.

19 It's My Show, Or, Shut Up and Laugh: Spheres of Intimacy in the Comic Arena and How New Technologies Play Their Part in the "Live" Act

Kélina Gotman and Samuel Godin

Kélina Gotman is a Lecturer in Theatre and Performance Studies in the English Department at Kings College London. An academic and theatre practitioner, she has worked as a dramaturge, director, actor, and artistic advisor on over two dozen productions in the US, the UK, France, Canada and Belgium. She writes regularly on science, philosophy and performance, and in 2006, published an English translation of Félix Guattari's *The Anti-Oedipus Papers*. She has taught writing and critical theory at Columbia University, Bard College, and The New School.

Samuel Godin is a composer, sound designer, keyboard player, and producer living in New York City. His original music can be heard on film and television soundtracks (Artisan, Mirimax, HBO, PBS), album releases and remixes (Polygram, Six Degrees, Schanachie) and television advertising (Pepsi, Cheerios, Gateway). He has performed in over 1200 live shows and concerts the world over including tours of Japan, Europe, 46 of the US states, Canada, Mexico and the Caribbean Islands.

Toward a Live Comedy of the Future: Degrees of Distance, Nexi, Nodes, and Expanded Arenas

Here is the scenario: right now, somewhere far far away, a comic is performing live to an audience of internet users via live video streaming, and no comedy club in sight. The comic cracks a joke, and folks laugh, heartily, or snortily, everywhere from London to Tokyo and Montreal; some of the humor falls flat, but the comic has only a webcam to look at for evidence that any of the humor is "landing." What happens to space and place, time and timing in the comic exchange where real-time performance is expanded to sites beyond the comedy club room?

In this chapter, we show that video shares, streaming, and other digital technologies are multiplying the sites for comic exchange; more importantly, the proliferation of performance sites creates a new nexus, a comic arena, where levels of distanciation and degrees of removal exacerbate the comic process as deferred audiences rewrite scripts in the comfort and privacy of their own homes. This comedic exchange and interaction—these economies of production and reception—are already at the core of live comedy performance. But what we show is that with the increased splintering of performance venues, from the stage to the computer screen, new degrees of audienceness are created. We are calling these primary and secondary audiences. The secondary audiences are deferred, in space and time, although occasionally (as in the work of Sasha Baron Cohen, whose acts we will discuss below) they are actually the intended primary audience of the comic performance. This layeredness in the comic process distends the spheres of production and reception, altering what it means to tell a joke live, when, where, and to whom. We show, finally, that the new generation of internet comedy (let's call it comedy 2.0) can be integrated into a broader narrative history of stand-up comedy, whereby: (1) technologies of diffusion (radio, TV) brought comedy to more people; (2) this removed the intimacy of the crowd; but, (3) more recent Web technologies have brought a certain element of intimacy—and a new sort of face-to-face relationship—back.

This new intimacy continues to complicate the crowd dynamics typically found in comedy clubs: whereas a performer normally holds the spotlight and works further to gain the approbation of the crowd by fending off aspiring performers seeking to upstage him or her as they try to grab the crowd's attention (through heckling or other commentary), in an online universe, these parallel acts proliferate far more dynamically—and powerfully—than ever before. Social cohesion is harder to create (and maintain), and that is double-edged. The degree to which stand-up comics risk losing face (or gaining positive exposure) in this expanded comic arena is untested at the time of writing, but we suspect the new world of interactive online comedy performance and audience reaction and response will serve further to expand, but also expose, the live act. Its controllability—and integrity—is at stake, amplifying the already dangerous spirit of self-exposure and vulnerability that have characterized live comedy from the start.

Liveness, Audience, and the Early History of the Technologies of Stand-Up Comic Diffusion

Although its roots can be traced to vaudeville acts of the 1920s, stand-up comedy as we know it today was born about sixty years ago in small, intimate clubs. Because a large percentage of audience members were other comics, the atmosphere of tension and creative competition was thick. This was when terms like "to kill" (to please a crowd) or "die" (to bomb a set) were born. It was the rawness, the uncertainty, and the bloodthirst that started attracting larger crowds to the comedy clubs. The attraction was and is that the average crowd member knows he or she would hate to be up there—it's terrifying. As Jerry Seinfeld noted in one of his routines, "According to most studies, people's number one fear is public speaking. Number two is death. Death is number two. Does that sound right? This means to the average person, if you go to a funeral, you're better off in the casket than doing the eulogy." The audience, for the most part, would rather die than be onstage. Then, when radio hit the comedy circuit, the comic's physical antics were removed from sight, but the audiences augmented considerably in number. LPs and TVs further contributed to the extended shelf life of jokes (and their neat packages). But this process was double-edged: on the one hand, it made comedy more popular because it was more accessible, but on the other hand, it rigidified the routines. Lenny Bruce, for instance, threatened his audience to shut them up and let him tell the jokes he wanted. At his 1961 Carnegie Hall show, he quipped: "People say to me, 'How come you don't do all the bits on the records?' . . . As soon as it becomes repetitive to me, I can't cook with it anymore, man" (qtd. in Double 52).[1] Even when he or she is working with a script, a comedian has to uphold the pretense of liveness, immediacy, and the non-scriptedness of the show. That's just the way live stand-up comedy works: if punch lines are preempted by overzealous fans, the joke is dead before it hits the stage.

Crowd Control: Socializing Unruly Audience Members in the Comedy Clubs

How an audience is controlled is up to a few people: (1) the comics themselves; (2) other audience members; and (3) club managers, who, as Robert A. Stebbins notes in *The Laugh-Makers: Stand-up Comedy as Art, Business, and Life-Style*, "often announce the norm of nonparticipation prior to the show": "[w]elcome to Foibles and an evening of terrific comedy entertainment. To enjoy our show to the fullest, we ask that you keep your talking to a minimum and your laughing and applause to a maximum" (56). It's kind of like being told to turn off your cell phone, be quiet, not kick your neighbors in the seat in front of you or put up your feet, and not eat your popcorn too loudly or slurp your Coke when you're at the cinema. It's a "socialization" process, as Stebbins says, destined to prevent offensive intrusions into the comic act. But even that does not always succeed, as offenders continue to perform their own heckling roles; the punishment for this "old school" approach to the live act is that they may be forced to leave if they fail to comply. This is not least because other audience members might follow their lead: something club owners may fear will cause the performance to disintegrate and the comic, or audience, to fail to return.

Sociologists and crowd theorists have long said that it takes just one leader for a crowd to form and follow. That is because crowds—by definition—not only imitate one another (resulting in their relative uniformity) but they also tend to imitate people who act out as leaders, even spontaneous ones. This is why some behaviors are considered to be contagious in a crowd setting and have to be monitored and controlled.[2] You can't just have one person making themselves visible, and therefore imitable, wreaking havoc on a show. It's just not cool to upstage the guy headlining the act—it's up to him to get the crowd going—and unless everyone sort of by a contagious feeling thinks he's bad (usually, if he really is), then the loudmouth gets turned against and heckled in their turn.

That's if the comic elicits sympathy from the floor—or even a sort of paternalistic pity, if the show is embarrassingly bad but not offensive. Choosing whose side to fight on is what the live comedy act is all about. It's not always funny, or right, but it creates a kind of cohesion. These attitudes and behaviors are a politics of the live stand-up comedy act all wrapped into what looks like just another night out.

Some comedians have their own tricks for making audience members shut up, such as ignoring them, talking back, or picking a fight. Lenny Bruce pulled a heckler up onstage and threw a cream pie in his face once, while Milton Berle jumped offstage and onto an anti-Semitic heckler who had called him, "Kike!" "Jew Bastard!" and said "Hitler's right," to set him straight (Double 115). But it's not always the comics who pick the fights. In another case Milton Berle recalls, an audience member attacked him after a show, grabbing him by the tie and sticking a plastic fork in his chin, saying, "I could kill you right this minute, you little rat bastard" (Double 114). Chris Rock told his audience to boo if they want to, they know he's right, at a critical juncture in his Bring the Pain show in Washington, D.C. in 1996. Richard Pryor insulted a group of audience members who stood up to go while he was performing: "I hate to see folks leave while I be talking. I hope y'all get raped by black folks with clap. And nothing worse than the black clap." He went on to tell a clap joke, then: "Moving right along. . . ." And he resumed his act. This kind of hostile retort is a way to deflect the insult, taking it as an opportunity to be funny, and to prevent other audience members from taking the lead provided by these rebels. It puts the other audience members back on the comedian's side, since he or she put the hecklers, or the walk-outs, down, and (as in all crowds or other settings where social cohesion is key) nobody wants to be friends with a loser.

Out-of-Town Audience Members Upstaging the Act at the Comic Strip Live in New York: Vying for Attention in the Comedy Club

Unfortunately, not all comedians are good deflectors of insults. At a show we saw at the Comic Strip Live in New York, strategies for coping with insults from the floor ranged from "Who am I, Oprah, you fuckin' asshole, don't scream out at me" to "Shhh, talk talk talk, do you think I'm a fuckin' VCR or something, I can hear you," to "'Scuse me, could you stop, you let me fuckin' talk, 'cause that's what I'm here for . . . so what else do I want to bitch about," to "She is still fuckin' talkin,' okay, just get some alcohol and get drunk" and "You know what fucked my delivery up: camera phone." These retorts were not so funny; in fact, they were a bit embarrassing because the comedians were obviously bothered by the interruptions in a way not unlike a grade school teacher might be by a screaming kid in class. It only made the situation (rather than the joke) funnier, and to some extent it even put us on the unruly interrupter's side.

One comic had a more creative solution, announcing: "You can say what you want, this is going to be interactive tonight." Great. Interactive. That's what comedy is all about, right? It's our show, not just yours? If you're bad, you know we can kick you screaming and crying off the stage? That's the contract, tacitly drawn, between comedians and audience members. Some audience members just know the rules better than others: they have been socialized, and know how far they can push.

Sometimes, the outcasts hardly intend to be so, they're just—inexperienced. Or out-of-towners, as we witnessed at the Comic Strip Live, which is also a popular venue for tourists: a group of extremely loud visitors from a state far less hip than New York (by New York standards) made such loud vocal interjections into the night's performance as to make a spectacle of themselves. We are convinced they were not consciously trying to upstage—or put down—the comics performing that night, or the MC, but they were the butt of audience members' private jokes, or so we could tell from our vantage point at a table not far from theirs, as locals snickered and scoffed at their incivility, rendering that (unfortunately) more memorable than the rest.

It is this audience-to-audience policing that keeps the show tight: good cops keep the rowdies in line. But the comic has to warrant their allegiance to him or her first so that to defend the space of performance becomes a valiant, self-enforced act of social cohesion, the friendlier face of this otherwise bloodthirsty sport.

Live Projectiles and Other Hazards of Oversized Venues

These areas of comic happening are present wherever a comedy club or venue is arranged such that audience members can see one another.

In a Wagnerian mega-venue, where all lights are onstage and the audience is sitting in neat rows, deprived of the social activity of most smaller clubs, namely, eating and (especially) drinking, and talking, the audience can hardly compete with the comic for other audience members' attention. This is not necessarily a good thing, since, as Steve Martin noted, performing to huge arenas really sucks. It's a rock star fame kind of performing, but without some interaction—some challenges—from the floor, you may as well be doing straight-up proscenium-style theater, or film, or other kinds of performance that are not so audience-dependent, i.e., dialogic (even if only rhetorically). The interactive element in these mega-club situations is almost entirely lost. There is still laughter (or its absence) to keep the comic in check and let him or her verify whether jokes are landing. But the power dynamic is so weighted in the comic's favor that it strips the situation of any real danger. (Physical danger is an exception, especially in non-traditional settings like rock shows, where a whole other level of rowdiness is the norm. Bob Goldthwait remembers having had shoes, beer-soaked jeans, and a live teenager thrown at him when he was opening for a Nirvana concert. He had to be rescued by security guards while Kurt Cobain "was laughing his ass off" in the sidelines; of course, Goldthwait was hired for the rest of the tour [19–21].)

What distinguishes live comedy from other theater arts is the role of this audience in the space and place of performance. Stanislavski defined the whole of modern theater as being characterized by a crowd of invisible audience members, with spotlights glaring in the performer's face so hard she can't see two feet in front of her. In his experience, it was like confronting a great chasm, oneself, because that is all one has up there; and, it's lonely (7).[3] Creating an organism, with the comic as leader of the crowd, is arguably the goal of any successful stand-up comedy night; the challenge is to relate to crowd members and put down any aspiring leaders—usurpers of the spotlight.

THE COMIC'S ETHOS: DEGREES OF INTIMACY, SELF-DEPRECATION, REAL OR FEIGNED VULNERABILITY

The question of personal attitude is central to live comedy. Woody Allen noted that it is the person onstage, not the jokes, that gets the audience going. You could say it's all about personality, not even character, persona, or the jokes or skits being performed. "[W]hat the audience want is intimacy with the person," he says. "They want to like the person and find the person funny as a funny human being. The biggest trap that comedians fall into is trying to get by on material" (qtd. In Double 61).

Sometimes, however, getting the audience to like you requires a certain dose of hostility, just to break the ice, and break down the wall that can rise up in a second the moment an un-funny gag is spoken. In fact, being likeable is often the worst way to be liked; it's off-putting if it's too saccharine, too needy, too desperate. Andy Kaufman famously worked hard at being un-funny (even anti-funny, or post-funny) when he threatened to read *The Great Gatsby* onstage if his audience didn't let him go on with his own jokes. He then went on actually to read from the book, while exasperated audience members filed out of the club in desperation.[4] The irreverence, and distinct lack of concern for pleasing the audience (as well as his play with duration), also made Kaufman a live, and a performance artist: comics generally have to pretend to be concerned with the audience response, even when they think or act like they don't.

The attitudes and personalities—the strategies—for coping with hostile audience members are endless. In the end, though, what's important, as Double remarks, is that there is an audience there to respond to, to talk to, to look at, and that will look at you, since, as he puts it, "[r]unning through the act without an audience is rather like leaving a message on somebody's answerphone; it's difficult to keep up the energy you need to express yourself, and you often end up collapsing into total inarticulacy" (106). The mixture of vulnerability and self-protection, actor, self, and persona, real or just feigned nakedness onstage, distinguish live comedy from the other theatrical arts: if an audience is not visible, and/or the show is not relatively interactive, the comedy act turns into proscenium theater. The comedy may still make the audience laugh, but the liveness is sacrificed, as the show is safer: interaction with audience members, for good or ill, rids the sport of its real, interpersonal, danger. It rids the show of its core vulnerability.

Borat: Candid Funny, and the Politics of "Secondary" (or "Deferred") Audiences

Distance can work in the comic's favor to foreground the politics of the comic arena. When the comic genius Sasha Baron Cohen, for instance, gets his immediate audience to laugh and clap and sing in the actual place of performance, the diffusion of this show to a secondary, deferred audience, later, somewhere else, shows that the act is also not funny at all in the larger scope of things. The complicity between him and his deferred audience is to be laughing at the initial situation: this doubling of laughter, and multiplication of comic layers, extends the nexus of performance in space, place, and time, playing to a range of types of affect. In Cohen's Borat skit, "Throw the Jew Down the Well!!!," he is dressed up as a Kazakh visitor to the US, performing at a country-and-western club in Tucson, Arizona, to a crowd of cowboy hat-clad men and women. His cameraman, meanwhile, and those of us later witnessing the show at a remove, stand in as his deferred (but also his actual intended) audience.

With the premise that the cameraman is following him to record this journey for the benefit of his compatriots back home, he performs a "traditional" Kazhak song, with a guitar, while wearing a cowboy hat—presumably to endear himself to his hosts; they are instructed by the MC to "show him how we do it here in Tucson, Arizona!" His song is quite simple, and follows a call-and-response model, inviting the audience to sing along. It is also made familiar by the presence of his back-up band, "the Astona-band," strumming along on a guitar in a very country-and-western vein. With mock goodwill for cultural understanding, he explains: "There is problem in my country, and that problem is transport. It take very, very long, because Kazakhstan is big. Throw transport down the well. C'mon! So my country can be free (So my country can be free!)." He continues like this, until "transport" is replaced by "Jew": "Throw the Jew down the well. So my country can be free." This is repeated after him by one enthusiastic audience member. Eventually, much of the audience joins in, howling and clapping and singing along, with evidently no idea that he is Jewish, or that his act is going to be diffused to an audience that will be shocked by this anti-Semitism. Cohen, in this performative doubling, has trumped the American melting pot dream on camera, and shown the dark, ugly underbelly of American prejudice to thousands of online viewers, for whom the skit was posted promptly.

The joke lands on these viewers a day, a month, a few months, later. This is a deferred viewership, and a kind of secondary audience. His joke, which is a kind of anti-joke, is performed at the expense of those having a good time right then and there. This doesn't mean that everyone on YouTube is shirking in horror at this display of anti-Semitism. On the contrary, some posts show support for his statements, a kind of deferred applause. philwoodcock3000 writes: "Borat, who is really Jewish, is being deceptive (what a typical Jew!). He's insidiously trying to portray Gentiles as racists and anti-Semites." Wawawaweewah! (as Borat would say). For a9clark, "That shit is funny so get the fuck out of my house nigger." Is he being serious? It's hard to tell.

Some postings defend Cohen's performance as showing ("outing") the racism still rampant in the US–Cohen was awarded a Forward 50 title by the *Jewish Daily Forward* for his attack on anti-Semitism—but there is little consensus as to the irony and intent of the whole affair. What do we do with this kind of deferred reaction? Is it even stand-up comedy anymore? Hardly. It is a kind of performance art, but it's also classic comedic strategy, dependent on quid pro quo (one person being taken for another onstage, with the complicit knowledge of the audience but not the characters themselves). Here, the misunderstanding is situated at the level of the immediate audience, not the actors. In this sense, Cohen's work is also a sort of invisible theater. [5] It is stand-up comedy in its dependence on the audience reaction (and punchline), but its use of character and misunderstanding are great enough, and sustained enough, to blend into theater.

This genre-bending work is, moreover, also possible because of the technologies of diffusion and discussion generated by the politics of the online world: Cohen expects gossip and scandal, reactions and dissent, confrontation and the danger of putting himself on the line. Even when Cohen is performing as Ali G, the baggy-pants gangsta from the East End of London, on *Da Ali G Show*, posing as an ignorant homeboy who just wants to "get" what's "happenin" in the political arena so he can share it with his "homies," he uses the playing dumb card to ask questions that would never be asked directly in a normal interview situation. And, with cameras in train, he makes his way into the offices of high-ranking policy makers, forcing them to engage in absurd conversations as shocking as uproarious to hear. Views and attitudes are exposed, to great deferred ridicule, as his interviews air to an HBO audience totally unlike what the interviewee thought he or she was addressing. In *Da Ali G Show* Episode 103, "Politics," for instance, Cohen pays a visit to Newt Gingrich in Washington, D.C., because, he says, "young people see da word 'politics' and dey immediately switch off. . . . So to bring politics into dis, da twentief century, me 'eaded down to Washin'ton, ai't." Having painstakingly copied down the spelling of Newt Gingrich's name, and practiced it—to Gingrich's muted exasperation, while the cameras were rolling—he goes on to announce his whereabouts to his viewers: "I is 'ere wit' my main man, his name be Newt Gingrich, and 'im was da leader of da 'ouse of Representatives." This is all performed with his hands out in front of him and cocked and kind of swaying in a mock hip hop style. What ensues is a side-splitting "conversation" about welfare, in which Gingrich tries to explain to Ali G that his main contribution to American politics was to phase out the welfare system, while Ali G, pretending totally to misunderstand him, goes on to ask repeatedly whether people on welfare shouldn't get more time the longer they stay, because it shows their commitment, like a raise on a job. Cohen's ability to completely transform himself allows him to take the classic stand-up technique of playing on "insiders" and "outsiders" to the next level, using the secondary or deferred audience as his witness.

COLBERT ROASTS BUSH

If Cohen's comic genius is to introduce a multilayered kind of funny into the comic arena by making use of his characters (with costumes, props, accents) to trump the direct address mode of performance classic in live stand-up comedy, then comic Stephen Colbert plays this card straight. In the widely-diffused "Colbert Roasts Bush" skit, Stephen Colbert was invited to perform at the 2006 annual White House Correspondents' Dinner, a venue traditionally employed for poking good clean fun at White House leaders. But the comic skit Colbert delivered was so virulent as to leave immediate audience members dumbfounded. Snickering could be observed, but most people present just had looks of stupor on their faces, as Colbert dug deeper into the open wound of the Bush administration and its flawed (and increasingly unpopular) policies on Iraq, health care, etc. Because Colbert knew, like Cohen, that he was playing to a secondary audience made up of television and internet viewers, he continued relentlessly to tear the President apart. Colbert was playing to his immediate audience—the journalists and other media personnel invited to the Correspondents' Dinner, and the White House members of the Bush administration—, but he was also, and especially, playing to the cameras, and blogs.

His use of humor was destined not so much to make his primary (or even his secondary) audience laugh, but to speak truth to the peanut gallery, like a modern-day jester, using the liberties granted live comics for saying what might not be said directly elsewhere.

Michael Richards aka Kramer "Dies" at The Laugh Factory in West Hollywood

If Colbert used his position of power as an invited guest at the Correspondents' Dinner to tear the President and his aides apart, he could do so because public opinion was on his side. He was safe. Not so Michael Richards, aka Kramer, from the television show *Seinfeld*, who destroyed his career in a manner of minutes while performing live at The Laugh Factory in West Hollywood in November 2006. Unnerved by insults shouted out at him by some African American men in the audience, he launched into a racist tirade. Because it was broadcast immediately on YouTube, the uproar was enormous. Within twenty-four hours, he was on the *Late Show with David Letterman* performing a public apology, visibly shaken, but not forgiven, if we are to believe the blogosphere. Countless spoofs were posted within days, building on his performance, repurposing it, remixing it, recuperating it into the online cultural landscape. One homemade YouTube spoof of the event, "What Kramer Meant to Say," ventriloquizes Richards's stance: "I went into a rage—I said some pretty nasty things—and I thought I could spin it into a Lenny Bruce/Bill Hicks kind of a thing, but I'm—uh—just not that good." This is near real time heckling. Michael Richards's victims also spoke out, something that was broadcast on YouTube as well. Interviews with The Laugh Factory owners were posted. An entire post-show conversation mushroomed in the online universe, taking the concept of post-show bathroom talk to a whole new level: this is audience gossip extended beyond the boundaries of the club, writing and rewriting the story of the show, adlibbing on the comic's line.

Whereas comedians normally can only imagine (if they care to try) what goes on at the bar or in cab rides home from the club, with online posting, anyone who wants to can listen in on that conversation. We suppose they do so at their own risk; it takes an extra strong will of steel to hear what people are saying about you when you have exposed yourself the way comics often do. The danger zone in the comedy act is that much wider, and it is in print—even if the print is ephemeral, as postings can disappear fast. We're not just talking about gossip among a few friends, and rumors that might deform an act briefly and only go so far, but the live coding, recoding and recording—as well as the archiving—of conversations that went on post-show.

Eddie Murphy had a joke about his jokes being retold wrong by an otherwise innocent audience member: "You're going to go to work tomorrow, and say something about how I said 'goonygoogoo,' or 'I'm Mr T: I'll rip your dick off with my ass,' and your buddy at work is gonna be like—yeah, right—very funny." Of course, the way he says it, it's hilarious, because of course it's hard to retell a joke right, and if we heard him tell his jokes himself up to that point, we can laugh at how terrible this rendition was.

In short, the "broken telephone" effect of comedy act repetition and disfiguration by audience members is transformed in the age of YouTube. Anyone who wants to can view an original performance, and anyone who wants to can edit it by offering comments and feedback, which the comic can integrate into what was already only a semi-prewritten script. If these revisions are like software updates, or a dynamic blog, or the Web 2.0, i.e., a new mini re-edition of the show, revisited from night to night, it is also double-edged: with the expansion of the volume and reach of reactions and comments, comics also have to reckon with the new heightened quality and availability of audience interaction. They may want the attention: we know their egos are on the line onstage; but this public dissection of performances normally held behind closed doors to an audience of up to a hundred viewers or so risks degenerating into a new culture of self-censorship. Yet, to date, comics don't seem to be exercising more care or circumspection in their acts; on the contrary, this heightened state of tension and interaction in the online comic arena exacerbates trends that led to comedy's boom in the first place. If comedy was censored in its early days (and continues to be so) because the cutting-edge material was too raunchy for TV, radio, and most live venues, that is also its appeal. HBO caught onto this when it first started to air crass, lewd, and socially unacceptable comic acts in the 1980s, with terrifically popular results.

Because the FCC regulations that apply to TV are meaningless online, anyone (for now) can post what they want, including the comics themselves. Dane Cook, for instance, on his website, allows fans to contribute videos: there is a great one of a twelve-year-old lip-synching to one of his routines. These sites are expanding the place and space of comic interaction exponentially. This is a new version—the next generation—of the type of audience interaction that made live comedy thrive in the clubs from the start, and has been absent from TV and even from some live comedy venues when they restrict or control audience participation.

More dialogue shouldn't cripple the performance, but enlarge the already voracious appetite for live comedy today—this has typically been a venue, like Speaker's Corner, for speaking out, whether it is well or ill received. And it does take a special breed to go out and do this—the nerves-of-steel breed, now taking on the blogging and remixing Gargantua.

Nostalgia and the Economics of Comic Diffusion

Most serious actors show respect for the best stand-up comics for the same reason most serious musicians show respect for the best jazz artists: it's really hard to improvise well, and it's even harder to do it in front of peers, with a live audience at arm's length, and no safety net, editing, or dress rehearsals in sight. But more and more stand-up comedians are emerging, especially in the past twenty years, thanks to the huge success of television programs like *The Cosby Show*, *Seinfeld*, and *Everybody Loves Raymond*, which swooped comics off the stage and dropped them into sit-coms loosely based on their acts. Big money in the form of records, radio shows, talk shows, sit-coms and sold-out-arenas is hard to refuse, especially when the comedian is used to being paid in drink tabs. For many of these comedians, though, something crucial is lost when they trade the small stage for the big script. That is why so many keep coming back to the small clubs, even when they clearly aren't doing it for the green—Jerry Seinfeld, Chris Rock, and Dave Chappelle are all cases in point. There is always a certain nostalgia; the comedy club, an original homeland of sorts, is still a vital platform and testing ground for new talent and new material.

Needless to say, we are streaming digitally in every direction—what you do and say can and will be held against you (or in your favor, if you're lucky). In this era of cell phone video uploads to YouTube and iPhones, you don't need to sign a contract to be (or cause) an overnight sensation. The best comics still have the qualities that were always crucial to stand-up: good material, the ability to improvise, a compelling personality (or personalities), and the ability gracefully to control a crowd. They, like their predecessors, need to be finely tuned to the world around them—a world that is multilayered, often deceptive and, thanks to the rapid growth of technology, speeding up the cycles of what is up-to-the-minute and what is out-of-date. Timing is everything—that's what they say in the biz. It's what "brings the funny." But comics also may discover the challenges offered by the new spheres of comedy audiences when a show is rebroadcast online. As comedy is booming, the venues, or locations (the sites), for the performance of live comedy are proliferating so fast the whole concept of the club act behind closed doors is being irremediably transformed. With that, the dangers of performing live in a club are relocated—re-territorialized—into the online comic arena.

"Live" Comedy Online: Re-territorializing the Live Comedy Club onto the Digital Screen

Websites are enabling comics to broadcast their work live to online viewers; this proliferates the sites of reception while undermining the real time, interactive audience-performer relationships found in live clubs. Here, audiences scattered beyond the club walls may view the show, but their deferred laughter (or derision) fails directly to contribute to the comic's act since the comic cannot always immediately respond. The simple posting of online shows presents a few challenges for the narrative history of live comedy: first, the comic may post a clip from a live show, where a primary audience viewed and participated in it directly; secondary audiences may see the show, and participate vicariously in the events that occurred that night. Other comics may choose to perform behind closed doors, solo, or for an audience of friends, and post that to the website for exposure and eventually comment. This option, which is safer, also allows aspiring comics to test the waters without being thrown into the deep end right away.

But what of a scenario—perhaps the live comedy act of the near future (the world of live comedy 2.0) —where webcams and microphones enable comics to show their faces and project their voices to an audience visible to them and to one another. It may be split into many boxes on everyone's screens, creating a live, digitized room where everyone can see and hear one another (really small, and perhaps without the mood lighting). This scenario suggests a live digitized show that might be performed in real time. It is different from rebroadcasting shows online via such sites as YouTube inasmuch as the liveness and opportunities for exchange are not just upheld but expanded, in real time, and actually interactively.

Conclusion: Technologies of Diffusion and Digital Manipulation in the Comic Universe

As live comedy gets more interactive, multilayered, and complex, with the advent of technologies of diffusion and digital manipulation, authorship and ownership are transformed. The shows are truly protean, and it is not just the comic who is in charge of the laughs. What was raw stuff produced by one man or woman can be recuperated, repurposed, near infinitely, to the delight of viewers exercising their own brand of creativity, engaging in co-authorship in the privacy of their own homes. Personality, persona, character are morphed in this new arena, and the voices really multiply.

This new polyvocality in the comic arena means views are received and jokes land upon a hyperactive, hyperlinked audience that does more than laugh or boo, but reuses the material as well. Jokes on unsuspecting (and faraway) audience members may become a new norm in classic stand-up comedy. Direct address is trumped with cameras in tow, and the peanut gallery online trumps the laughter of consent (or contestation) often found in a comedy club. Connecting to the audience is a temporal affair that extends beyond the shelf life of the live joke, dividing for and against the comedian long after his or her act was first delivered. The degree to which comics and producers control a crowd is at stake in the diffusion of live acts online: where it is less controllable because of a relative physical distance, the comic is safer, and yet more vulnerable to the judgment of internet commentators. Because comics respond to crowd moods and energies—they "feel the room"—the live show is all the more difficult online because of the crowd's facelessness and relative silence. But, post-show commentary can be used for comic effect.

Blogosphere critics delight in the possibilities afforded them in the way of posting and reposting, chatrooms and popularity charts. *TIME* named "you" person of the year in 2006 in recognition of the power of these online communities, from craigslist to YouTube to flickr. The amount of time between a punchline landing on stage, and an audience member's reaction ending up online is continually shrinking. That reaction may involve heckling from the front row, silent texting from a back table, or someone watching live remotely on the other side of the world, posting a comment on their blog. The technology of the twentieth century helped to bring stand-up comedy from its birthplace in small clubs to wide audiences (in the form of albums, television and film), but in doing so it lost the crucial element of direct audience participation. The technology we have seen so far this century is still bringing stand-up comedy from the clubs to these wider audiences (online, at a much greater scale), in a way that may actually be much truer to the interactive origins of the genre.

Yet, we still believe there is something magic to being in a room where a comic dies, or kills, regardless of what happens after. Laughing is a very physical thing, and to laugh in concert is priceless. But laughter comes in many guises. We have laughed in concert writing this chapter together, even if some of that laughter was deferred over email, hypertexted and hyperlinked, webcammed, skyped, purposed, and repurposed as we exchanged notes, morphed some ideas into others, listened, agreed, disagreed, and worked together as each others' audience. If laughter is being splintered in living rooms and cafés all over the world, as screens give way to—and complement, or expand—live stages, degrees of intimacy morph. As we have argued, these degrees of intimacy constitute an expanded interface that reconfigures what it means to perform or attend a "live" act. Here, "live" isn't just in the flesh; it is also reterritorialized onto screens and mobile devices that reproduce and transform the laughter as quickly as it hits the circuit.

Notes

1. Media and performance theorist Philip Auslander argues that "[w]ith the stand-up comedy boom of the 1980s . . . , comics and comedy club owners discovered that audiences were only too happy to come to a club to hear the same jokes they had already heard on a comic's cable television special. . . . In these cases, the traditional privileging of the 'original,' live performance over its elaborations and adaptations is undermined and reversed: . . . the mediatized performance has become the referent of the live one." In short, "live performance is now a recreation of itself at one remove, filtered through its own mediatized reproductions." Philip Auslander, *Liveness: Performance in a Mediatized Culture* (London and New York: Routledge, 1999): 31.

2. See, for example, Gustave Le Bon, *Psychologie des foules* (Paris: Félix Alcan, 1895): 105 ff. On imitation as a prime mover of social interaction,

see especially Gabriel de Tarde, *Les lois de l'imitation* [1890] (Paris: Éditions Kimé, 1993) and *Les lois sociales: esquisse d'une sociologie*, 8th ed. (Paris: Librairie Félix Alcan, 1921). Gilles Deleuze and Félix Guattari riff off of Tarde's theory in *Capitalisme et schizophrénie 2: Mille Plateaux* (Paris: Les Éditions de Minuit, 1980): 267. On group psychology, see William McDougall, *The Group Mind* (New York and London : G. P. Putnam's Sons, 1920) and Sigmund Freud, *Group Psychology and the Analysis of the Ego* [1922] (New York and London: W. W. Norton & Company, 1989). For a more recent analysis, see, for example, Paulo Virno, *A Grammar of the Multitude* (New York: Semiotext(e), 2004).

3. See also Nicholas Ridout, *Stage Fright, Animals, and Other Theatrical Problems* (Cambridge and New York: Cambridge University Press, 2006): 35 ff.

4. Philip Auslander calls Andy Kaufman's brand of post- or anti-stand-up comedy "conceptual comedy" for dealing with comedy in the same way "conceptual art" deals with art, that is to say, making its production politics visible. In *Presence and Resistance: Postmodernism and Cultural Politics in Contemporary American Performance* (Ann Arbor: University of Michigan Press, 1992): 139 ff.

5. "Invisible theater" is a practice developed by the Brazilian theater-maker and civic leader Augusto Boal in Argentina in the 1970s. The goal is to perform live in settings not framed as traditional theater spaces, such as subways, subjecting unsuspecting audience members to a live show in which everyday conflicts are played out. This is intended to encourage civic awareness of, and involvement in, a variety of political issues.

WORKS CITED

Double, Oliver. *Getting the Joke: The Inner Workings of Stand-Up Comedy*. London: Methuen, 2005. Print.

Goldthwait, Bob. "The 200-Pound Heckle." *I Killed: True Stories of the Road from America's Top Comics*. Ed. Ritch Snyder and Mark Schiff. New York: Crown Publishers, 2006. 19-21. Print.

Jerry Seinfeld Live on Broadway: I'm Telling You for the Last Time. Writ. Jerry Seinfeld. Dir. Marty Callner. Perf. Jerry Seinfeld. HBO Home Video, 1999. DVD.

Live and Smokin'. Writ. Richard Pryor. Dir. Michael Blum. Perf. Richard Pryor. MPI Home Video, 1971. DVD.

Stanislavski, Constantin. *An Actor Prepares*. Trans. Elizabeth Reynolds Hapgood. London: Methuen, 1988. Print.

Stebbins, Robert A. *The Laugh-Makers: Stand-up Comedy as Art, Business, and Life-Style*. Montreal and Kingston: McGill-Queen's University Press, 1990. Print.

20 High Time for Humor

Andrea Fraser
(in conversation with Judy Batalion)

Andrea Fraser is an artist whose work has been identified with performance, institutional critique, and context art. Her major projects include installations for the Berkeley Art Museum (1992); the Venice Biennale (Austrian Pavilion, 1993); the Whitney Biennial (1993); and the Bienal de São Paulo (1998). She has created performances for the New Museum of Contemporary Art, New York (1986); the Philadelphia Museum of Art (1989); the Wadsworth Atheneum (1991); inSITE, San Diego/Tijuana (1997); and the MICA Foundation, New York (2001). Fraser is also an essayist and her essays and performance scripts have appeared in *Art in America, Afterimage, October, Texte zur Kunst, Social Text, Critical Quarterly, Documents, Artforum*, and *Grey Room*. The Kunstverein in Hamburg produced a twenty-year retrospective of her work in 2003. Her recent books include *Andrea Fraser: Works 1985–2003*, available from DuMont, and *Museum Highlights: The Writings of Andrea Fraser*, edited by Alexander Alberro and with a foreword by Pierre Bourdieu, released by MIT Press in 2005. She is currently on the faculty of the Whitney Independent Study Program and Professor in the Department of Art, University of California, Los Angeles.

Fraser's foundational work, *Museum Highlights*, was performed at the Philadelphia Museum of Art in 1989. Performing as the docent "Jane Castleton," she gave tours of the museum in a parody of gallery talks that called into question the foundations of the art institution, addressing the politics of collecting, the meaning of artistic value, and even the architecture of the bathroom. She has gone on to create several similarly institutional-critical performances that have addressed the "framing" and meaning of art practice, including versions of opening remark speeches (including *Inaugural Speech* in Chapter 21 in this book). In the following conversation, Fraser discusses her use of humor, the hybrid nature of her audiences, and the ways comedy has influenced "high" art practice.

Judy: This book addresses comedy audiences and live comedy entertainers. You're a "high" art comedy entertainer. Or, actually, I don't know if you're an entertainer or if you'd consider yourself to be an entertainer at all? You are, though, unique in being a very funny performance artist. What do you see as the relationship between performance art and comedy?

Andrea: No, I would never describe myself as an entertainer. When I started working in the early 1980s, cultural studies was still pretty low on the horizon in the US. I was struggling with the old high culture/low culture divisions which, in the Greenbergian and Adornian traditions I absorbed in art school, oppose the radical negations of avant-garde art to the conservative affirmations of popular kitsch. At the same time, I was absorbing critical thinking about art and art institutions that came out of feminism and conceptual art, which questioned the elitism of such cultural hierarchies. So I began looking to humor and comedy as a popular form of subversion and radical critique. I grew up with Warner Brothers cartoons, *Saturday Night Live*, and Woody Allen. I watched Marx Brothers movies as a child. Certainly, in popular culture, it seemed to be in the arena of comedy that one generally found the most formal experimentation and the most transgressive content, and I would say that's still true today. Now, when I'm teaching younger art students about ideology critique, Barthesian secondary mythification, or the Brechtian alienation effect, all I have to do is mention *The Daily Show* or *The Colbert Report*, and they say, "oh, ok, I get it" [laughs]. And that's absolutely fine with me.

Within an art history context, the artistic strategies that form the background for the work I do, like most of the critical strategies that developed in art in the twentieth century, primarily come out of Berlin Dada. Those artists were appropriating popular cultural forms of satire and caricature that came out of traditions of carnival, cabaret, and vaudeville. At a certain point I realized the opposition between radical avant-garde critique and popular culture was based on a pretty questionable historical myopia.

In the 1980s in New York, the dominant form of performance art was cabaret-based and monologue-based. Much of that work was engaged in a critical examination of identity in and through those forms in ways that corresponded quite closely with the "pictures" art of the period and was broadly influenced by feminist strategies of the 1970s, even when the work itself was not particularly feminist. There were a number of figures in that scene who crossed over between art and comedy, theater, film, and television. I'm thinking of Eric Bogosian and Ann Magnison and Spalding Gray. Andy Kauffman went in the other direction: a comedian whose work leaned heavily toward a kind of performance art, confounding some of the expectations of comedy. Art world people today, oddly enough, often think of New York in the 1980s as a time when there wasn't much performance art, which demonstrates the degree to which gallery-based performance art has almost completely split off from stage and club-based performance art. Indeed, the most famous artists of the late 80s may have been the NEA Four—Karen Finley, Tim Miller, John Fleck, and Holly Hughes—all of whom were stage-based performance artists. Before the 1980s, and again in the 90s and 00s, most performance art in New York was more closely allied with sculpture, such as body art, and was gallery-based. Californian and much Canadian performance art has always had a much stronger interface with popular culture, from General Idea and Mr. Peanut in Canada to Ant Farm and Paul McCarthy in L.A.

Judy: What roles does humor play in your work?

Andrea: The performance of mine that comes the closest to political satire and stand-up comedy is *Inaugural Speech* from 1997 (Chapter 21). It's funny. I wrote it to be funny—rather desperately, in fact. It was a performance for the opening of an exhibition along the San Diego/Tijuana boarder called *inSITE*. Because it was a very politicized context, with half the funding coming from the Mexican government, politicians where scheduled to give speeches at the opening. These turned out to be a US politician reading a letter from President Clinton and a Mexican politician reading a letter from President Zedillo, both congratulating everyone on the "cross-border cooperation." But most of the audience of about two thousand had paid tickets to see Laurie Anderson, who was performing after the speeches. I was sandwiched in between, with an agenda of elaborating a critique of anti-immigration policies as well as neo-liberalism and economically driven globalization and their relationship to international exhibitions of contemporary art. Most of the two thousand people in the audience had no idea who I was. Why on earth would they listen to me for twenty minutes? It was terrifying. I just HAD to be funny.

Pierre Bourdieu, in *Language and Symbolic Power*, rejects a purely linguistic model of the performative. He argues that it is the institution that acts from certain positions of speech, and this functions through a delegation of authority and legitimacy in which the audience participates with its own acts of recognition and legitimation. In that context, I had no authority, I had no legitimacy. The audience had no reason to recognize or receive my speech. So comedy—being funny—was a very self-conscious, strategic way of securing the attention of the audience. It was a strategy to keep people listening to me for twenty minutes. There were hecklers toward the end, but it was my one performance when I really felt the power of having so many people laughing with me, of holding their attention, and I thought, wow! I could really get into being a demagogue!

It was an interesting experience in all sorts of ways. The audience itself was extremely stratified. In the front rows, there were the invited guests—patrons and critics and so-forth. In the middle, there were the people who had bought tickets for Laurie Anderson. The artists in the exhibition were seated all the way in the back. I could feel the different parts of that audience responding to me in different ways. There were some people who laughed and applauded with me, while other people applauded against me when I was saying things that were clearly ironic, who applauded against the irony. It was a very interesting dynamic and seemed to demonstrate that the performance was quite successful in activating the audience, transforming their applause from the pretty passive recognition of political authority one heard during the official speeches to an active articulation of various positions. It was a great experience. I've been trying to do something like that again ever since, but no one has been willing to give me the opportunity.

If the politicians in that situation enjoyed the authority delegated them by political institutions, you could say Laurie Anderson enjoyed the authority of her reputation and people's past experiences with her work, but she is also very much of an entertainer. Entertainment can be an end in itself and being entertained can be an enjoyably passive experience. Of course, forms of entertainment can also be a means for conveying all sorts of content, including critical content. What seems particular to comedy, however, is the degree to which it can function, not only as a vehicle for critical content (just about anything can) but also as a critique or subversion of form and the relations produced and reproduced through various forms. And it often does so in ways that are very immediate, even site-specific, and also self-reflexive. So, in addition to all the specific content I mentioned above, what *Inaugural Speech* was REALLY about was the institution of the speech itself, as a ritual form, and the relations of delegation, recognition, and legitimation that structure and bind the hierarchies of power at work in the political and cultural context of its performance. To that extent, the comedy was not just a means to convey content or even to expose contradictions or hidden agendas, but quite inseparable from the aim of the performance to shift those relations around. I think the pleasure manifest in laughter came directly from that operation—as is usually the case with that kind of comedy—from the release of latent hostility toward authority.

But that's just one kind of laughter. My vision when I started dealing with humor, even with *Museum Highlights* [the gallery-talk performance], was less of the kind of satire or parody familiar from political comedy than of the grotesque. Bakhtin describes the grotesque somewhere as the collapsing of irreconcilable representations or ideas. It's when identities, or ideas, or representations that seem opposed are mashed up together. That's what I wanted to do. I wanted smoke to be coming out of people's ears. I wanted to short-circuit people's brains in a way that was about the breakdown of identity or a kind of liberation from signification, and that might provoke laughter or also tears or just a kind of open blankness. Recently, I have come to think more about the collapsing or confrontation of opposing impulses and affects, like love and hate, in terms of engaging ambivalence, but the result there is more likely to be anxiety than laughter. There are lots of different kinds of laughter. There are kinds of laughter I would not want to provoke.

Judy: Which kinds of laughter would you *not* want to provoke?

Andrea: Well, there's a kind of ego-consolidating laughter that's about externalization—the kind of relief you feel when you're able to externalize a bad idea or feeling—to project a bad object onto someone else, in psychoanalytic terms. I do not want to provoke that kind of laughter. I think a lot of the pleasure parody and irony allow—certainly racist jokes and sexist jokes—is about that kind of externalizing. That would be a Kleinian perspective on jokes.

For Freud, laughter is a manifestation of pleasure and all pleasure is a release of the tension produced by libidinal energy. According to Freud the various techniques of jokes correspond quite closely with the kind of condensation and displacement at work in dreams. And through such techniques, like dreams, jokes manage to circumvent the forces of repression and release repressed ideas and affects, producing pleasure. Well, maybe pleasure for some people; anxiety for others. Freud's model for humor was largely based on what he calls "tendentious jokes." Freud focuses on obscene jokes, which he suggests originated as seductive remarks by men addressed to women. In his narrative, when the women responded with "go fuck yourself," [laughs] a displacement occurred. Instead of addressing such remarks to women, men addressed them to other men, about women. The structure of such a joke, then, is that of a displaced address from a second term to a third term, in which the original addressee is transformed into an object, a third term, whose exposure or denigration the teller and new addressee enjoy together. In this scenario the original erotic impulse also becomes mixed with and to some extent transformed into an aggressive or destructive one.

This Freudian model of the tendentious joke also works for aggressive jokes. It was a revelation for me when I realized most avant-garde art has the structure of an aggressive joke in some sense. The aggression is filtered through irony and satire and various techniques of dissimulation—above all the extreme self-consciousness that defines art more than anything else. While avant-garde traditions largely have been defined as the critique or subversion of power, what we find over and over is the displacement of that critique. For example, if the avant-garde aimed to reintegrate art and life in a critique of bourgeois art institutions, what we find over and over again is that "life," people, and the popular are transformed into an object of often aggressive appropriation and become objects of exchange between artists and their patrons.

Avant-garde artists often claimed to be engaged in a critique of those in positions of power in the art world and in society. Historically, however, it's clear that most often that critique ended up being experienced as such by those in a more dominated position, while the dominant have easily appropriated it. I think one of the mechanisms at work there is a displacement of address similar to that in the structure of jokes. For example, there has been a romance in art with the idea of the guerrilla intervention, of taking people by surprise, so they don't even know what they are experiencing is art, as if that somehow makes the critical or subversive aspect of art more effective. I sometimes call this the candid-camera school of performance art and it's a perfect example of this joke structure of displaced address in operation. The people, on whose behalf we are supposedly subverting or exposing the powers that be, become, in effect, the objects, the butt of the joke, at whose credulousness or naiveté we laugh with other insiders, other people in the know. So what we're really doing in those instances is reaffirming our insider status, our privileged in-the-knowness, which should rather be foremost among the structures of power we aim to critique. I set up my early performances, like *Museum Highlights*, with that kind of ambiguity. When I realized the insiders were just watching the supposed outsiders, and not taking themselves as the object of the critique, I changed tactics—I did not want to provoke that kind of laughter. Since then, I always start my performances as myself, as Andrea Fraser, an artist. I then go through different voices and positions. My hope is that this levels the playing field for the audience.

However, if Freud is right and laughter represents pleasure in the discharge of affective energy, then distinguishing between different kinds of laughter is problematic. For Freud, pleasure is quantitative, not qualitative, and all that laughter indicates is that some barrier of repression has temporarily been suspended. Maybe then the question becomes, what is the structure of the discharge? Or, what are the ideas or representations with which that energy is bound up? Or, what are the origins of those forces of repression? I don't know. This makes it difficult to put a political value on jokes and humor. Of course, there are a lot of really vicious sexist and racist and classist jokes out there. The knife cuts both ways. You could take a position that would be, perhaps, a more psychoanalytic one, that repression is always bad, that repression always fails, that repressed ideas always come out in some form as symptoms, displaced, and that any kind of lifting of repression is, if you want to put a kind of political value on it, a progressive and liberatory thing. Maybe to a certain point. On the other hand, maybe it would be better if people who were racist and misogynist didn't express their racism and misogyny in jokes because that form of expression is actually a way of protecting that racism and misogyny from a direct response, a direct engagement, a direct confrontation. This is not unlike a lot of the aggression in avant-garde art. In this sense, jokes themselves can be seen as symptoms. Of course, thinking of them that way rather ruins the fun, doesn't it?

Works Cited

Bakhtin, Mikhail M. *Rabelais and His World*. Trans. Hélène Iswolsky. Bloomington: Indiana University Press, 1993. Print.

Bourdieu, Pierre. *Language and Symbolic Power*. Cambridge, MA: Harvard University Press, 1999. Print.

Freud, Sigmund. *Jokes and Their Relationship to the Unconscious*. Trans. James Strachey. London: Penguin, 1991. Print.

21 Inaugural Speech

Andrea Fraser

INTRODUCTION[1]

Inaugural Speech was prepared as my contribution to *inSITE97*, the third installment of a bi-national exhibition of public art works commissioned for the San Diego/Tijuana area. That fact that the federal government of Mexico contributed half of the exhibition's budget was largely responsible for the unusual (in the United States) scheduling of official public opening ceremonies, complete with speeches by public officials. *Inaugural Speech* was delivered on September 26, 1997 at the San Diego opening of *inSITE97*. The Tijuana ceremony took place the following evening. The San Diego opening, which included a performance by Laurie Anderson, was sponsored by Anheuser-Busch Companies, Inc. A loading dock at a factory-turned-cultural-center in downtown San Diego was transformed into a stage for the occasion. The street was blocked off and seating for two thousand set up. Speeches by officials included the United States Attorney for Southern California reading a letter from President Clinton and the Undersecretary of Foreign Relations for Mexico reading a letter from President Zedillo—both letters congratulating the organizers and participants in the show. One of the co-directors of the exhibition introduced me, the last of the speakers, saying: "I am now happy to introduce an artist participating in *inSITE97*, Andrea Fraser, who is, as her contribution to *inSITE97*, making a speech. Thank you very much."

INAUGURAL SPEECH

Thank you.

Thank you. Thank you very much.

On behalf of the participating artists—who have, actually, been seated way in the back . . . Hi! [The speaker waves.]

Good evening and welcome to *inSITE97*.

As an art exhibition, *inSITE97* is focused on the exploration and activation of public space.

I think I can speak for all of the artists when I say that this is an extremely important aim. Especially now, when here and throughout the Americas all aspects of the public sphere are under attack; when the public sector is being downsized, public services privatized, public space enclosed, public speech controlled, and public goods of all kinds exchanged for the currency of private goals, be they prestige, privilege, power, or profits.

Public art cannot forestall the forces foreclosing on our public lives. But it can remind us of what we are losing, like the casual democracy of everyday encounters, when we find ourselves equal before places and things that needn't be paid for and can't be purchased; or the practical democracy of forums of public speech, where differences of status do not determine our places at the podium.

1.

All the more reason why it is such a *special* opportunity for me to address you here this evening.

This is a perfect example of what makes *inSITE97* so rewarding for its artists. As an exhibition of public artworks and community engagement projects, it gives us the opportunity to address people who would otherwise never stop to look or listen. There are all of you here this evening, but that's just the beginning. There are the tens of thousands of people expected to tour the exhibition sites. There are the hundreds of thousands who will just happen upon our work, unawares, in their parks and plazas, on their streets.

You will encounter our work as you walk along beaches, sit in cafes, go to elementary schools or see adult films, wait for buses, get tattoos, fish, cruise and, of course, cross the border.

You are residents, tourists, students, sailors, migrants; you are young and old, gay and straight, US, Mexican, and Chicano; you are upper-, middle- and working class, you are unemployed; you live in walled estates, gated communities, condominiums, trailer parks, shanties, and doorways.

inSITE97 depends on the active involvement of its audiences. You are our audience this evening, and it is with great enthusiasm that I thank you for your participation.

Finally, I think I can speak for all of the artists when I express my gratitude for the tremendous support we have received from the exhibition's organizers.

Thanks to them, we will achieve a new level of recognition—locally, nationally, and internationally, within the art world, and beyond. [The speaker turns to her right.] Thank you. [She turns back to the audience.]

2.

Thank you very much.

Thank you.

And thank *you*, Andrea, for that thoughtful introduction.

As one of the exhibition's organizers, I can say that Andrea is truly exemplary of the artists participating in this event. An internationally recognized and emerging talent, she has delved into the commotion and poetic pause of this discontinuous urban sprawl, probing, digging, tracking, traversing and intervening in public space, discerning domains of dialogue and reverie.

And, Andrea is only one of over fifty artists and authors from eleven countries participating in our exhibition and events. As a group they represent the most influential cultural figures of the Americas. It is their extraordinary achievements that we celebrate here this evening.

We find ourselves this evening in a restlessly metaphoric place. It's a place of conflict and contradiction, disparity and division, rift and entanglements, all poised at a juncture of economies, labor forces, languages, artistic cultures and urban communities.

It is a matrix of forces that tends to strain relationships and threatens to pull us apart.

This exhibition demonstrates the enormous potential in working together. The participation and support of so many federal, state, and municipal agencies, national foundations, and international corporations demonstrates a shared belief that the arts are a uniquely powerful means of promoting understanding across borders, of building bridges between groups and discovering common ground in a multicultural and increasingly transnational society.

This is indeed the terrain in which the new arrangements of "global culture" are being formed.

It isn't possible to thank all of the many people who have contributed to this event. But we do want to say a special word of thanks to our board of trustees. They are a deeply devoted group of individuals who have generously volunteered their time, knowledge and wealth, networking, promoting, opening their homes for exclusive parties.

Who could forget that evening! A black-tie benefit gala that equaled the raw creativity, exuberance, and international flavor of the exhibition itself. There was music, dancing, live performance and superb cuisine, all in a lavish and dramatic setting.

And that's just one example of the many ways our trustees have marshaled their extensive resources in support of our project. In their long and distinguished careers they have served as directors, executive vice presidents, state appointees, partners, brokers, planners, director generals, secretary generals, consul generals, vice-presidents of development, co-founders, chairmen, owners, significant shareholders, registered principals, chief financial officers, chief executive officers, and presidents throughout the Americas.

[The speaker turns to her right.] To our trustees I would like to say, we are all deeply in your debt, and I thank you. [She turns back to the audience.]

3.

Thank *you*.

Thank you *so* much and thank you from the bottom of my heart for this. . . .

I am privileged…

I am truly privileged.

Working with such an accomplished and multi-talented group of artists and art experts has indeed been a rare and rewarding experience. This warm evening is an apt metaphor for how I feel about these wonderful creative people.

I am very proud of them and what they have done for us.

For us, this event is a unique opportunity to step up to the world stage. We want people to realize there is a *lot* going on down here.

We're home to many internationally respected institutions, to Nobel Prize winners, authors, artists, celebrities, custom ocean view homes, boutiques, luxury, charm, sophistication, and jet setters from around the globe.

If you don't believe me, just look around this evening. This is *not* your regular crowd. This is *very* cutting edge. This is very much *big* time, on an *international* level!

We are *not* provincial.

We're the gateway to the Pacific and Latin America. We're the information hub of NAFTA. We're a major center for high tech, software, media and financial services.

We should also be a major center for art.

Our bi-national strength can help to get us there.

But first we have to put aside parochial interests and realize that our power lies in the relationships we forge and the common goals we establish.

Citizenship and national origin have never stood for much in our cosmopolitan community. In this new age of global culture and capital, they mean less and less.

As more and more of our Latin American friends are joining our museum boards and country clubs and purchasing estates in our neighborhoods, we are discovering that we have more in common than art, golf and horsemanship. There are also political and economic interests that we share. Through cooperative projects such as this we are testing the soil for new hybrids, planting seeds that will blossom into beautiful joint ventures, election victories, and influence policy throughout the hemisphere.

Of course, we could not approach these goals without the support of governments here and abroad. That is why I want to say a special word of thanks to our friends at city, state and federal agencies who have helped to make this effort a success.

Representing our public sponsors this evening, I am delighted to introduce a man who was elected and overwhelmingly reelected by a small minority of the voting age population.

Throughout his career, he has shown optimism and courage.

He is the national leader in the drive to stop illegality.

He has made tough choices necessary, cutting our income taxes.

His toughness was proven yet again when, recovering from a burst appendix, he was wheeled onto the floor to cast a tie-breaking vote on budget reduction.

He enjoys reading history and cheering for the Chargers.

I think that we all owe him a vote of thanks. [The speaker turns to her right.]

Thank you. [She turns back to the audience.]

4.

(Applause.)
Thank you.
(Applause.)
Thank you.
Won't you all sit down, please?
Thank you very, very much. Thank you.

It is a high honor and a rare privilege for me to join you in kicking off this tremendous effort.

And, I have to say that I am quite intrigued with many of the art projects I have seen so far.

But I can only begin by acknowledging my wife. A "career volunteerist," she is a shining example of just how much one woman can achieve—and achieve with grace, with style and with class. She's been so active, in fact, that I haven't seen her in months. It is wonderful to have her with us here this evening.

Gayle and I are strong supporters of the arts, and we applaud you for your efforts to bring quality art reflecting our diverse cultures into all of our lives. It is our exciting and distinctive art that keeps us on "the cutting edge." And there is no better place to be on "the cutting edge" than here.

Our region is a diverse region, populated by many different kinds of people. There are people who work in our fields and flower shops, hotels and factories. There are people who vote. There are people who pay taxes. There are people who establish foundations. There are people who send their children to public schools. There are people who vote.

And yet, despite this diversity, we are held together by our belief in diversity. We are devoted to that myth. It's our myth. It's all that many of us have.

Throughout our history, we have always answered *ad*versity with a dream.

West! Over desolate prairie and frozen mountains, we risked our lives crossing the mighty, until one day we found ourselves gazing down from the heights upon a golden valley of promise, inviting us to partake of the good life.

Quality communities, quality lifestyles, prime location. Benches and landscaping. Family-friendly neighborhoods and vibrant, multipurpose districts. California Casual, Renaissance England and Palazzo Italiano in forty-nine different colors. *Multi*level. Stunning.

Within the next three years, no single race or ethnic group will make up a majority of this region's population.

We know what we'll look like. Just look around at this crowd tonight!

Yes! That's right!

I'm the redneck son of a poor dirt farmer! But even I can understand the benefits of the cultural diversity of our new global society.

With just five percent of the world's population, but twenty percent of the world's income, we must sell to the other ninety-five percent just to maintain *our* standard of living.

Because we are drawn from every culture on earth, we are uniquely positioned to do it.

We will meet the challenge of building the first society to embrace every ethnic group on the planet.

We will share a common future.

We will invent that future—and export it.

We are now the world leader in television set production and golf course design—117 golf courses in our city alone. That's good news!

We have made your lives more livable, with tougher penalties for graffiti taggers. We now prohibit young people from loitering in public places. There's the Juvenile Curfew Enforcement Policy and the Anti-Cruising Ordinance.

We confine demonstrations to parking lots!

We listened to what you wanted. We heard what you said: Stop the raw sewage flows that have plagued our residents!

We are now an advocate for business, not an adversary. We cut business taxes in half and then in half again.

Ours is a growth economy, built on the low-wage labor of people motivated to perform. With little or no unemployment and welfare benefits, a job is their only chance for survival. That equals a savings to you of up to eighty percent on your labor costs.

Our success is because of you. You: business, hotel and restaurant owners, investors and professionals.

Legitimate members of the community.

You are the ones who have made it happen and I thank you.

Our corporate sponsors also deserve a special word of thanks for our success.

Representing our corporate sponsors this evening, I have the honor to introduce to you a man whose outstanding leadership at the helm of a remarkable organization is deserving of special praise. Thanks to his vision, his competitive spirit, his tenacity and his uncompromising commitment to excellence, he has made this flagship Enterprise a global champion.

We are proud to count him as one of us. [The speaker turns to her right.] And I thank you. [She turns back to the audience.]

5.

Thank you.

Good morning! And welcome to those of you who are from out of town. I'm happy to see so many of my old friends here today. It's also exciting to see so many new faces.

I must say that I swell with pride and satisfaction in your accomplishments. Too many of us have been told, "You can't, you shouldn't, you won't." But you found a way around those obstacles. You can, you should, and you did!

Increasingly, as public expenditures are reduced, corporate philanthropy is being called on to support the building blocks of our diverse communities. We view our contributions as an investment in regions where our company has a presence.

The globalization of culture makes this an especially favorable time for us. Films, TV programs, music, sports and classic products are proliferating and spreading around the world.

We must maximize our tie-ins with culture.

We may be the world's largest, but the world market still offers tremendous potential for growth.

We must act aggressively, making inroads with a strong presence and significant investment.

But in our zeal for global success, we must also be willing to discover and appreciate the uniqueness of each market. In this we have been able to draw on the diversity of our work force, people who understand *other* cultures and who speak *other* languages.

We have hired *local* people. We have developed *local* partnerships. We clearly picked the right partner in Mexico, in Brazil. Argentina is growing rapidly. Our partner is the leader in Chile.

And, as personal incomes rise in developing countries, more and more people will be able to spend money on "luxury" items, like ours.

We will work to transform regional identities, indigenous cultures and stable communities into differentiated markets.

We will work to create the future that we imagine, a future in which everywhere around the globe, we will symbolize the good things in life.

We are the world . . . 's beer company—"*la compan'a cervecera del mundo.*"

Gracias!

Note

1. *Inaugural Speech* has been reprinted courtesy of the artist.

Works Cited

Primary Sources (by section):

1.

inSITE94 exhibition catalog.
inSITE97 press releases.
inSITE97, Guide/Guía.

2.

inSITE94 exhibition catalog.
inSITE97 press releases.
inSITE97, Guide/Guía.
The Rockefeller Foundation, *Annual Report*, 1996.

3.

inSITE94 exhibition catalog.
inSITE97 press releases.

inSITE97, Guide/Guía.
Fodor's 97: San Diego. "Biography of Governor Pete Wilson."

4.

"Biography of Gayle Wilson, First Lady of California." California Arts Council, "Message from Governor Pete Wilson," 1997.

"Remarks By President Ford, President Bush and President Clinton at Luncheon," Philadelphia, Pennsylvania, April 28, 1997.

Governor Pete Wilson, "California: Forging America's Future," second Inaugural Address, Sacramento, California, January 7, 1995.

Iris H. W. Engstrand, *San Diego, Gateway to the Pacific: A Christopher Columbus Quincentennial Commermorative*, 1992.

President Bill Clinton, "Remarks By The President At University of California At San Diego Commencement," June 14, 1997.

Mayor Susan Golding, "The City of Infinite Possibility," fifth State of the City Address, San Diego, California, December 4, 1996.

Alfa Southwest Corporation, "Maquila Workers at a Tijuana Electronics Assembly Plant Are Typical of the Efficient Employees Who Characterize the Industry."

5.

Thomas d'Aquino, "Globalization, Social Progress, Democratic Development and Human Rights: The Responsibility of An International Corporation," address delivered to the Academy Of International Business, Annual General Meeting, Banff, Canada, September 27, 1996.

Sol Trujilo, "American Hispanic Population: Reaching New Heights, Seeking New Horizons," address delivered to the US Hispanic Chamber, Denver, Colorado, September 20, 1996.

BankAmerica Foundation, *Report,* 1992–1993.

Anheuser-Busch Companies, Inc., *Annual Report,* 1996.

Inaugural Speech 289

Figures 21.1, 21.2, 21.3 Andrea Fraser, *Inaugural Speech*, video stills. Courtesy of the artist.

About the Editor

Judy Batalion is a writer, performer, and independent scholar. She has written and performed stand-up, sketches, improv, one-woman shows, short films, and comedy theater in her native Canada, throughout the UK (where she spent a decade), and in the US. Her academic work has appeared in publications including *Contemporary Theatre Review*, and her journalism and personal essays have been published in newspapers, magazines and blogs, including the *Washington Post*, the *Jerusalem Post*, *Salon*, the *Forward* and *Nerve*. She has a BA from Harvard in the History of Science, and a PhD from the Courtauld Institute of Art, University of London, in Art History. She currently resides in New York City.

www.ingramcontent.com/pod-product-compliance
Lightning Source LLC
Chambersburg PA
CBHW030130240426
43672CB00005B/91